AS WIDE AS THE WORLD IS WISE

AS WIDE AS
THE WORLD
IS WISE

Reinventing
Philosophical Anthropology

Michael Jackson

Columbia University Press
New York

Columbia University Press
Publishers Since 1893
New York   Chichester, West Sussex
cup.columbia.edu
Copyright © 2016 Columbia University Press
All rights reserved

Library of Congress Cataloging-in-Publication Data
Names: Jackson, Michael, 1940– author.
Title: As wide as the world is wise: reinventing philosophical
anthropology / Michael Jackson.
Description: New York : Columbia University Press, 2016. |
Includes bibliographical references and index.
Identifiers: LCCN 2016000265 (print) | LCCN 2016013034 (ebook) |
ISBN 9780231178280 (cloth : alk. paper) | ISBN 9780231541985 (e-book) |
ISBN 9780231541985()
Subjects: LCSH: Philosophical anthropology. | Anthropology—Philosophy.
Classification: LCC BD450 J233 2016(print) | LCC BD450 (ebook) | DDC 128—dc23
LC record available at http://lccn.loc.gov/2016000265

♾

Columbia University Press books are printed on permanent and durable acid-free paper.
This book is printed on paper with recycled content.
Printed in the United States of America

COVER DESIGN: Catherine Casalino
COVER IMAGE: © Dimitri Otis / Getty Images

The logocentricism of Greek metaphysics will always be haunted . . . by the "absolutely other" to the extent that the Logos can never englobe everything. There is always something which escapes, something different, other and opaque which refuses to be totalized into a homogeneous identity.

—JACQUES DERRIDA, *DECONSTRUCTION AND THE OTHER*

Contents

Contents

Acknowledgments

Between 2009 and 2015, I had the good fortune to participate in conversations and collaborative projects with colleagues in Denmark and the United States on how philosophers and anthropologists might enter into productive dialogue and perhaps find common ground. During this same period I was engaged in ethnographic fieldwork in Sierra Leone and Europe on issues of well-being, migration, ethics, and social justice. While this fieldwork was the dominant influence on my thinking and writing, I was well aware that my existential anthropology ran parallel to the work of many others, so when Wendy Lochner expressed interest, in November 2014, in a book that would explore the interface between philosophy and anthropology, I was mindful of the three books on this theme that I had already had a hand in producing, and wondered what more I could possibly say on the subject. (Those books are *The Ground Between: Anthropologists Engage Philosophy*, ed. Veena Das, Michael Jackson, Arthur Kleinman, and Bhrigupati Singh; *Anthropology and Philosophy: Dialogues on Trust and Hope*, ed. Sune Liisberg, Esther Oluffa Pedersen, and Anne Line Dalsgård; and *What Is Existential Anthropology?*, ed. Michael Jackson and Albert Piette.) As I took stock of my ongoing research, I realized that some of its recurring themes and most pressing concerns had not found adequate expression in the essays I had contributed to these collaborative volumes. In this respect, my situation exemplified the Sartrean paradox of the singular universal that I explored in my *Between One and One Another*, namely that the singular "I" is never completely occluded in any collective activity and the collective has no reality apart from the people who constitute it. As Sartre observes in *The Family Idiot*, every individual is at once universalized by his or her location in a historical moment yet "singular by the universalizing singularity of his [or her] projects."

This perspective offers a novel way of examining the relationship between philosophy, which tends to universalize its subject, and ethnography, which tends to singularize it, and touches on anthropology's oldest dilemma—how to reconcile a focus on particular cultures, people, and lifeworlds with a fascination for concepts that transcend such particular identifications: the human condition, the global, or life itself.

It is in this spirit, responsive to others yet solely responsible for my own thought, that I acknowledge the following individuals and friends, and celebrate the convivial occasions when we came together to discuss what Heidegger called "the end of philosophy and the task of thinking": Anne Line Dalsgård, Veena Das, Kate DeConinck, Robert Desjarlais, George Gonzalez, Ghassan Hage, Chris Houston, Tim Ingold, Arthur Kleinman, Joshua Jackson, Michael Lambek, Sune Liisberg, Marc Loustau, Francine Lorimer, Hans Lucht, Cheryl Madingly, Roberto Mata, Joseph Méar, Anand Pandian, Esther Oluffa Pedersen, Albert Piette, Devaka Premawardhana, Bhrigupati Singh, Jason Throop, Sebastien Tutenges, Mattijs van de Port, Thomas Schwartz Wentzer, Souchou Yao, and Jarrett Zigon.

AS WIDE AS THE WORLD IS WISE

Introduction

If philosophy has always intended, from its point of view, to maintain
its relation with the nonphilosophical, that is the antiphilosophical,
with the practices and knowledge, empirical or not, that constitute
its other, if it has constituted itself according to this purposive *entente*
with its outside, if it has always intended to hear itself speak, in the
same language, of itself and of something else, can one, strictly
speaking, determine a nonphilosophical place, a place of exteriority
or alterity from which one might treat *of philosophy*?

—JACQUES DERRIDA, *MARGINS OF PHILOSOPHY*

On the first day of spring 2015, shortly after completing the penultimate
draft of this book, I flew to Kansas City and thence to St. Louis to give
a keynote address at a theology conference on the theme of borders and
boundaries.[1] It was only when I was well into the flight, reading George
Eliot's *Middlemarch* and reflecting on my own writing, that I realized
how directly the theme of this conference spoke to my recent preoccupations, including the question as to how one might cross the disciplinary
borders between philosophy (or theology) and anthropology without
feeling that one was trespassing in fields far beyond one's limited experience and expertise. I also realized how closely connected my new project
was to my earlier work on storytelling, art, and ritual, where my focus
had been not on the intrinsic meaning of any story, rite, or work of art
but on the *process* of creating objects that went beyond oneself, connect-
ing one with others and providing a transitory sense of mastery over difficult experiences and degrading events. I approached thinking in a similar way, drawing on psychological studies of primary intersubjectivity to
explore how human beings "learn to use their mental capacities to know

meaningfully about the world," reflecting on and responding to their own and others' changing thoughts, intentions, moods, and desires.[2]

Human beings do not simply think *about* themselves and others; they think *through* them. The same is true of events and objects or natural and supernatural phenomena; they are not only subject to thought but are the conditions of the very possibility of thought. This is why thought is always going on, even when we are not consciously thinking. By deconstructing the academic conception of philosophy as a uniquely European form of knowing, I hope to show that thinking is just one among many techniques humans have evolved for comprehending and negotiating the space between themselves and the world at large. Claude Lévi-Strauss asks why we readily accept the great antiquity of our species yet do not grant humanity a "continuous thinking capacity during this enormous length of time." He sees no reason why thinkers of the caliber of Plato and Einstein did not exist two or three hundred thousand years ago, though they were, of course "not applying their intelligence to the solution of the same problems as these more recent thinkers; instead, they were probably more interested in kinship!"[3] While I agree with Lévi-Strauss, my interest is less in the epistemological or logical status of any form of thought than in its ethical and "magical" capacity to transform experience, play with reality, and give a person a sense of having a say in, and a degree of control over, the world's workings. Like art, dreaming, ritual, and storytelling, thinking carries us to the margins of our immediate and empirically particular world, generating simulacra of the real, repertoires of images, words, plots, patterns, and ground rules that provide seemingly secure oases in the world's wastes.[4]

As I was pondering these matters, I found myself distracted by the young woman in the window seat beside me. She had opened up a large drawing book on her tray table and was painstakingly copying an image of Lisa Simpson from the screen of her iPhone. Her concentration was remarkable, and though I had initially wondered why anyone would dedicate herself to such a banal project, I now become captivated by that dedication—as intense and compulsive as Casaubon's academic labor on his Key to All Mythologies or Dorothea Brooke's bedazzled attachment to her husband's delusional project.

After completing an outline of her subject, the young woman opened up a plastic pencil case containing a variety of color pencils. Beginning with the yellow of Lisa's skin, she gradually filled in the blank spaces, not crossing any line and maintaining a constant pressure on her pencil in order to guarantee perfect coverage. Minor imperfections were corrected with an eraser, or smoothed away by a soft scraping of her fingernail. Though I resumed reading *Middlemarch*, I glanced at her drawing from to time to see how she was faring. At one point she emblazoned the words "Congratulations, Sis!" across the top of the page, like a banner, with little hearts instead of full stops. Observing her focus and devotion, I felt that the drawing was less important than the drawer; what mattered most was what the process of drawing consummated in her mind and might enable her to accomplish in her world. From this perspective, her labor of love was essentially no different from my own writing or the work of any philosopher. If there was any comparison to be drawn between these modes of "mentalization," all of which operate in a subjunctive or "pretend mode,"[5] it would have to be based not on the moral character of a single person but on the *relationship* between an intentional agent and a suffering moral patient.[6] In this intersubjective perspective, morality is not simply a question of one's good intentions; it is a matter of at least two people's moral responsiveness to each other and of the good or harmful repercussions of any action for both oneself and others. Not only did I see no harm in the devoted labor of this naïf, but I found it admirable that it was done for a beloved sister; this caused me to think of the priority that West African villagers give to thought that serves the common weal and their distrust of thinking that takes place in the darkness of a single mind or dwells on the metaphysical. Wasn't this why I had felt compelled to bring anthropology and philosophy together—a desire to see thought in existential terms, as one technique among many for negotiating and renegotiating our relations with others, and with the wider fields of being in which our own individual being is embedded so that no one would be able to claim on a priori grounds that his or her thought was necessarily or intrinsically more worthy of the name philosophy?

The One and the Many

In *Phenomenology of Perception*, Maurice Merleau-Ponty observes that the "one" or "we" is inevitably apprehended through the "I" and that the questions of "how the word 'I' can be put into the plural," how "a general idea of the *I* [can] be formed," or "how I can speak of an *I* other than my own" are basic to philosophical anthropology.[7] Echoing this view, Bernard Stiegler points out that individuation is a process whereby the self emerges in a context of other selves. Accordingly, the *"existential* dimension of *all* philosophy, without which philosophy would lose all *credit* and sink into scholastic chatter, must be analyzed through the question of the relation of the *I* and the *we*, in which consists this psychic and collective individuation."[8]

Merging these insights with Jean-Paul Sartre's notion of the singular universal and Hannah Arendt's paradox of plurality (all human beings are at once unique *and* members of a single species), I propose a tripartite conception of philosophical anthropology that includes our multiplex relationships with ourselves, with others, and with life itself.

Whether we think of these relationships sociologically (the dialectic of self and other), logically (the relation of part to whole), epistemologically (the interplay between microcosm and macrocosm, the human and the extrahuman, the local and the global), existentially (the connections among *eigenwelt*, *mitwelt*, and *umwelt*) or theologically (via the Upanishadic dictum *tat tvam asi*, "thou art that," or the Christian mystery of our relationship with God), we encounter them as perplexing and incommensurable. This may be because all these modalities of relationship are refractions of primary intersubjectivity, which, though informed by phylogenetically given behaviors that are common to many species, finds expression in human ontogeny as modes of reciprocal interaction that remain ambiguous, fraught, and only partially realized. As Helmuth Plessner argued, individual human beings and entire societies are continually bound up in an ebb and flow wherein they withdraw from others one moment only to open themselves up to them the next.[9] Accordingly, human existence involves a never-ending struggle, both intellectual and practical, to "take a stand," "find one's footing," or work out some kind of "positioning" that reconciles one's own perspective with the perspectives of others. We strive for an acceptable balance between being actors and being acted on, speaking and being spoken to, having and not having, giving and getting, and accepting things as they are even as we strive to improve our lot. Although thrown into a world we neither made nor chose, we inhabit it as a field of instrumental possibilities that are open rather than closed to us, affording us the means of making the world our own.

The question of positioning is also central to the relationship between philosophy and anthropology (or psychology) for, as Merleau-Ponty notes, "A science without philosophy would literally not know what it was talking about"; moreover, "A philosophy without methodical exploration of phenomena would end up with nothing but formal truths, which is to say, errors."[10]

Descending from Olympus

There is an escapist strain in human life that finds expression in fantasy and philosophy alike—a yearning to retreat from the vicissitudes of everyday existence, to have others tell us what to do rather than accept responsibility for our own lives, to conjure imaginary realms we may rule without distraction, to dream of utopian states, or to become lost in thought. For some, such otherworldly imaginings come to eclipse their sense of and interest in quotidian reality, like the gambler who plays not to win but to stay in a "zone where nothing else matters."[11] But what some individuals regard as impediments to peace of mind are, for others, grist to their mill, and minor epiphanies are found in the mundane that, like ripples on the still surface of a pond, fractally replicate the original ripple as they encompass ever-widening circles and finally touch on remote shores.[12] Following in the steps of Walter Benjamin, I take the road away from Plato by giving primacy to empirical particulars rather than eternal ideas, convinced, like Benjamin that "the eternal is more like lace trimmings on a dress than like an idea."[13]

While many philosophers have distanced themselves from worldly affairs in their quest for intellectual clarity, anthropologists have typically immersed themselves in the stream of everyday life, as if preferring immanence to transcendence. Though this preference has not prevented many anthropologists from claiming to know far more than they can possibly show, the promise of ethnography was that it would enable us to hear, see, and understand the world of others rather than oppress them with our own preformulated agendas and professional ambitions. This may account for the aporetic character of anthropology, which often appears to be in perpetual doubt as to whether it is a way of advancing one's academic career or committing oneself to some amelioration or deep understanding of the lives of those who make one's career possible in the first place.

Such uncertainty also reflects the oscillation in ethnographic practice between participation and observation and anthropology's dual fascination with thinking as it has been understood in the history of Western philosophy and thinking as it might be understood in the lives of ordinary people, whether at home or abroad.[14] Not surprisingly, this diversity of methods, points of view, and voices makes it impossible for any one person to claim the last word in the conversation of humankind and implies that our conception of truth is inescapably social, reflecting the contrary opinions and curious affinities that arise in all intersubjective encounters. Thought is never wholly intrapsychic, even when the thinker cuts himself from the world to think clearly. No one is immune to the historical and social conditions that shape one, which is why both anthropology and philosophy are relational and dialogical, despite the impression we sometimes have that great thinkers or theorists attain a transcendent position that is neither entirely solipsistic nor divinely inspired but has liberated them from the subjective singularities that, like gravity, bind us to this earth.

Although Immanuel Kant gestured toward a "philosophy in the cosmopolitan sense of the word,"[15] it was Kant's student and subsequent rival, Johann Gottfried Herder, who proposed that philosophy fully metamorphose into anthropology,[16] so initiating the line of descent through Alexander von Humboldt, Georg Wilhelm Friedrich Hegel, Wilhelm Dilthey, Gustav Klemm, and Edward Burnett Tylor that culminated in Alfred Kroeber's seminal 1917 essay, "The Superorganic," and laid the groundwork for modern American cultural anthropology.

That Herder's anthropology was conceived as a philosophy for the people (*Popularphilosophie*) rather than academic or metaphysical speculation (*Schulphilosophie*) reminds us that the tension between synthesizing or summarizing the bewildering variety of human experience and sustaining a sense of experience as something *more* than can be contained in concepts or consolidated in language has always vexed philosophers. It is for this reason, perhaps, that anthropologists have felt more kinship with such "edifying" thinkers as Theodor Adorno, Arendt, Gilles Deleuze, Jacques Derrida, John Dewey, Michel Foucault, Martin

Heidegger, William James, Merleau-Ponty, Sartre, and Ludwig Wittgenstein than with "systematic" philosophers searching "for universal commensuration in a final vocabulary." As Richard Rorty puts it, "The [whole] point of edifying philosophy is to keep the conversation going rather than to find objective truth."[17]

Such edifying thinkers are critical of philosophy's attempts to separate itself from common sense or its dismissal of experiences on which one can gain little intellectual purchase; several go as far as saying that philosophy in its traditional form has reached the end of its useful life. Thus, Arendt questions the view, "at least as old as Parmenides, that whatever is not given to the senses—God or Being or the First Principles and Causes (*archai*) or the Ideas—is more real, more truthful, more meaningful that what appears, that it is not just *beyond* sense perception but above the world of the senses."[18] For Alain Badiou, philosophy's malaise lies in its thralldom to its past, its fixation on its own genealogy.[19] In a slightly different vein, Adorno argues that "philosophy is no longer applicable for mastering one's life. At the same time, by abstaining from all definite content, whether as a formal logic and theory of science or as the legend of Being beyond all beings, philosophy declared its bankruptcy regarding concrete social goals."[20] More recently, Jonathan Lear has taken to task the professions of philosophy and psychoanalysis (he might well have included anthropology in his critique) for their tendency to deploy thought as a defense against an openness to life. To resist professionalization, Lear argues, we must return to the fundamental question posed by Socrates: in what way should one live?

It is my conviction that anthropology can play a meaningful role in realizing this Socratic idea and "bring some life into the [disciplines] which lie at the heart of our humanity."[21] Not only does ethnographic research enable us to *fully* realize Kant's cosmopolitan ideal by encompassing *all* world societies, past and present; it also helps us see that thinking is not the sole property of European philosophers but an inalienable aspect of every human being's psychic life and everyday existence. In this sense, it is hard to see much merit in Heidegger's comment that the analysis of *Dasein* among "primitive peoples" may be facilitated by the "often less concealed and less complicated" character of "primitive phenomena," though ethnology must wait for "the ontological labours of philosophy to be done" before this research can make a start.[22]

I cannot embrace any project to unconceal the nature of being without reckoning with the fact that so many human beings are, philosophically, left out of sight and out of mind, rendered invisible, as Ralph Ellison put it, by the objectifying, pathologizing, and othering language we use of them.[23] Moreover, how can the question of being be raised without immediate reference to the particular being who finds this question so imperative? What kind of upbringing, background, or life situation might account for a person prioritizing such a question over, say, the questions of everyday life—struggling to make ends meet, caring for a child, enduring loss, or coping with racism? Not only can we not separate the question of being from actual beings, but all beings must, as a matter of principle, be placed on a par, and no Supreme Being be evoked, either divine or human, to lend authority to any one ontology. As Donna Haraway argues, philosophy must seriously reckon not only with the human condition but also with the myriad other-than-human life-forms whose existence is deeply implicated in our own.[24] Is a lion protecting an antelope calf from another marauding lion any less thoughtful than the actions of the Good Samaritan, and is Hegel's *Phenomenology of Mind* any more "thoughtful" than the music of Johann Sebastian Bach or Thelonious Monk, the Kuranko stories of Keti Ferenke Koroma, or Francisco de Goya's painting *The Colossus*? All involve mastery of a medium. All engage both body and mind. All emerge from and speak to a specific moment in history, a specific place, a specific question. Why do we insist in singling out one medium and thinking of it as "thinking" when all are equally viable ways of addressing our human need to comprehend ourselves through things seemingly beyond ourselves, whether those media are objects, words, images, ideas, other people, or our own bodies and senses? Most problematic, however, is the weighting we have tended to give verbal-cognitive thought and our neglect of the kinds of visual-spatial thinking that are, after all, critical to *social* nous and *social* adroitness (reading nonverbal cues, divining intentions, judging the moods and need of others). Have academics focused on one mode of thinking because social engagement and sensitivity is secondary in their own lives? To what extent have we disparaged so-called primitive thought because its emphasis on social skillfulness and practical experience are forms of virtuosity that our tradition has come to devalue?

Purely philosophical conceptions of anthropology, from Plato to Heidegger, have been informed by a desire to bring truth out of the darkness and into the light. The Renaissance image of holding up a mirror to nature and capturing "our glassy essence" (or "intellectual soul") reflects Plato's conviction that the objects and figures that enter our fields of vision are mere shadows, mimicking an ideal form or abstract idea that is never immediately apparent to us. Many things are red, but the idea of redness holds true for all and is thus the greater reality. In Plato's well-known allegory of the cave, light and shadow serve as metaphors for this difference between reality and mere appearance. A group of chained prisoners have, from the day they were born, known only the shadowy shapes of animals and objects thrown by firelight on the cavern walls. Unable to go out into the daylight or see the fire that is burning in the depths of the cave or encounter the creatures they hear moving about in the darkness, the prisoners assume the shadows to be real and give them names, ponder their attributes, and debate their worth. However, if the prisoners were free and saw the fire or went out of the cave into the light of day, they would, after a period of adjustment, reach a very different understanding of the world. They would see "that it is the sun that produces the seasons and the course of the year and controls everything in the visible world, and moreover is in a way the cause of all that [they] used to see."[25]

From Plato's idealistic standpoint, art and poetry do not get us beyond appearances. "A stick will look bent if you put it in the water, straight when you take it out, and deceptive differences of shading can make the same surface seem to the eye concave or convex; and our minds are clearly liable to all sorts of confusions of this kind."[26] But, says Plato, reason and calculation can save us from mistakenly supposing that such magical effects are real and enable us to render the world truly intelligible.

What Plato overlooks is that *both* art and reason have a place in our lives. Sometimes we draw insights from the shadows; sometimes we need the blinding light of day to see things clearly. Sometimes illusions help us get through hard times; sometimes they are obstacles to lucid understanding. Sometimes objects appear to possess a life of their own; sometimes they seem alien and antagonistic.

Rather than define magical and scientific worldviews in terms of their intrinsic differences, I find it more edifying to explore the conditions under which these different perspectives arise. Consider the thought that finds expression in the figures depicted in Magdalenian caves. Rather than decide whether the animals on the walls are real or illusory, let us ask what compelled people to periodically retreat from the outside world into spaces that sunlight could not penetrate and then, among shadows cast by handheld torches, reanimate in painted images the creatures they hunted in the icebound forests and whose bones and skulls the hunter-painters would also bring into their subterranean sanctuary. If the origins of art and shamanism can be traced back to the Magdalenian cave paintings of late–Ice Age Europe, so too can the origins of philosophy. These are all means by which we create external images of worlds within or internal mirrors of the world without.

If philosophy is a process of illumination, a way of artificially bringing to life presences that have been repressed, forgotten, or otherwise lost, then there is a connection not only between contemporary and Stone Age artists but also between art and philosophy, whose longstanding preoccupation has been to hold up a mirror to nature, and so capture "our glassy essence," albeit in words rather than paint.[27]

My own preference, however, is for those thinkers whose work has explored the penumbral regions *between* illumination and shadow.[28] "Light," Mark C. Taylor writes, observing how the dawn light touches a mountaintop before descending gradually into a valley of shadow, "is never merely light, for illumination creates a residual obscurity more impenetrable than the darkness it displaces but does not eliminate."[29] In this vein, Wittgenstein's claim that while philosophy has nothing to *say* it nevertheless has something to *clarify*, Adorno's reminder that concepts never do justice to the experiences they purport to cover, James's focus on transitive and transitional phenomena, Derrida's insistence that philosophy is always engaged with the nonphilosophical, and Karl Jaspers's notion of limit situations continue to summon us to the task of making philosophy answerable to experience rather than some extra-empirical standard. This is Hannah Arendt's rationale for focusing on the *vita activa* rather than the *vita contemplativa*. "The active way of life is 'laborious,'" she writes, while "the contemplative way is sheer quietness; the active one goes on in public, the contemplative one in the 'desert'; the active one is devoted to 'the necessity of one's neighbor,' the contemplative one to the 'vision of God.'"[30]

Such a conception of philosophical anthropology implies that the pursuit of enlightenment has often entailed not simply retreating from the world but losing touch with life. This is not an argument for a vulgar utilitarianism, in which the good of philosophy is measured according to the suffering it alleviates or the social justice it secures. Rather, it is an argument, first, for treating thought as an emergent property of *relationships* rather than as a singular property of individual minds and, second, for treating thought as a mode of critique, as understood by Karl Marx and by the Frankfurt School that built on his work.

This critique questions the *epistemological* assumption that truth is only accessible to a clear-sighted few; it refuses to accept the *social* entailment of this assumption—that ordinary human beings are blind to the truth of their own condition. By implying that rationality is a distinctly European possession, the inequalities of power and wealth that have historically divided the West from the Rest are given spurious legitimacy, and those who live beyond the European pale are likened to the benighted souls in Plato's cave who mistake the shadows cast by a fire they cannot see for reality.

Though compelling philosophical arguments have been made against this traditional model of philosophy—that the mirrors we hold up to nature are distorting mirrors; that our personal or historical position always determines our pictures of reality; that thought, by its very nature, cannot capture the complex and fluid character of existence—the ethnographic case against philosophy is that it is incorrigibly Eurocentric, deploying pejorative distinctions that make reason superior to superstition, science superior to religion, history superior to myth, and literacy superior to illiteracy. Though these terms betray the complexity of empirical reality, they tend to be retained as a discursive currency because they serve the interests of power elites. As James Scott remarks in his critique of high modernism, we have to learn to stop "seeing like a state."[31] In a similar vein, Michael Herzfeld shows that there is an unsettling connection between the exalted place of theory in social science and statist discourse in political life. The distinction between *anthropos* and *ethnos* (interpretive generalizing and ethnographic particularizing) in anthropology both mimics and reinforces the unequal power relations between centralized states and marginalized peoples (the first associated with civilized virtues, the second with folkloric customs).[32]

These invidious separations pervaded classical Greek thought and social organization alike. The distinction "between vegetative, animal and rational souls was, when applied to men, a formulation and justification of class divisions. . . . Slaves and mechanical artisans living on the nutritional, appetitive level were for practical purposes symbolized by the body—an obstruction to ideal ends and as solicitations to acts contrary to reason. . . . Scientific inquirers and philosophers alone exemplified pure reason . . . *nous*, pure immaterial mind."[33]

One might ask if anything has really changed over the last two thousand years and whether philosophy and ethnography might now join forces in effecting a radical break from discursive conventions that effectively divide humanity into superior and inferior realms. This is not merely an academic matter of questioning the idealism of Plato or Kant or deciding which philosophers are on the side the angels and which have gone over to the dark side; it is a matter of shifting our focus from logos to life and of anchoring philosophical debates in the immediate and pressing issues of everyday existence.

In making this move, it is no longer possible to sustain the distinction Iris Murdoch makes between philosophy, which "involves a disciplined removal of the personal voice" (Plato "is our best philosopher"), and literature, defined as "a disciplined technique for arousing certain emotions."[34] Analogous notions of rationality and irrationality, or science and religion, must also be set aside. Neither academic philosophers nor the so-called common man are given special privileges. By ridding ourselves of the view that certain people, by virtue of their genius for enlightened thought, have the wisdom and the right to govern those who are allegedly at the mercy of ungovernable emotions and appetites (and good for nothing but menial or mechanical roles in the service of ruling elites), discourse becomes democratic, and we can no longer assume that certain classes of people—peasants, primitives, laborers, women— are intrinsically less capable than philosophers in possessing wisdom or knowing how to live.

This is not simply a caution against the hubris of what Bourdieu calls scholastic reason—the "bedazzled identification with great heroic roles" that makes us readily fall prey to what Arthur Schopenhauer called "pedantic comedy"—"the absurd pretension of believing that there is no limit to thought, of seeing an academic commentary as a political act or the critique of texts as a feat of resistance, and experience revolutions in the order of words as radical revolutions in the order of things."[35] The case is against academic aloofness, to be sure, but also against the claims of intellectual and political elites that they best know how to speak on behalf of the oppressed or decide what the masses need for their well-being. Consider, for example, Diana Allan's compelling ethnography of Shatila Camp in Beirut. In this Palestinian "refugee" lifeworld, the exigencies of everyday life and local loyalties take precedence over the rhetorical abstractions that pervade the mediatized metanarratives of the PLO and, by extension, Middle Eastern politics. Allan shows that people's quotidian struggles to find work, keep healthy, educate their children, and maintain a household make talk of a traumatic past or utopian visions of return a luxury they can ill afford. Rather than focus on *resistance*, her attention is engaged by people's everyday *existence*.[36] Rather than buying into a *dominant* discourse, Allan bears witness to the *demotic*. Lotte Buch Segal's sensitive exploration of the conflicted emotions of Palestinian women whose husbands are long-term detainees in Israeli jails leads her to a similar conclusion: while faithful both to the "martyrs" and to Palestinian narratives of national becoming, these women's everyday reality is "keeping the household and the family together despite frequent destitution," and "being exemplary" is often experienced as a "burden" one cannot easily bear.[37]

This is not to say that any one discursive perspective is intrinsically right or wrong, only that every perspective reflects specific situations and interests. A corollary of this view is that if thought does not transcend the situation of the thinker, whether this is defined in terms of personality, gender, culture, ethnicity, or class, then thinking might be best understood as techne rather than episteme. Thinking may appear to make the world more intelligible, but the ends of thinking must include questions of what makes life livable, not simply meaningful. By defining thought as a means of *working* on the world rather than a means of acquiring symbolic capital, the worth of philosophy is measured by the degree to which it militates against social inequality, increases human conviviality, and enhances well-being. This is why Veena Das finds Pierre Hadot's notion of philosophy as a kind of spiritual exercise "scandalous," for in the lifeworld of which she writes, thought is not a matter of "scaling heights" or about "the profundity of philosophy." Rather, it is all about the "small disciplines that ordinary people perform in their everyday life to hold life together as the natural expression of ethics."[38] As such, these "disciplines" can be placed on a par with storytelling, ritualization, experimentation, and dialogue as forms of art and science—ways of transforming one's immediate experience in order to make life more bearable and fulfilling, a way of creating models or homologues of reality that allow one to momentarily disengage from everyday situations the better to reengage with them, a way of making the world one's own.

In bringing thought down to earth, John Dewey noted that "thinking is not a case of spontaneous combustion"; it does not occur just on "general principles." There is something specific that occasions and evokes it, namely "some perplexity, confusion, or doubt."[39] In this pragmatist understanding, truth happens to an idea. Rather than evaluate an idea in terms of some prior state or hidden motive, or assign it some abiding value, we explore its practical effects and repercussions when it is brought to bear on a life situation, noting how it may be subject to doubt or revision or cast aside in favor of another idea as people endeavor through trial and error to work out a modus vivendi with one another and with their changing situations.

For this grounded and engaged conception of philosophical anthropology to be realized, we need a method that continually refers thought back to the everyday situations in which it originates, to which it speaks, and from which it can never entirely escape. This was the call of Michel de Montaigne, who cautioned that a philosophizing that presumes a view from afar risks estranging us from the experiences to which it is attempting to do justice. After observing that "study and contemplation draw our souls somewhat outside ourselves . . . a state which both resembles death and which forms a kind of apprenticeship for it," Montaigne goes on to say that "the labor of reason must be to make us live well"— to create pleasure rather than pain.[40] Accordingly, one might argue that the question of the relationship between anthropology and philosophy must be couched in such a way as to encompass the less obvious question as to how these academic disciplines may be made more experience-near and less experience-distant—edifying and enjoyable rather than dull and deadening. In other words, the question of writing ethnography comes to the fore—the question of how we can do anthropology or philosophy in ways that enable us to see ourselves and the world from new vantage points, transforming our understanding without promulgating yet another paradigm.

The power of ethnography lies in its insistence that understanding cannot be reached through distancing oneself from the world but by engaging with it. Concepts or analytical categories that have emerged from the experience of others at other times are set aside or invoked depending on how well they enable us to grapple with the situation at hand. In this process the ethnographer is sorely tested not only because the security blanket of preconceived ideas must sometimes be cast aside but also because the value of any knowledge wrought from his or her engagement with others is decided by whether it does justice to what was *socially* at stake for those people at a particular time and in a particular place, not by whether it corresponds to some so-called objective reality or achieves coherence according to a set of prescribed discursive rules. John Dewey makes this point well. In spelling out this "test of the value of any philosophy," he asks: "Does it end in conclusions which, when they are referred back to ordinary life-experiences and their predicaments, render them more significant, more luminous to us, and make our dealings with them more fruitful? Or does it terminate in rendering the things of ordinary experience more opaque than they were before, and in depriving them of having in 'reality' even the significance they had previously seemed to have."[41]

Recesses of the Ordinary

If, as Veena Das argues, we must learn to understand violence as an irruption neither from within the depths of the psyche nor from some foreign quarter but as inherent in everyday life, then might not the same be said of thought? This "descent into the ordinary," which Das treats as an ethical guide for anthropological research, draws us away from abstract philosophical pronouncements on how things ought to be, or how a phenomenon might be systematically explained, and demands a direct engagement with life as it unfolds as a series of *critical events*.[42]

Although Kant's categorical imperative states that we should never act in such a way that we treat humanity, whether in ourselves or in others, as a means only but always as an end, the fact is that we often treat the other as a means or argue that the end justifies the means—torturing a prisoner in order to extract information that will allegedly protect our nation's borders, exploiting or abusing a migrant because his illegal status excludes him from our moral code, lampooning the Prophet because a gang of criminals killed three thousand of our citizens in his name. Morality always involves a *relationship* between agent and patient, actor and sufferer, as well as between espoused ideals and lived situations. Rather than lay down moral laws for how people ought to think and behave, we must describe the *existential* imperatives at play in any social context.[43] In a 1957 letter to Karl Jaspers, Hannah Arendt wrote that Kant's "vast experience of the world is equaled only by his completely impoverished experience of life," and though he had great powers of the imagination, these powers "left him in the lurch as far as life is concerned."[44]

The argument here is not against philosophy's retreat from life per se but against the dangers inherent in any view of the world that is not continually tested against its gritty and gruesome realities. Obviously, there will be times when our capacity for seeing the other as ourselves in other circumstances is severely challenged, and our anxieties will bring the focus of our attention entirely onto ourselves. It is then that we throw up defensive barriers against radical others (terrorists, infidels, criminals, illegals) and withhold our definition of the human from them.[45] Reciprocally, the other sometimes treats us as a means—of taking revenge for some humiliation he or his people have suffered at the hands of our government or making one of us the scapegoat for what others of our color, class, or gender have done to him.

Emmanuel Levinas's ethics of the face is no less problematic than Kant's categorical imperative. As Joshua Greene puts it, "It's a lovely sentiment . . . but the moral laws within us are a mixed blessing."[46] For myself, I have absolutely no quarrel with Levinas's claim that "a first philosophy" is neither "traditional logic nor metaphysics, but an interpretive, phenomenological description of the rise and repetition of the face-to-face encounter, or the intersubjective relation at its precognitive core; viz., being called by another and responding to that other."[47] Indeed, as I write, I recall a vivid description by an American doctor, Kwan Kew Lai, of her first shift in a Liberian Ebola treatment center in October 2014. Having donned with difficulty her protective suit and goggles (PPE), she attended to a patient in triage called John:

> Either he was too weak to get up to walk or he was absolutely petrified at the sight of us in our full PPE. With the dark ominous rain clouds hanging very low in the sky, harbinger of a severe rainstorm; we must look like hovering specters or apparitions. We helped him into the ward, pants soiled with loose stool, changed and cleaned him. He was breathing fast and looked dehydrated, a definite glint of fear in his eyes. We gave him a bottle of oral rehydration solution and the night shift would start an IV. What was it like to be cared for by us all dressed up in hazmat suits when the comfort of human touch was gone? As we departed, the rain came pelting loudly down on the tinned roof offering little solace to this lonely man covered by a white sheet sick as he was, left in a strange blue-tarped Spartan room lit by a squiggly energy-saving bulb. Deep in my heart I feared the worst for him. Death lurked around the corner. The fear in his eyes foretold his fate.

> [The next morning], I stuck around, rubbed his back and squeezed his shoulders to convey the message that he was not alone. I had felt the need for human touch and kindness when I was sick. I could not imagine the profound loneliness and tremendous fear this man had to face by himself—to fight for his life without any of his family members by his side, in a totally alien place. I wished we had morphine or IV valium to ease his feeling of hunger and anxiety. But there are no such medications here currently.
>
> In the afternoon, we learned that John passed away. His Ebola sample still sat in the fridge, missed by the morning delivery. He was 42 years old.[48]

Despite being deeply moved by this doctor's responsiveness to her patient, her description highlights our everyday recourse to masks as ways of defending or hiding ourselves from one another. Even philosophy can serve as a defense against the refractoriness and stressfulness of life. There are, moreover, always limits to anyone's capacity for responding to the needs of strangers. These limits are not just logistical or conceptual; they are political and existential. Consider Aristotle's ethic of friendship (*philia*), for example. Though acknowledging that friendship between unequals (rulers and subjects) is different from friendship between equals, Aristotle does not help us solve the problem of so-called corrupt regimes, for while he claims that they are corrupt because no friendship exists in them, we tend to criticize such regimes precisely because they *are* based on friendship or kinship (i.e., nepotism).[49] The problem is only complicated, as Arendt points out, by the impossibility of making *philia* the basis for organizing relationships within a modern nation-state. "Because of its inherent worldlessness, love can only become false and perverted when it is used for political purposes such as the change or salvation of the world."[50]

These allusions to masking or feigning affective virtue bring us to consider psychological studies of primary intersubjectivity (Aristotle's parental "friendship") in which love and hate are always copresent potentialities. As with gestalt figure-ground illusions, our perceptions of the other (particularly the mother) are, from early infancy, inherently unstable. The mother/other may be responsive one moment, only to appear inexplicably unresponsive the next. Intersubjective relationships typically oscillate between presence and absence, engagement and disengagement, responsiveness and unresponsiveness. Accordingly, ambivalence and uncertainty would seem to be the primary ethical condition under which copresence is experienced. A similar critique may be made of Edmund Husserl's notion of intentionality. Often, consciousness is aimless or vague, or a person is of two minds about what he or she wants or feels toward another.[51] As such, Merleau-Ponty's definition of consciousness as an "I can" is always in tension with a sense of "I cannot." Indeed, every face-to-face encounter, whether with another human being, an animal, or a machine, is so precarious that it is almost impossible to sustain the illusion that our intersubjective negotiations, conversations, and interactions are governed by any a priori moral imperative or mind-set; rather, our lives unfold as a series of essays at understanding in which we deploy rough and ready guidelines based on previous experience to the same extent that we take cognizance of new information in working out a modus vivendi with others or with otherness. This is the gist of Jane Bennett's argument against reducing ethics to "a code to which one is obligated, a set of criteria to which one assents or subscribes," and for exploring the ways that ethics is "responsive to the surprises that regularly punctuate life."[52] It is in such "minor experiences" and spontaneous actions, which Knud Løgstrup calls "sovereign expressions of life," that our humanity is realized.[53]

By implication, our humanity is often compromised by moral codifications, religious dogmas, and the generalizations and abstractions of social science and redeemed by a return to the particular. Freedom from the autarky of concepts does not simply consist in realizing that concepts are the end product of reification; it means *remembering* the nonconceptual soil from which concepts spring in the first place.[54] Inasmuch as that soil may be said to be our common humanity, the task of philosophical anthropology is to *re-cognize* that oneself and the other are of a kind—humankind—regardless of any specific morality, law, or concept of human rights. This challenge implies an ethics before ethics whose quintessential expression is love—one's capacity to set one's ego aside in order to enter into the situation of someone else, to see the world from his or her standpoint. There is an uncanny parallel here between Løgstrup's notion of the "sovereign expressions of life" and Husserl's notion of the phenomenological standpoint. If the "natural standpoint" implies a world of facticity and presence "in which I find myself and which is also my world-about-me," the "phenomenological standpoint" implies a world of pure consciousness in which my presuppositions about fact and fiction, or truth and falsity, are bracketed out.[55] But rather than emphasize "pure consciousness," I find it more interesting to explore how the epoche entails a movement toward the consciousness of the other—a suspension not only of one's taken-for-granted *ideas* about the world *but of one's own sense of self*. The epoche thus implicates what we call empathy. Husserl's intentional "consciousness of something" becomes "consciousness of another,"[56] though this "other" is *a suppressed dimension of one's own many-sided self*, occluded or held *in potentia*, as one inevitably inhabits a social milieu that privileges one mode of being at the expense of all other possible modes of being.

Anthropology is, in this sense, unavoidably phenomenological. It assumes the possibility of going beyond oneself and entering into the lifeworlds of others. Where anthropologists differ is in their understandings of whether this project is one of knowing the other, experiencing the world as the other experiences it, achieving a modus vivendi with the other, or achieving a quasi-transcendent position that enables one to penetrate the hidden forces that explain the other's behavior, motivations, values, and consciousness. Whatever the emphasis, however, anthropology remains, for the most part, a body of theories and methods for having something interesting to say about worlds that lie outside the worlds of privilege and power to which most anthropologists and philosophers belong.[57] For this reason, anthropologists struggle to suspend their own worldviews and enter into the lifeworlds of others; they also struggle with the gap between haves and have-nots, either by seeking to use their knowledge to ameliorate the conditions under which the other lives or by bearing witness, in their writings, to the humanity of the other. Unfortunately, an anthropology that is focused on the practical ingenuity and social vitality that may be found in even the most poverty-stricken societies is sometimes criticized for deflecting attention from the work that must be done to improve living conditions in these societies. One riposte is to criticize the anthropological focus on global processes and political economies that construe the poor as victims of social violence, wholly lacking the wherewithal to live, thus reinforcing, albeit inadvertently, the implicit tendency in modern societies to write off the lives of billions of human beings as insignificant, even undeserving of life.

A balance may be struck, however, between these extremes of testimony and indignation. In his ethnography of "Vita," a "zone of social abandonment" in southern Brazil—where the mentally ill, the sick, the homeless, and the unemployed are left by relatives, neighbors, hospitals, and the police—João Biehl steers a course between a critique of the society that condemns so many of its citizens to social death and the ethical struggle of the *abandonados* to "hold onto the real," to "articulate their experience," and to "transmit [their] sense of the world and of [themselves]."[58] Similarly, in her study of a slum known as Annawadi near Mumbai airport, Katherine Boo underscores the need to alleviate poverty while testifying to the life that nonetheless finds expression in this place where, for all the evidence of hopelessness, hope springs eternal—often in minor things. Slum dwellers would speak "of better lives casually, as if fortune were a cousin arriving on Sunday, as if the future would look nothing like the past," and Boo was struck "by the ethical imaginations of young people, even those in circumstances so desperate that selfishness would be an asset. . . . It is easy, from a safe distance, to overlook the fact that in under-cities governed by corruption, where exhausted people vie on scant terrain for very little, it is blisteringly hard to be good. The astonishment is that some people are good, and that many people try to be."[59]

In the Buddhist view, we cannot avoid pain, but suffering is another matter since suffering arises from our desire to avoid pain. It is not death that causes us the greatest anxiety but our fear of the pain of dying. As Shalom Auslander puts it, "It isn't the fire that kills you, it's the smoke."[60] The insight is crucial. It echoes Husserl's distinction between the natural and phenomenological standpoints and suggests that human beings have a hard time distinguishing between the emotions and moods of the moment and the stories they have learned to tell themselves about their histories and their lives. It is not easy to dump the conceptual baggage we carry and subtract our conception of pain from the pain itself. Yet in poor and affluent societies alike, people struggle to define what can and cannot be changed, accepting that life is always lived within limits, defined by our mortality, our vulnerability to illness and loss, the vicissitudes of human relationships, and the struggle for fulfillment in work or recognition from peers.

At any given moment, our understanding of the other must be provisional, and this should, arguably, also be the case with our academic understandings of the ways that others understand one another. Rather than name or claim to know the other or create a static description that classifies or identifies a person, our ethical mandate is to hold the tension and accept the contradictions between alternating states of consciousness or modes of action, refusing to allow our anxieties over not comprehending or controlling the world to lead us into making generalizations that effectively bring the world to an end, much as psychological or biological experiments on laboratory animals often lead to their deaths.

In repudiating philosophy's search for a transcendent grounding outside the chaos and confusion of our worldly existence and invoking ethnography as a method for involving us more deeply in the existential situations that condition the way we think, our emphasis effectively passes from a concern with legal codifications and moral ideals to a paranomic realm of ethical negotiation in which ideals are subverted, rules are bent, laws are broken, and ex post facto rationalizations have greater force than rational choice. By beginning and ending our essays in understanding in medias res, in the shifting sands of human relationships, we move away from abstract categories, whether of the person, the nation, or the tribe; we regard bounded entities—genders, classes, cultures, ethnicities, individuals, groups—as figments of the academic imagination rather than intrinsically real and reject systematicity as our intellectual goal and dialectic reason as our methodology. Relationship becomes key—relations that hold in tension both antagonistic and empathic potentialities, in which subjects become objects and vice versa as the dynamics of interaction change, and in which consciousness is never fixed in a single steady state but is always oscillating between a sense of identity and difference, patiency and agency, constancy and inconstancy, transcendence and immanence, free will and determinism, belief and experience, person and type, life and concept, being and nothingness.

Between Poles

Although each chapter in this book evokes a binary, I resist ontologizing the terms, and seek, rather, to explore the modes of experience they signify, and the space between them, where they are, by turns, given definition and dissolved. My focus is, therefore, on the transitive, the contingent, the fugitive, the fragmentary, and the fleeting rather than substantives as such. I am fascinated by what Adorno calls "constellations," in which unflagging oscillations, lines of tension, temporary alignments, and indeterminate positions render questions of constancy and order absurd.[61] Unlike Claude Lévi-Strauss, who demonstrated how binaries are mediated, I share Adorno's view that resolution, synthesis, and mediation may be perfectly possible in the myths and models of reality that artists and intellectuals so brilliantly and diligently create, but lived reality rarely admits of this as a permanent possibility. This is a recurring leitmotif in the chapters that constitute this book, and it is first broached in chapter 2. In preparing the ground for this perspective, however, chapter 1 addresses the ubiquity and scope of analogical reasoning, calling into question the ways we conventionally distinguish between modern and premodern thought and, by extension, distinguish between philosophy and common sense.

Chapter 2 considers the seemingly incompatible perspectives of philosophy and ethnography. While philosophy has traditionally presumed to make universal claims about the human condition, modern sociocultural anthropology has, for the most part, avoided such claims, preferring a vision of human diversity, ethnic distinctiveness, and moral relativism. The challenge for reinventing philosophical anthropology is working out how we can accommodate both these orientations, recognizing difference and sameness, dissonance and consonance. I evoke Arnold Schoenberg's atonal music, Adorno's negative dialectics, and John Keats's negative capability in taking up the question of how it is possible to do justice to *both* our empirical knowledge of the linguistic, cultural, and individual *diversity* of humankind *and* our quest to identify modes of thought, action, and being that are *common* to all humanity and, in many cases, are shared with other life-forms.

Chapter 3 explores the recurring problem in both philosophy and anthropology of doing justice to what William James called the "unsharable feeling which each of us has of the pinch of his individual destiny as he privately feels it rolling out on fortune's wheel." Is it possible to bracket out such a priori, abstract, and transpersonal terms as "the social," "the cultural," or "the customary" and avoid what A. N. Whitehead called the fallacy of misplaced concreteness—treating such analytical constructs as though they were lived realities and, as a corollary, treating lived realities as though they were a veil camouflaging unconscious forces that required scientific expertise or intellectual genius to uncover and arcane coinages to describe?

Chapter 4 further explores the indeterminate relationship between being and thought. Can thought ever transcend the limits of a thinker's particular situation, let alone comprehend the lifeworlds of animals or the nature of the material universe? Is an abstract language possible, or is all language grounded in bodily, material, and social imagery and experience? Theodor Adorno speaks of the illusion "that the concept can transcend the concept" and "thus reach the nonconceptual." This remains "one of philosophy's inalienable features and part of the naïveté that ails it."[62] Arguably, however, this naïveté is also a necessity, for what human being could live without the illusion that thought or language, number or knowledge, can enable him or her to encompass, demystify, and even master the world?

My focus in chapter 5 is on human-animal relationships, specifically the ways in which the life of one passes into the other and one makes the other thinkable. After elucidating how this interchange of being is understood in various societies, I propose an existential theory of ritual that explores the proposition that many myths and rites are informed by an urge to redistribute *life itself*, which always tends to be perceived as unequally distributed. Life-forms are constantly moving, both physically and imaginatively, from where life is scarce to where it is more bountiful, and these life-forms are also in constant competition with one another for the scarcest of all goods, life itself. These actual or virtual redistributions of life are typically justified by moral dogmas that determine which life-forms are more deserving of life (including eternal life) and which have less urgent claims on the right to live. For if life is to be taken from one person, creature, or place and incorporated into another, then some kind of moral rationale will be needed to justify why one being's right to life is greater than another's.

This theme is taken further in chapter 6, which explores the conditions under which certain beliefs and behaviors seem so incommensurable and inexplicable that we are led to conclude that those who hold these beliefs or exhibit these behaviors are alien to us, even scarcely human. While philosophers have occasionally wrestled with the question as to whether beliefs and practices are intrinsically rational or magical, moral or immoral, ethnographers have sought to explicate the social and practical *functions* of worldviews. But is it possible to go beyond relativism and claim that there are epistemological, logical, psychological, or ethical criteria that hold true in all human societies and at every period of human history?

Chapter 7 considers the relationship of persons and types in both philosophical and anthropological discourse. My starting point is F. Scott Fitzgerald's observation in his story "The Rich Boy" that "there are no types, no plurals," only individuals, and his warning against the literary tendency to begin with individuals only to create types, for types offer us "nothing." Although Fitzgerald has in mind the stereotypes with which the poor depict the rich and the illusions the rich have about themselves, his comments apply equally to the glib contrasts we draw between men and women, good and evil, old and young, and modern and premodern. Not only do we tend to believe that these category distinctions reflect empirical reality, but we become convinced that one category is superior to the other and that we who deploy these antinomies with greatest aplomb are more rational and clear-sighted than those who occupy the inferior positions in our equations.

Chapter 8 is a critique of the notion of agency. Rather than make a philosophical case for either agency or patiency, I consider two modes of thinking. The first emphasizes an active, disciplined, focused application of thought to being; the second stresses a more passive, attentive, open-minded approach in which the thinker simply registers or channels thoughts that appear to come from elsewhere. In critiquing any kind of ontologizing of cultural representations of self and other and sweeping generalizations concerning intrinsic cognitive or epistemological differences between primitive irrationality and modern rationality, "them" and "us," I focus not on fixed mind-sets or mentalities but on the existential conditions under which thinking is experienced either as a process that is undertaken consciously and intentionally or as a process that simply happens to people without their choosing.

Chapter 9 explores the theme of fatality and freedom as a fact of experience—as something to be lived through rather than simply thought through. My existential bias implies that the compatibilist resolution of the so-called free-will problem in philosophy perpetuates the view that this problem is a logical one that can be resolved by some kind of intellectual legerdemain when in fact it must be treated as a recurring and often unresolvable existential issue.

The leitmotif of chapter 10 is alienation. Though Marx broached this subject in his critique of the capitalist mode of production—which alienates the worker from the fruits of his labor and undermines his capacity to determine his own destiny—and French existentialism made fashionable cognate ideas of aloneness and estrangement in mass society, my focus is the imperfect fit between our lived experience and the ways we conceptualize, narrate, and represent it. Building on Adorno's negative dialectics, Derrida's method of deconstruction, and James's radical empiricism, I explore this aporia between words and worlds, *nomos* and nature, through the vernacular medium of Kuranko storytelling. Storytelling, I argue, may be conceptualized as an alternative sovereignty, a negotiated form of ethical and social life that lies at the margins of the state—a space outside of domestication.

My concluding chapter returns to the theme with which this book begins—the oscillation between intimacy and estrangement, participation and observation, immanence and transcendence, and the contrary roles that anthropology and philosophy have traditionally played in academic discourse. Life involves a perpetual oscillation between engaging with the world and seeking distance, respite, or release from it. What we call philosophy is only one of many adaptive strategies that human beings have devised for working out a modus vivendi with other human beings and with the extrahuman world that envelops them. As such, ideas emerge, spread, metamorphose, mutate, and die out in the same way that other traits do, and all are as potentially vital to our continuing existence as the tools we use, the genes we carry, the families we create, the homes we build, the clothes we wear, the land we farm, and the minerals we mine.

1. Analogy and Polarity

It may be that universal history is the history of the different intonations
given a handful of metaphors.

—JORGE LUIS BORGES, "THE FEARFUL SPHERE OF PASCAL"

If there is any mode of thought common to all people, in all societies, at all periods of history, it is analogy.[1] The ubiquity of analogical reasoning makes it a useful point of departure for critiquing what are often alleged to be radical differences between modern and premodern thought and for calling into question the binaries of abstraction and concreteness, rationality and irrationality, on the basis of which these distinctions have typically been drawn. As George Eliot puts it, "we all of us, grave or light, get our thoughts entangled in metaphors, and act fatally on the strength of them."[2] It is in this vein that I argue, in this chapter and throughout this book, that human differences are best regarded as circumstantial, not essential; matters of ideology and interest, not of ontology.

The Order of Things

Even though this chapter is a critique of the kind of intellectualist, discourse-based approach to the history of ideas that Michel Foucault's work so brilliantly exemplifies, his *Les mots et les choses* offers an entrée into how we might understand analogical reason without invoking the kinds of historical or cultural continuities on which his gaze was focused.

Up until the early seventeenth century, knowledge was principally a matter of discovering similitudes in the order of things. As Foucault explains, "To search for a meaning [was] to bring to light a resemblance.[3]

To search for the law governing signs [was] to discover the things that are alike. . . . The nature of things, their coexistence, the way in which they are linked together and communicate [was] nothing other than their resemblance."[4] Within this tangled "semantic web" of resemblances that constituted knowledge in Western culture, Foucault identifies four main forms of similitude. First, *convenientia*, in which things are supposed to be alike because they occur together or occupy the same space. Here are two examples, the first from Giambattista della Porta's *Magie naturelle* (1650), the second from my Kuranko ethnography:

> As with respect to its vegetation the plant stands convenient to the brute beast, so through feeling does the brutish animal to man, who is conformable to the rest of the stars by his intelligence; these links proceed so strictly that they appear *as a rope stretched from the first cause as far as the lowest and smallest of things*, by a reciprocal and continuous connection; in such wise that the superior virtue, spreading its beams, reaches so far that *if we touch one extremity of that cord it will make it tremble and move all the rest.*[5]

> The interdependence of members of the community is compared to the network of ropes that are tied over a rice farm when the crop is nearing maturity. One end of the rope is always tied to the foot of the bird-scaring platform where children sit with slingshots to keep birds from scavenging the rice. When this main rope is tugged, all of the tributary ropes shake. This scares away the birds. It is sometimes said that "one's birth is like the bird-scaring rope" (*soron i la ko yagbayile*) or "like a chain" (*soron i la ko yolke*) because one's fate is always inextricably tied to the fate of others.[6]

Foucault's second mode of similitude is *aemulatio*, the relation of emulation whereby things mirror or "imitate one another from one end of the universe to the other without connection or proximity."[7] Paracelsus likened this relation to the relation between identical twins; one could never be said to be the original and the other merely a duplicate or reflection. An ethnographic example of *aemulatio* is immediately suggested by the Nuer conception of twinship.

> The Nuer assert "that twins are one person and that they are birds" . . . because twins and birds, though for different reasons, are both associated with

Spirit and this makes twins, like birds, "people of the above" and "children of God," and hence a bird a suitable symbol in which to express the special relationship in which a twin stands to God. . . . In respect to God twins and birds have a similar character.[8]

A third mode of similitude is *analogy*, whereby the microcosm is shown to correspond in every detail to the macrocosm. "Man's body is always the possible half of a universal atlas": his flesh is glebe, his bones are rocks, his veins great rivers, his bladder the sea, and his seven principal organs the metals hidden in the shafts of mines.[9] The Dogon of Mali provide a contemporary ethnographic example of this painstaking elucidation of correspondences between the human body and the body of the world. According to Geneviève Calame-Griaule, the Dogon conceive the world in its totality as a gigantic human organism, and parts of the Dogon world reproduce this image on a greater or lesser scale.[10] Thus the village is conceptualized as a person, lying north-south, the smithy at his head, shrines at his feet, while the Dogon house is an anthropomorphic representation of a man lying on his side and procreating.[11] Moreover, a symbolic geology of the human body is recognized, with different kinds of minerals corresponding to different bodily organs, various earths being organs "within the belly," rocks being assimilated to the "bones" of the skeleton, and a family of red clays made to represent the blood. Different rocks and stones stand for different parts of the body so that one rock balanced on another is the "chest" and small white river pebbles are "toes." The Dogon also maintain that each of these phenomenal correspondences "speaks" to people, auguring or signifying something that must be deciphered if they are to flourish. Words are likened to grain, speech to germination, and divination to winnowing. Moreover, body parts have analogues in parts of the grain (heart = cotyledon, nose = germ, and so on) as well as in intonations of the voice.[12]

Foucault's fourth mode of similitude, *sympathy*, is really a corollary of the other modes, as suggested by the Dogon view that things that are analogous *also influence one another*. Foucault takes an example from Porta's *Magie naturelle*, where it is observed that mourning roses that have been used at obsequies can, simply from their former adjacency with death, render all who smell them "sad and moribund."[13] Sympathy, which transforms things "in the direction of identity," is, however, complemented by its twin, antipathy, which "maintains the isolation of things." Anthropologists are familiar with these notions in the form of sympathetic magic and pollution beliefs. Among the Kuranko, pregnant women sometimes bind a strip of antelope skin around their wrists so that the child they bear will be imbued with the antelope's litheness and grace. Among the Fang of Gabon, squirrels are prohibited for pregnant women because squirrels shelter in holes of trees and a future mother who ate their flesh would run the risk of the fetus imitating the squirrel and refusing to leave the uterus. As Günther Tessmann notes, "The worst danger threatening pregnant women is from animals who live or are caught in any sort of hole (in the ground, in trees). One can positively speak of a *horror vacui*. If a pregnant woman eats an animal of this kind, the child might also want to stay in its hole, 'in the belly,' and a difficult birth is to be expected."[14]

The sixteenth-century episteme was characterized by what Foucault calls a "teeming abundance of resemblances"—limitless, plethoric, and indiscriminate.[15] This preoccupation with similitudes, analogies, and correspondences had two important consequences.

In the first place, distinctions between "magic" and "science" had little currency in the sixteenth century. Observations and discoveries that we would recognize as "scientific" *were* made, to be sure, but they were often accidental or incidental to the overriding passion for divining the internal harmonies of the world. Consider, for example, an observation from Pierre Belon's *Histoire de la nature des oiseaux* (1555) in which the wing of a bird is likened to the human hand: "The pinion called the appendix which is in proportion to the wing and in the same place as the thumb on the hand; the extremity of the pinion which is like the fingers in us."[16] It so happens that these correspondences between the wing of a bird and the upper limb of a human being provide an excellent example of what biologists call homology, an organic or structural connection that derives from a similar phylogenetic prototype, that is, a connection that reveals common descent. But Belon's comparative anatomy was neither "scientific" nor "magical." It was just one of the innumerable correspondences that the world revealed to the fascinated human mind, no more or less significant than the connection assumed, say, between apoplexy and storms.[17]

One is reminded of Taoist thinkers whose spiritual desire to discern the unity of nature led, almost inadvertently, to alchemical experimentation, healthy skepticism toward preconceived theories, disinterested observations of the natural world, a search for hidden causes, and what we would now call an attitude of "scientific naturalism" that brought the Taoists "intuitively to the roots of science."[18] Joseph Needham draws an analogy between the Taoists and Paracelsus:

> Standard-bearer of alchemy applied to medicine, proponent, against all opposition, of mineral drugs, first observer of the occupational diseases of miners, he was an experimentalist and a theoretician. . . . Paracelsus had much in common with the Taoists. Indeed it can be shown that his alchemical medicine derived ultimately from the elixir concept of China mediated through Arabic and Byzantine culture.[19]

It is because the thought that we sometimes disparage as "mystical" or "magical" often goes hand in hand with experimentation and exhaustive observations of the natural world that Claude Lévi-Strauss argues that it must be regarded as a different but parallel mode of scientific thought. This "science of the concrete," through its meticulous and methodical classification of things on the basis of similitudes and sensible properties (hard/soft, sweet/sour, long/short, and so on) makes possible discoveries of a practical and theoretical kind in rather the same way that many scientific discoveries are made by accident, not design (such as Alexander Fleming's discovery of penicillin and Friedrich August Kekulé's discovery of the benzene ring[20]):

> Not all poisonous juices are burning or bitter nor is everything which is burning and bitter poisonous. Nevertheless, nature is so constituted that it is more advantageous if thought and action proceed as though this aesthetically satisfying equivalence also corresponded to objective reality. It seems probable . . . that species possessing some remarkable characteristics, say, of shape, colour or smell give the observer what might be called a "right pending disproof" to postulate that these visible characteristics are the sign of equally singular, but concealed, properties. To treat the relation between the two as itself sensible (regarding a seed in the form of a tooth as

a safeguard against snake bites, yellow juices as a cure for bilious troubles, etc.) is of more value provisionally than indifference to any connection.[21]

A second important consequence of the sixteenth-century preoccupation with resemblances was a passion for divining and deciphering the system of signatures that were their visible form. As in hermetic philosophy, where the natural world was spoken of as the "book of God,"[22] the sixteenth-century episteme saw the world as bristling with signs, blazons, omens, and figures, that is to say, *as a text*. Erudition was a matter of making the signs speak, of elucidating their cryptic meanings, of revealing the laws that governed the connections between them. Renaissance knowledge was, in a word, hermeneutic.[23]

Measurement and Difference

In the early seventeenth century, the intellectual quest for synthetic resemblances began to give way to analytical methods for establishing identity and difference. Galileo sought intelligibility through deductive reasoning—an abstract mathematization of the world (*mathesis universalis*)—that avoids the confusing testimony of the senses.

René Descartes attacked the indiscriminate habit of seeing resemblances everywhere and of losing sight of essential differences. The "proper order of things," he wrote in 1637, could only be worked out through rational means, particularly mathematics and geometry: "Those long chains of reasoning, simple and easy as they are, of which geometricians make use in order to arrive at the most difficult demonstrations, had caused me to imagine that all those things which fall under the cognizance of man might very likely be related in the same fashion."[24]

As reason became sundered from the senses, so "man" the rational subject became separated from nature. As Maurice Merleau-Ponty points out, this split not only entailed a radical separation of mind and body; it reinforced the doctrine of philosophical transcendence, creating a rupture between philosophical models "and the obscurity of the 'there is.'" Because thought is part and parcel of our embodied being, "it cannot, by definition, really be thought [conceived]. *One can only practice it, exercise it, and, so to speak, exist it; yet one can draw nothing from it which deserves to be called true.*"[25] Indeed, this view calls into question the very idea that metaphors comprise tenor and vehicle or subject and object, for just as intersubjective relations involve one person's perception slipping or dissolving into the other's in "consummate reciprocity" so our relations with ideas and things often blur the lines we suppose to exist between them.[26] In this sense abstraction is a misnomer or, rather, yet another metaphor, for as the etymology of the word suggests, abstraction is not a purely cognitive process but a social and physical action of "drawing away from," or withdrawing from someone or something.

Numerous examples can be adduced in support of Hannah Arendt's claim that "all philosophical terms are metaphors, frozen analogues, as it were, whose true meaning discloses itself when we dissolve the term into its original context."[27] Thus, the ostensibly abstract concept of time derives from the Latin *tempus*, originally denoting a "stretch," and cognate with *tempora*, "temples of the head"—perhaps because the skin stretches and corrugates as one ages. In a similar vein, the Chinese character meaning duration, *jiu*, was explained by the Han lexicographers as derived from the character *ren*, man; hence *jiu* was a man stretching his legs and walking, moving from one event or location to another.[28] As for the concept of knowing, the word is cognate in all Indo-European languages, with words meaning "king," "kind," "kin," "generation," "knee," and "can."[29]

Although Enlightenment thinkers sought to avoid metaphor in the same way they tried to expunge intuition and affect from their work, men like Francis Bacon and John Newton remained under the influence of magical, alchemical, and Hermetic traditions.[30] Most alarmingly, however, the new scientists fostered negative attitudes toward anyone who allegedly failed the test of rationality.[31]

The dramatic difference between Renaissance and post-Enlightenment attitudes is shown by the following characterizations of "primitive" peoples by Michel de Montaigne, writing in the 1570s, and John Locke, writing ninety years later. Montaigne is speaking about the South American Indians he had met in Le Havre:

> I find (from what has been told me) that there is nothing savage or barbarous about those peoples, but that every man calls barbarous anything he is not accustomed to; it is indeed the case that we seem to have no other criterion of truth or right-reason than the example and form of the opinions

and customs of our own country. There we always find the perfect religion, the perfect polity, the most developed and perfect way of doing anything![32]

Montaigne expresses irritation that Plato had no knowledge of these people and assumes that Plato would have appreciated them for their "conceptions and yearnings of philosophy."[33] In complete contrast with Montaigne's romantic view, consider the benighted attitude of John Locke in his *Essays on the Law of Nature.*

> Anyone who consults the histories both of the old world and new world, or the itineraries of travellers, will easily observe how far apart from virtue the morals of these people are, what strangers they are to humane feelings, since nowhere else is there such doubtful honesty, so much treachery, such frightful cruelty in that they sacrifice to the gods and also to their tutelary spirit by killing people and offering kindred blood. And no one will believe that the law of nature is best known and observed among these primitive and untutored tribes, since among most of them there appears not the slightest trace or track of piety, merciful feeling, fidelity, chastity, and the rest of the virtues; but rather they spend their life wretchedly among robberies, thefts, debaucheries, and murders.[34]

History and Critique

The possibility of a discursive anthropology that draws contrasts, as Foucault does, between Renaissance and Enlightenment thought is grounded in a notion of order based neither on the perception of similitudes nor on the privileged status of the rational subject. Rather, its foundation is history and a sense that both order and reason, and even the appearance and disappearance of the human subject, are historically determined. This is the episteme of the nineteenth century, of Hegel, Marx, Darwin, and Nietzsche—despite their different opinions as to whether history is a structured whole or open-ended, or whether truth is relative to time and circumstance. It is also the episteme of the social sciences and anthropology, despite the ahistorical tenor of functionalism and the reluctance of structuralism to address history except as "mere contingency." It is the episteme in which we are still caught up, despite ourselves, and that leads us to distinguish modern and premodern societies on the spurious grounds that the latter are not simply societies without reason but societies without history.

Foucault's work is predicated on the assumption that the history of thought is marked by radical and unpredictable discontinuities (epistemic breaks, paradigm shifts). But how comprehensive are any of these discursive regimes, and how complete is the displacement of one by another over the course of historical time? As Foucault notes, "The episteme is not a motionless figure that appeared one day with a mission of effacing all that preceded it."[35] Rather, it would appear to entail, as Ernst Cassirer insists, a shift in "the ideal center of gravity of all philosophy," in which new trends coexist with rather than supplant the old.[36] In the work of Jean Bodin and Montaigne, as we have seen, the importance an individual attaches to reason anticipates the Enlightenment fetishization of it, while seventeenth-century scientists like Bacon and Newton often fall back on magical thought while at the same time seeking to reconcile natural philosophy with divine authority.

Clearly, science does not necessarily bring about the demise of religion, and religion does not necessarily eschew science. Alchemical and physiological imagery abound in supposedly "rational" economic discourse to this day (markets crash, hemorrhage, hurt, are volatile or nervous and suffer wounds). Nor does reason foreshadow the end of poetry. And despite attempts by the *philosophes* to expunge mythical thought from their well-reasoned treatises, anthropomorphism and magic continue to pervade the way we think and act. Is it not empirically truer to say, therefore, that any human society, at any epoch, contains many potential ways of thinking and of acting, and that though these potential forms may cluster more densely among certain classes, ethnicities, or personalities, they are so various that any one may emerge in any particular setting at any time? Foucault's view is nominalist and therefore biased against the empirical.[37] It is a view, moreover, from afar. It overlooks the specific existential contexts in which thought emerges as a form of savoir faire, and it fosters the illusion that discourse has a life, not only a logic, of its own.

The ethnographic critique of Western philosophy reverses the common philosophical assumption that primitive thought is irrational or purely pragmatic by showing that even Western intellectualism cannot escape the impress of sensory, bodily, and mundane realities and that so-called primitive thought can, theoretically, encompass ideas that Western thinkers have typically considered their own. A singularly compelling example of this thesis is Jadran Mimica's study of the "being of number" among the Iqwaye of Papua New Guinea. Demystifying the Enlightenment distinction between mythos and logos, Mimica argues that the prescientific world is *the very ground on which the possibility of science rests*, and he demonstrates how counting on the fingers and toes can generate the "abstract" notion of infinity that we tend to associate exclusively with the formal logico-mathematical systems that have emerged in the West.[38] Yet Iqwaye have no use for "infinity," and their theory of number is organically assimilated to a complex cosmology that ties the unity of human beings "to the unity of the cosmic being, the creator, Omalyce. In the Iqwaye lifeworld the being of number is the corporeal man."[39] One may conclude, therefore, as Ludwig Wittgenstein does, that while "in one sense mathematics is a branch of knowledge [it] is also an *activity*."[40] Thus, Helen Verran's research on teaching math and logic to Yoruba schoolchildren led her to identify a mode of thought in which quantity was not absolute but relational and in which certainty derived from cultural practices such as tallying goods or conceptualizing social groupings rather than from abstract logic. Resisting the fetishizing of "natural number" as a universal category (by virtue of it being "abstract" rather than "concrete"), Verran argues that *both* European and Yoruba systems of numeration reflect specific cultural, historical, and practical contexts, not some transcendental standpoint. Deciding which logic we should use is therefore a pragmatic matter of what questions we are asking and what problems we are trying to solve.[41] Recent cognitive approaches to religiosity argue along similar lines, that the seemingly extraordinary, exotic, or metaphysical concepts that we associate with religious worldviews are "natural" products of "aggregated *ordinary* cognitive processes."[42]

These studies suggest that thought is always analogical, drawing comparisons between different "forms of life."[43] Contrary to George Lakoff, who sees metaphors as concrete images of abstract ideas, such as time, love, emotions, and relations, I prefer to bracket out the distinction between the concrete and the abstract and ignore the question as to whether metaphors should be taken literally or figuratively. Phenomenologically speaking, metaphors are not necessarily a way of saying one thing "in terms of" or "by way of" something else (implying a distinction between subject and object, tenor and vehicle); rather, metaphors effect a "consummation of identity," as when we speak of our life's journey or love's labor's lost. Indeed, worldviews exist in which sensations, thoughts, and feelings are regarded not as ethereal but as substantial—as "impersonal substances with independent causal efficacy, so that senses and feelings are in fact experienced as 'forces' or 'things' that move into and between people." Carla Stang notes that even "an idea or concept for the Mehinaku is not an intangible production of an intangible mind, each is a concrete and specific 'thing' that is not differentiated in its substantial 'thingness' from the other things that constitute the Mehinaku worlds."[44]

The advantage of this view for Mehinaku is that it provides "a way of interacting with things in a very palpable way."[45] Pragmatically speaking, metaphors make it possible to communicate and converse with others even if they exist on what we might think of as an illusory, spiritual, or ethereal plane. As such, the value of these substantivized images does not lie in their capacity for capturing abstractions in concrete form but in actually mediating relationships, whether these are social or (in our terms) "merely" symbolic.

Gregory Bateson also makes a case for evaluating analogies in terms of what they do for us rather than what their epistemological status might be. In one example, he proposes an edifying comparison between two modes of social life (one in which a group secedes from the parent society and goes away to be different, the other in which the new community migrates but retains the values of the original one) and two different organisms—radially symmetrical animals like the jellyfish or sea anemone and animals with transverse segmentation like earthworms, lobsters, and humans. The value of the analogy lies in breaking free of "the sterile rigidity of formal thought," though this is not to disparage strictness, which is equally necessary to creative thought.[46]

If philosophy cannot claim to have developed a nonfigurative language for describing and analyzing reality, then all that differs from one historical epoch, or one human society, to another are the metaphors that are given pride of place in its dominant discourse. But alternative metaphors always abound, which is why a vast array of agricultural and horticultural images continue to figure in the discourse of industrial and postindustrial societies and why scientific understandings of the cosmos never entirely displace pre-scientific ones.

If all thought is rooted in images of everyday life, then no thinker and no society can claim to possess a philosophy that transcends the limits of the human condition. All that can be claimed is that one possesses a more alluring metaphor that allows new conversations to take place concerning the dilemmas and difficulties of being human. Thus, having shown that Western philosophy from its pre-Socratic beginnings has depended largely on metaphors of thinking-as-seeing (systematic thought mirrors the nature of the world in the same way that systematic theology mirrors the nature of God), Richard Rorty concludes that ocular metaphors are no more edifying than any others and suggests that we might have more interesting conversations if we dream up new metaphors. To this proposal I would add another: that such conversations might benefit from using the metaphors in circulation in societies outside the Western hemisphere, and placing these on a par with our own rather than writing them off as ill suited to sophisticated thought. For what really matters is whether a figure of speech improves our ability to cope with life and find fulfillment in it, not whether it corresponds to some formal set of rules.

For Aristotle, metaphor was a matter of giving one thing a name that belonged to something else—a kind of *lateral* comparison that did not necessarily imply a vertical relationship between an immanent object and a transcendent idea. Moreover, Aristotle regarded mastery of metaphor to be "a sign of genius, since a good metaphor implies an eye for resemblance."[47]

In this spirit, let us explore some sensory metaphors for thinking that get us away from the visualist imagery that has informed so much philosophical discourse.

Senses of Meaning

In formulating the empiricist canons of modern social science, John Locke wrote, "The perception of the mind is most aptly explained by words relating to the sight."[48] This ocular metaphor goes back to the Greeks. Xenophon pictured God as a sphere and, as James Edie notes, "Even the later and more technical term for sight, the one adopted by Plato and Aristotle for philosophical contemplation, *theorein*, was not originally a verb but a noun, *theoros*, meaning 'to be a spectator,' from which it derived its later meaning of 'looking at,' ultimately 'to contemplate.'"[49] Accordingly, seeing as an optical phenomenon and thinking as an intellectual phenomenon were, in effect, conflated. As Richard Rorty puts it, "It is pictures rather than propositions, metaphors rather than statements, which determine most of our philosophical convictions. The picture which holds traditional philosophy captive is that of the mind as a great mirror."[50] Hence the plethora of terms in our Western epistemological vocabulary that evoke the notion of knowing as seeing (*eidos*, eidetic, idea, ideation, intuition, theory, theorize) or refer to optics as a metaphor of understanding (reflect, speculate, focus, view, inspect, insight, outlook, perspective).

This visualist bias has the effect of distancing subject from object, and seeing them as discontinuous entities. John Dewey explains the process:

> The theory of knowing is modeled after what was supposed to take place in the act of vision. The object refracts light to the eye and is seen; it makes a difference to the eye and to the person having an optical apparatus, but none to the thing seen. The real object is the object so fixed in its regal aloofness that it is a king to any beholding mind that may gaze upon it. A spectator theory of knowledge is the inevitable outcome.[51]

Visualism also implies a *spatialization* of consciousness in which knower and known are located at several removes from one another and regarded as essentially unalike, the one an impartial spectator, the other an object at which he gazes. For this reason, visualism tends to deny coevalness.[52] The alienating effects of visualism may also be related to the impact of perspective and literacy on human consciousness. As Sigfried Giedion notes, perspective (lit. "clear-seeing") becomes the principal Western conception of space from the early fifteenth century and has the immediate effect of privileging the way things appear from a fixed, detached point of view—that of the observer. "With the invention of perspective the modern notion of individualism found its artistic counterpart. Every element in a perspective representation is related to the unique point of view of the individual spectator."[53]

Perspective, however, is atypical of the preliterate worldview, as I discovered in 1970 when administering psychological tests for distance perception among Kuranko villagers, who often regarded objects at a distance as being as small as they appeared. A vivid example of how the world appears to someone for whom seeing is not believing is Christine Helliwell's phenomenological description of life in a Dayak longhouse in Kalimantan Barat (West Borneo). The "flow of sound and light is crucial," she writes. "The longhouse community as a whole is defined and encircled more by these two things than by anything else." Whereas previous ethnographers compared Dayak longhouses to *lines* of privately owned, semidetached houses along a street, Helliwell concentrates her attention on "lived space," drawing on her own field experiences and emphasizing what is heard and felt as much as what is seen:

> I recall, while living in the Gerai longhouse, writing letters back to Australia in which I constantly referred to the longhouse as a "community of voices," for I could think of no more apt way to describe the largely invisible group of which I found myself to be a part. Voices flow in a longhouse in a most extraordinary fashion; moving up and down its length in seeming monologue, they are in fact in continual dialogue with listeners who may be unseen but are always present. As such they create, more than does any other facet of longhouse life, a sense of community.[54]

My experience of living in a Kuranko village is very similar. The Kuranko image of a community as a cluster of common centers connected by paths is grounded in the physical layout of the village itself, which is made up of open spaces called *luiye* around which are grouped circular thatched houses.[55] The *luiye* are interconnected by a labyrinth of narrow lanes and dusty paths along which people move in the day-to-day round of village life. In a Kuranko village, there is no main path leading to a privileged vantage point where one can take up the position of spectator or observer. On the contrary, the structure of the village enforces participation. Even from a hammock on a veranda, looking out into a *luiye* half-hidden by the low eaves of the house, one is part of the goings-on in the village, immersed in its sights and smells and sounds: the feel of a cracked mud wall against the palm of one's hand, the pungent odor of cassava leaf and dried fish sauce, the fetid smell of bodies, the cries of children, the rhythmic thud of mortars pounding rice, the crowing of a rooster, the raised voices of men debating some vexed issue in the court *gbare*.

Not long after beginning fieldwork in Firawa in 1969, I climbed the hill overlooking the village *to get things into perspective*. From the hilltop, I surveyed the village, took panoramic photographs, and achieved my bird's-eye view, believing that my superior position would give me *insights* into the organization of the village when, in fact, it was making me lose touch with it. Ten years later I was living in Firawa with my wife and daughter. One evening my daughter, Heidi, and I climbed the hill above the village. No one else ever did. There were no paths, only tall brakes of elephant grass, granite boulders, and acacias. At the crest of the hill I found the gnarled and charred *lophira* tree where I had taken my photographs of Firawa in 1969. I asked Heidi what she thought of the view. "It's all right," she said, "except you can't see anyone in the village from here." And indeed, there was no human movement visible; only the smoke from cooking fires.

Those ten years had seen me cease to be a detached observer and become a part of Firawa. I recognized the village as a second home. The transition was, I sometimes thought, like the transition that occurs in a friendship. At the time of first meeting you are somewhat guarded; you try to get a sense of the other person through exchanging views and experiences. But to *live* with another person or to *go through* difficult experiences with him or her gives rise to a different kind of understanding, one that suspends the sense of separateness between self and other and evokes the primordial meaning of knowledge as a mode of being-with.

My sketch of the Kuranko village as *lived space* replaces a perspectival model with a topoanalytical model that emphasizes one's sense of being-in-the-world, experiencing it from all sides, moving and participating in it rather than remaining on the margins like a voyeur. But striving for this radically empirical point of view brings one hard up against the limitations of literacy. Marshall McLuhan argues that perspective derives unconsciously from print technology.[56] Like perspective, literacy privileges vision over the other senses, abstracts thought from social context, and isolates the reader or writer from the world.[57] "If oral communication keeps people together," observes David Riesman, "print is the isolating medium par *excellence*."[58]

Because philosophy and literacy are so closely interwoven, they tend to produce similar ways of constructing reality. Both have the effect of separating us and our ideas from the world of lived experience. They also predispose us to think of social experience in sequential, lineal terms. Consider the notion of lineage or lineal descent. The Polynesian notion of *whakapapa* (Proto-Austronesian, *fakapapa*) may be translated as "genealogy" or "family tree," implying a "line" of descent. But the etymology suggests a different picture:

> "Papa" is anything broad, flat and hard such as a flat rock, a slab or a board. "Whakapapa" is to place in layers, lay one upon another. Hence the term Whakapapa is used to describe both the recitation in proper order of genealogies, and also to name the genealogies. The visualization is of building layer by layer upon the past towards the present, and on into the future.[59]

Applied to most African societies, the term *lineage* is also misleading. Even when one finds an indigenous word that is nearly identical to our word *lineage*, there may be an indefinite relationship between the word and what it appears to designate. For example, for the Tiv of Nigeria the word *nongo* means literally "line" or "queue," though it "refers primarily to the living representatives of a lineage," a grouping without any real genealogical depth. A more inclusive term, *ityo* (patrilineage), that one might expect to suggest a descent "line," conjures up for the Tiv an image of "the father's path" or the father's way of doing things rather than a "line" of succession and ancestry.[60] This is reminiscent of the way the Kuranko speak of their relationships with both contemporary kin and forebears as networks of paths or ropes.

Meyer Fortes's ethnography of the Tallensi provides a superb example of how relationships are conceptualized spatially and temporally in terms of images of a house and a begetting. Somewhat surprisingly, given his fascination with West African "lineage systems," Fortes notes that "the Tallensi have no term for the lineage."[61] Yet he proceeds to assimilate their metaphors to his own:

> A lineage of any order is designated the "house" (*yir*) or the children (*bus*) of the founding ancestor. . . . In contexts where the emphasis is on the lineage considered as a segment of a more inclusive lineage, it is commonly described as a "room" (*dug*) of the more inclusive "house" (*yir*). . . . As this nomenclature shows, the internal constitution of the lineage is modelled on that of the polygynous joint family.[62]

What Fortes calls a lineage is, for Tallensi, a house or household (*yidem*), a group of people who feel they share "one blood" or "one begetting." These metaphors of dwelling and "common birth" are widespread in Africa and suggest that Vico's notion of a *nation* (lit. a natal group) may better capture the experience of being a family than "lineage" or "descent group."[63] This is borne out by E. E. Evans-Pritchard's account of how the Nuer figure a lineage system: "When illustrating on the ground a number of related lineages they do not present them the way we figure them . . . as a series of bifurcations of descent, as a tree of descent, or as a series of triangles of ascent, but as a number of lines running at angles from a common point." Nuer see the "lineage system," Evans-Pritchard goes on to say, "primarily *as actual relations between groups of kinsmen within local communities rather* than *as a tree of descent*, for the persons after whom the lineages are called do not all proceed from a single individual."[64]

But the problem with the concept of lineage is not only its bias toward a linear perspective. It gives rise to reified *models* of segmentary social organization that effectively eclipse the senses in which a lifeworld is understood by those who actually inhabit it. In effect, map is confused with territory and the structure of discourse conflated with the structure of experience.[65]

The Anthropomorphic House

For Martin Heidegger, the etymological connections between our conceptions of dwelling, thinking, and being disclose something so fundamental about our being-in-the-world that even language may be said to "house" our being.[66] But though Heidegger uses metaphor, he distrusts it. Is it philosophy's longstanding infatuation with the metaphysical that explains this resistance to the physicality of thought? Certainly this is Derrida's view: "concept is a metaphor, foundation is a metaphor, theory is a metaphor; and there is no meta-metaphor for them."[67] Having already adduced African examples of how houses are metaphors for the people who dwell in them (households), let us now consider comparable examples from elsewhere in order to further develop a phenomenological understanding of analogical reason.

Among the Maori of Aotearoa (New Zealand), the experience of community solidarity is concretized in the *wharenui* (big house) or *whare whakairo* (carved house) on one's home *marae*. This is not a dwelling house but a community hall—a gathering place for critical events such as births, deaths, marriages, family reunions, political negotiation, and dispute resolution. These big houses are typically carved inside and out with images of tribal ancestors and usually named after a heroic forebear or mythological figure. Different parts of the house, moreover, refer to different parts of the ancestral body so that to enter the house is to become one with all those who trace their descent to this eponymous figure. The *koruru* at the apex of the front gable is a stylized portrait of the ancestor's head. The *maihi* (bargeboards) signify arms; the ends of the *maihi* are fingers (*raparapa*), while the *tāhuhu* (ridge beam) represents the backbone and the rafters the ribs (*heke*).

It is not simply that the house is *depicted* or *constructed* as an ancestor; it is *experienced* as a proto-parent, a source of security and warmth. And it holds ancestral events within its body as the human mind holds memories. Even we sometimes say of a house, "If only these walls could speak," as if a dwelling place had absorbed traces of what had transpired there and of the lives of those who had lived there. That haunted houses figure so often in our collective imaginings is surely because the buildings in which we spend our lives somehow participate in our existence; when they are ruined or destroyed, something in us dies, and when those who dwelt in them die, something of their spirit remains, a ghostly presence like a memory in the vacant spaces.

It is in the phenomenology of Gaston Bachelard that we find one of the most eloquent arguments for approaching the house as an ontological metaphor—an embodiment and objectification of our actual experience of being-in-the-world. As Bachelard points out, the immediate and intimate microcosm we call "home" is the basis on which we construct, conceptually and physically, our understanding of the wider, encompassing social macrocosm we call the world. It is in the home environment that the child learns basic orientations like up and down, near and far, threshold and horizon, or how to move in space—realizing his or her bodily capacity to reach out, point, grasp, express intentions, communicate needs, or experience attachment to certain people, places, and objects. None of this learning is mediated by concepts. As Yi-Fu Tuan puts it, "Sensorimotor intelligence precedes conceptual grasp, sometimes by several years."[68] In other words, before we consider a house as an object that can be named or *thought of* as homely or inhospitable, or assigned a value, it is primordially inhabited as if it were one's own body. And it is this sense of being at one with one's most immediate and intimate environment that gives rise to the anthropomorphic image of the house as a human being.

In this vein, one might remark that both Karl Marx and Sigmund Freud had recourse to anthropomorphic images of buildings when they constructed their respective models of society and the psyche: for Marx, the contrast between *Überbau* (state, religion, philosophy, ideology) and *Basis* (means of production, productive labor); for Freud, the contrast between attic (superego), living rooms (ego) and doorways (where censoring occurs), and basement (unconscious, libido). But Marx and Freud, like Heidegger and Bachelard, are European thinkers, and the question arises as to how far one can generalize their models of being to other societies, or, for that matter, to every human being regardless of his or her particular circumstances.

For the Warlpiri of Central Australia the verb "to be" is the same as the verb "to sit"—*nyinami*. Here dwelling is not associated with building or being housed. Warlpiri regard walled dwellings as cages or prisons, and when Australian government welfare services provided them with houses, they ignored the buildings as places to live, using them, if at all, as places to store possessions. For Warlpiri, the crucial anthropomorphic connection is not one between oneself and a camp or windbreak or shelter, for these are temporary, but between oneself and the *country* to which one belongs. And this connection is spoken of in kinship terms, much as sedentary people speak of having a motherland or fatherland. The country from which one's father hailed is called father; the country of one's mother and her family is called mother. Just as a person has deep ties to both parents, so he or she has deep ties to both their natal countries.

"All great, simple images reveal a psychic state," writes Bachelard. "The house, even more than the landscape, is a psychic state, and even when it is reproduced as it appears from the outside, it bespeaks intimacy."[69] As one example of this intimate connection between self and house he cites children's drawings. If a child is happy she will draw a snug, protected house built on firm foundations. An unhappy child, by contrast, will draw houses that communicate her inner distress. Children who suffered the cruelties of the German occupation during World War II drew narrow, cold, closed houses. As one psychologist observed, the houses were lifeless and motionless, like the traumatized children who drew them. But for Warlpiri, landscape, not house, is a psychic state, and one may discern in their extraordinary production of acrylic paintings of traditional country, some of which fetch huge prices on the international art market, a poignant desire to keep a connection alive that enforced displacement jeopardized and almost destroyed, a nostalgia for a psycho-physical link with something wider than self, which they call the Dreaming (*jukurrpa*) and we sometimes call our heavenly home.

Thinking Through the Sensorium

Understanding the world through senses other than sight is not simply a courtesy we pay to the ways in which others perceive the world; it affords us a means of seeing our world in a new light.[70] Let us briefly consider three societies where the five senses are given different emphases and meanings than in the modern West: the Suya of central Brazil; the Kuku-Yalanji of southeast Cape York, Australia; and the Northern Yaka of Zaire.

Among the Suya, seeing is *not* believing. "The eyes are literally the seat of antisocial power" and associated with witchcraft. Witches possess extraordinary vision but hear and speak badly. Hearing and speaking are the "eminently social faculties," and the ear and mouth are the most important organs. Thus, while the Suya decorate the ears and lips with disks, the eyes and nose are left unornamented. At the same time, different *odors* signify social distinctions. While initiation is said to rid men of their pungent odor, women "by their very sexuality are strong-smelling" and elderly men and women "are both pungent."[71]

This use of olfactory metaphors for social and moral realities is reminiscent of Kuku-Yalanji uses of body odor to mark moiety divisions. Sea people (*jalunji*, lit. "of the sea") are said to have a fishy smell (*bikarr*); they carry the odor of saltwater and sea fish. Land people (*ngalkalji*, lit. "away from or outside the sea") have a strong marsupial smell, though it is not as strong as the smell of strangers. When a woman marries, she acquires the smell of her husband's group, just as my wife and I lost the smell of white people (which is likened to the slime of an eel), and acquired the same odor as the people with whom we camped. And it is one's body odor that communicates to the spirits of a sacred site one's identity as kinsman or stranger.

Among the Yaka, somewhat different sensory emphases exist. Social interaction is construed as a kind of weaving or intertwining. One powerful expression of this is dancing, which lustfully celebrates the flow of vital force (*m-mooyi*) between human beings and between people and nature. Dancing is compared with sexual intercourse and commensality that likewise create reciprocity through physical copresence and intertwining.[72] For Yaka, social relations involve "exchanges of feeling," and in this process the senses of touch and smell are paramount.

> Eating, drinking, and procreating, which involve olfactory and tactile contact, are the acts that constitute the domestic zone and that generate symmetrical reciprocity. . . . As the Yaka say, "By its very nature, eating must be shared" (-*diisasana*). Eating circumscribes a space of physical co-presence "where bodies intrude on one another" (-*dyaatasana*). Procreating is spoken of as "causing one another to intertwine legs" (-*biindasana maalu*). . . . Olfactory contact . . . "puts oneself beside oneself" and inserts the individual into the social and natural domains. Procreation, by which the sexes and generations are mediated and differentiated, is symbolized and concretized among the Yaka as "smelling one another": sexual partners "induce each other to secrete smell and to take in each other's smell" (*fyaasana, -nyuukisana*). In other words, smelling constructs a liminal process between the procreators: it provides a bodily matrix for a reciprocal interaction in which the poles (inner/outer, self/other, giver/receiver) are joined and set apart.[73]

The Yaka feel illness to be a disturbance in this symbolic interweave of self, society, and cosmos—"a bad smell"—and therapy is a way of revitalizing social and cosmic connections, as well as giving rebirth to the sick individual through bodily metaphors of hunting, weaving, and sexual regeneration.

If there are so many "paths toward a clearing," so many ways that life can be understood, suffering can be alleviated, and well-being can be sought, then is it possible to ever ascertain on a priori grounds which path is wisest? And should we decide to prioritize existence over episte-mology—"reasons for being" (raisons d'être) over rules of discourse—what is to be gained by claiming that any one theory or mode of praxis is more reasonable than any other? When it comes to deciding between going to a doctor or a diviner, a shaman or a scientist, a philosopher or a sage, the question of which worldview is *epistemologically* superior may be less urgent than which one offers the best cure or the greatest conso-lation. Life is an ongoing improvisation, and people everywhere appeal to different ways of thinking and acting in their struggles to make their lives worth living. There seems little point in making claims for either karmic or genetic explanations for why certain traits occur and recur through many generations when both have the potential to help us al-leviate what Hindus call *dukkha*, the "unsatisfactoriness of existence."[74] And though philosophy gave Boethius great consolation during his im-prisonment at Pavia and "moral medication" in the face of execution, other philosophers have found no such comfort in enlightenment.

In 1826, John Stuart Mill began to suffer severe doubts about the phi-losophy to which his father had introduced him: "I now saw, or thought I saw, what I had already before received with incredulity—that the habit of analysis has a tendency to wear away the feelings: as indeed it has when no other mental habit is cultivated, and the analyzing spirit re-mains without its natural complements and correctives."[75] Mill felt that his intellectual upbringing had made "precocious and premature analy-sis the inveterate habit of [his] mind," "undermining" and "weakening," as he put it, a feeling for nature and for "pleasure and sympathy with human beings." This sense of alienation immobilized him for more than two years, and he describes himself as living in a state of "dry, heavy dejection," performing his intellectual tasks "mechanically." Gradu-ally, however, his malady lifted, first through his resolve not to make happiness a direct goal or necessary precondition of his existence and second through cultivating what he called "passive susceptibilities." In this endeavor, William Wordsworth's poetry, which Mill first read in the autumn of 1828, was a revelation, reawakening a lost love of "rural objects and natural scenery" and helping him recover that disposition of mind that John Keats called "negative capability." Mill described Wordsworth's poems as "a medicine."

> They seemed to be the very culture of the feelings, which I was in quest of. . . . I needed to be made to feel that there was real, permanent happiness in tranquil contemplation. Wordsworth taught me this, not only without turning away from, but with a greatly increased interest in, the common feelings and common destiny of human beings.[76]

Cat's Cradle

Just as Nietzsche considered untruth to be "a condition of life" so might we consider philosophy and anthropology.[77] Whether they are magical or real may be less important than the consolation they provide that the world may be grasped, if not in practice then in the imagination. And just as gifts are sometimes poisons, so the things we consider true are sometimes necessary illusions.

Mendacity, make-believe, and gainsaying are constitutive of our humanity. The linguistic and mental ability to recognize "the thing which is not," to create counterworlds—a dissociative skill that George Steiner describes as a capacity for "alternity"—is what lends us the belief that we may determine our own lives to the same extent that they are determined by forces that lie beyond our grasp.

> Whatever their bio-sociological origin, the uses of language for "alternity," for misconstruction, for illusion and play, are the greatest of man's tools by far. With this stick he has reached out of the cage of instinct to touch the boundaries of the universe and of time.
>
> At first the instrument probably had a banal survival value. It still carried with it the impulse of instinctual mantling. Fiction was disguise: from those seeking out the same water-hole, the same sparse quarry, or meagre sexual chance. To misinform, to utter less than the truth was to gain a vital edge

of space or subsistence. Natural selection would favor the contriver. Folk tales and mythology retain a blurred memory of the evolutionary advantage of mask and misdirection. Loki, Odysseus are very late, literary concentrates of the widely diffused motif of the liar, of the dissembler elusive as flame and water, who survives.[78]

Are philosophy and anthropology not also ways of creating appearances—whether of order or of understanding—that provide us with a sense of purchase on the elusive face of human existence? And are not philosophers and anthropologists the cousins-german of the trickster heroes who figure in all traditions?

The Maori trickster Maui was the inventor of the cat's cradle (variously called *he whai, huhi,* and *maui*). As with any discourse, the cat's cradle is stretched, tensed, and held between the poles of reality and make-believe. With a single endless loop of string, the Polynesians could illustrate stories, depict mythological scenes and people, or suggest the forms of houses, weapons, articles of clothing, canoe and adze lashings, landmarks, flora, and fauna.[79] Can our discourse be likened to these string figures, a game we play with words, the thread of an argument whose connection with reality is always oblique and tenuous, that crosses to and fro, interlacing description with interpretation, instruction with entertainment, but always ambiguously placed between practical and antinomian ends? If so, truth is not binding. It is in the interstices as much as it is in the structure, in fiction as much as in fact.

2. Identity and Difference

In philosophy we literally seek to immerse ourselves in things that are heterogeneous to it, without placing those things in prefabricated categories. We want to adhere as closely to the heterogeneous as the programs of phenomenology and of Simmel tried in vain to do.

—THEODOR W. ADORNO, *NEGATIVE DIALECTICS*

While philosophical anthropology has traditionally presumed to make universal claims about the human condition, modern sociocultural anthropology has, for the most part, avoided such claims, preferring a vision of human diversity, ethnic distinctiveness, and moral relativism. The challenge for reinventing philosophical anthropology is working out how we can accommodate both these orientations, recognizing difference and similarity, dissonance and consonance. In this chapter, I evoke Arnold Schoenberg's atonal music, Theodor Adorno's negative dialectics, and John Keats's negative capability in addressing the question of how it is possible to do justice to both our empirical knowledge of the linguistic, cultural, and individual *diversity* of humankind and our quest to identify modes of thought, action and being that are *common* to all humanity and, in many cases, are shared with other life-forms.[1]

That this question has haunted the entire history of anthropology is perhaps less compelling than that variations of it occur in every society and in every human life. That is to say, it makes its appearance as an existential question before it is taken up as a philosophical problem. Sometimes it is experienced as an inescapable ambiguity, born of the fact that all other human beings—and, to varying degrees, all other life-forms—resemble us both in their general appearance and their particular behaviors yet manifest characteristics with which we simply cannot identify.

This paradox of pluralism arises from the simultaneous recognition that while each of us is unique (*ipse*), we are identical (*idem*) with all other human beings—singular yet at the same time similar.

When confronted by this paradox of pluralism we typically have recourse to one of two strategies. The first is to focus on differences, as when the racist suppresses the traits that he has in common with the abhorred other, regarding any resemblances as purely coincidental or a matter of mistaken identity, or when the rugged individualist acts as if he is a law unto himself, or when the anthropologist focuses on distinguishing or differentiating features (different kinship terminologies, different systems of inheritance or succession, different economies, different ways of understanding the relationship between animals and humans) with the result that shared features are played down or completely disappear. The second strategy is the polar opposite of the first. It minimizes differences, celebrates shared traits, and thereby creates the appearance of human universals. Particular differences are read as variations on a universal theme. Or it is proposed that we are all equal in the sight of God, or that it is categorically imperative that under no circumstances should we act in such a way that we treat humanity, whether in ourselves or in others, as a means rather than as an end. Despite evidence that in stressful circumstances it is often almost impossible to do unto others as you would have them do unto you and contrary to political claims that the means will justify the end—torturing a prisoner, for example, to extract information that might safeguard one's nation—the universalist sticks to his guns, fearing that any compromise will throw us into relativism and anarchy. That anthropologists have wavered between these extremes of universalism and particularism may be taken as a sign not of intellectual failure but of the inescapable ambiguity of the human condition, regardless of whether it is considered cognitively, culturally, ethically, or personally.

In what follows, I explore this paradox of pluralism in the work of three major figures in the history of anthropological thought and suggest that the apparent contradictions in their work reflect their lived situations as much as the philosophical or cultural tenor of their times. My argument is against reifying any mode of thought as a distinctive epistemology or ontology; rather, I maintain that we should see worldviews as ever-present potentialities whose actualization depends on the exigencies of concrete existential situations and events rather than culturally, historically, or politically predetermined formations. Finally, I provide some empirical examples of this situational approach to the problem of thinking across cultures.

First, then, to Émile Durkheim's *The Elementary Forms of Religious Life* (1912), which provides a striking instance of an unresolved tension between widely held views of the primitive in early twentieth-century Europe and Durkheim's more liberal persuasions.

While admitting that "even the crudest religions that history and ethnography make known to us are already so complex that they do not fit the notion people sometimes have of primitive mentality," Durkheim refers to Aboriginal societies of central Australia as "simple," "archaic," and "primitive." And though he writes that these societies "display not only a luxuriant system of beliefs but also such variety in principles and wealth in basic facts that it has seemed impossible to regard them as anything but a late product of a rather long evolution," he also speaks of them as "belonging to the beginning of history." Moreover, Durkheim's avowed fascination with religious experience is immediately occluded by a focus on religious "belief and ritual." Despite drawing a distinction between "individual states that are wholly explained by the psychic nature of the individual" and "collective representations" that are widely shared, and saying that "one can no more derive the second from the first than one can deduce the society from the individual," he insists that society is the "highest reality," one in which "the individual naturally transcends himself, both when he thinks and when he acts." Thus, Durkheim tends to collectivize *consciousness*, implying that "human mentality" is a by-product of "collective representations" and ignoring the various ways collective representations are taken up, glossed, or acted on by individuals in everyday situations.[2]

A similar tension between perceiving the other as oneself in other circumstances and perceiving the other as essentially unlike oneself pervades Bronislaw Malinowski's *Coral Gardens and Their Magic* (1935).[3] Central to Malinowski's "ethnographic theory of language" was a prioritizing of the instrumental over the expressive. For Malinowski, the most compelling thing about language was not its capacity for articulating thoughts, ideas and feelings, but its pragmatic capacity for making things happen. "Speech is . . . equivalent to gesture and motion," he writes. "It does not function as an expression of thought or communication of ideas but as a part of concerted activity . . . Speech . . . is primarily used for the achievement of a practical result."[4] At times, Malinowski makes it clear that he is "not speaking here only of the Trobriand language, still less of native speech in agriculture" [but] "the character of human speech in general," and he observes that the advertisements of modern beauty specialists like Helena Rubenstein and Elizabeth Arden would make interesting reading if collated with the formulae of Trobriand beauty magic, reproduced in chapter 13 of *Argonauts of the Western Pacific* (1922) and in chapter 11 of *Sexual Life of Savages* (1929).

> I smooth out, I improve, I whiten.
>
> Thy head I smooth out, I improve, I whiten.
>
> Thy cheeks I smooth out, I improve, I whiten.
>
> Thy nose I smooth out, I improve, I whiten.
>
> Thy throat I smooth out, I improve, I whiten.
>
> Thy throat I smooth out, I improve, I whiten.
>
> Thy neck I smooth out, I improve, I whiten.[5]

In these passages, Malinowski argues that in both Trobriand gardening magic and Western cosmetics, it is *the effect on the user's consciousness* that is at stake. Although their spells are seemingly directed at anchoring and filling the yam house, the Trobrianders are under no misapprehension that it is the belly of people that is the real object of the spells, for, logically, if bellies remain empty the yam house will be full.[6]

> In the majority of cases indeed, magic refers to human activities or to the response of nature to human activities, rather than to natural forces alone. Thus in gardening and in fishing, it is the behaviour of plants and animals tended or pursued by man; in the canoe magic, it is the carver's magic, the object is a human-made thing; in the Kula, in love magic, in many forms of food magic, *it is human nature on to which the force is directed.*[7]

But while these ethnographic observations effectively narrow the gap between Trobriand thought and European thought, Malinowski overrides his own insights by insisting that Trobriand Islanders have no interest in or capacity for the kind of abstract analytical thought that his own work exemplifies, and that while spells inspire hope, bolster confidence, and concentrate the mind, their principal function is to satisfy a need for social integration. It would seem that Malinowski's confessed "failure to integrate myself" is less of a moral fault than a methodological difficulty to accommodate a view from within and a view from afar. As his field diaries make clear, he was often too close to his informants for comfort, and this oppressive intimacy, together with the stresses of isolation from his family and friends, sometimes drove him to distance himself from the Trobrianders, denying coevalness and disparaging the natives as radically other. But after leaving the field, distance lent enchantment, and he celebrated commonalities, "writing his life through the other."[8] In other words, Malinowski's varying image of the other reflected different situations in his own life—being in the field or being out of it, feeling in control or out of control of his emotions.

Something similar can be said of Claude Lévi-Strauss. Despite arguing that all human beings share a propensity to regard the universe as "an object of thought," not simply a means of making a livelihood, Lévi-Strauss slips quickly into proposing that premodern and modern thought are different. While the former "postulates a complete and all-embracing determinism," the latter is more sensitive to the differences between analogy and homology, contingency and necessity, cause and coincidence.[9] "Primitive" thought is allegedly "imprisoned in the events and experiences it never tires of ordering and re-ordering" through an interminable process of bricolage, while science employs new hypotheses and techniques in order to create new events and experiences.[10]

Despite his insistence that magic is not "a timid and stuttering form of science" and that it shares with scientific thought a compulsion to bring intellectual order to the world, rendering it intelligible, Lévi-Strauss's determination to distinguish magic (which is "supremely concrete") and science (which is "supremely abstract") prevents him from seeing that these alternative modes of thought can readily be found in all human societies, tied not to different mentalities but to different problems or situations.[11]

These oscillations ("contradictions" is perhaps too strong a word), in the thought of Durkheim, Malinowski, and Lévi-Strauss reflect a paradox that continues to trouble the anthropological project. For while an anthropologist's deep immersion in another lifeworld may foster a sense of commonality both at the level of everyday coexistence and in patterns of thought, familiarity may sometimes breed contempt and exacerbate a sense of radical difference, particularly when the ethnographer is under stress. As George Devereux showed, anxiety in fieldwork may lead an anthropologist either to extoll the humanity of his hosts, particularly when their goodwill helps him sustain his sense of self-worth, or to exaggerate the otherness of his hosts, particularly when their food proves unpalatable, their language is incomprehensible, and their customs seem barbaric.[12] Although anthropological paradigms may oscillate historically between a bias toward difference and a bias toward similitude, these alternative perspectives are psychologically copresent for every anthropologist in the field. They are always potentialities, though which one will be brought to the fore and which will be thrust into the background depends on the changing situations—of sickness or health, ennui or excitement, loneliness or conviviality—in which the anthropologist finds himself. Rather than stereotype different lifeworlds in terms of such abstract antinomies as concrete versus abstract, rational versus irrational, or scientific versus magic, my preference, therefore, is for exploring the phenomenon of *selective attention*, whereby different modes of thought, being, and acting are brought into focus depending on an individual's social position and perspective.[13]

The Tristan Chord

My argument is against seeing any culture or any one person as a seamless whole or reducible to a single story. Radically different possibilities of action and of thought coexist within every social formation and every personality.

For many theorists of music, a key moment in the transformation from traditional tonal harmony to atonality was Richard Wagner's opening chord of *Tristan and Isolde*, composed between 1857 and 1859. The so-called Tristan chord holds in unresolved tension both romantic hope and tragic inevitability. Its initial sounds, the first uplifting, the second downcast, capture not only the unresolvable dilemma of the two lovers in Wagner's drama but also the composer's own conflicted personality.

Unlike Lévi-Strauss, who celebrates Wagner as "the undeniable originator of the structural analysis of myths,"[14] I see the great German composer both as embodying the paradox that soul-stirring art and malignant ideas can emerge from the same mind and as presaging Theodor Adorno's negative dialectics, with its echoes of Schoenberg's atonal music[15]—pioneering forms of art and philosophy that dispense with harmonic resolutions or artificial syntheses and cultivate what John Keats called a "negative capability" for accepting discord, or holding contrasted voices in tension.

For Lévi-Strauss, human thought is analogical but not necessarily tied to economic ends. Natural species figure in human cosmologies not because they are "good to eat" but because they are "good to think."[16] But while Lévi-Strauss regards the end of thinking to be the creation of order (whether imaginary or empirical) and the resolution of contradictions, I am fascinated by the contrary tendencies in human thought—for creating order and disorder, raising Cain and raising children, idealizing and demonizing the other, embracing strangers and making them scapegoats for one's misfortunes. Rather than analyze how these contrary tendencies are resolved in myth or discourse, I am more interested in how they are differentially expressed in what Malinowski called "contexts of situation."[17]

The ambivalence I discern in the work of Durkheim, Malinowski, and Lévi-Strauss reflects an all-too-human inability to make up one's mind about the status or intentions of the other—whether they are compatible with or inimical to one's own narcissistic sense of self. But human attitudes toward self or other are notoriously unstable. While social psychological research has shown that we share with all human beings a primary, unreflective mode of seeing other forms of life, especially other human beings, as similar to us, we learn to focus on differentiating traits, sometimes bringing these into the foreground and pushing common features into the background.[18] This tendency explains not only the origin of racist mind-sets but also the tendency in anthropology to focus on distinguishing or differentiating features to the exclusion of underlying commonalities. This gestalt oscillation between different ways of construing our relation with others—same as or different from—reflects changing external environments, both social and physical, and changing inner moods, emotions, or states of health. Typically, we attend selectively to different traits in others, depending on whether they threaten or support our sense of self. This is why, when our personal or group integrity is in jeopardy we seek to both affirm our own privileged right to life *and* deny that right to the other.

Am I Charlie or Not Charlie or Both?

When the World Trade Center in lower Manhattan was destroyed on September 11, 2001, people reacted as if they were bereaved. Everyone, in his or her own way, struggled to make sense of what had occurred, obsessively watching replays of the event on television, calling family long-distance, e-mailing friends, attending teach-ins, standing together in solidarity and silence, and, through the exchange of anecdotes and stories, reclaiming a sense of shared certainties and meanings. Identical reactions were seen in France when gunmen killed seventeen people in raids on the offices of a satirical newspaper, *Charlie Hebdo*, and a kosher supermarket in Paris on January 7, 2015. The slogan *Je suis Charlie*, seen everywhere in the aftermath of the atrocities, affirmed French values (particularly democracy and a free press), and two million people assembled in Paris on January 11 in a rally of national unity. But in the aftermath of both these critical events, an intense demonstration of togetherness was accompanied by an equally intense vilification of Islamic fundamentalism—the latest expression of Europe's and America's historical need for a radical other against which to define their own senses of identity.

Whenever a notion of "either you are for us or against us" takes hold, it becomes difficult, if not treasonable, to criticize this binary logic or express any other view. As Susan Sontag observed in 2003, "It is hard to defy the wisdom of the tribe, the wisdom that values the lives of its members above all others. It will always be unpopular—it will always be deemed inappropriate—to say that the lives of the members of the other tribe are as valuable as one's own."[19] Within days of the killings in Paris, similar reservations were expressed, most succinctly by the graphic artist Joe Sacco. "My first reaction," he wrote, "was sadness. People were brutally killed, among them several cartoonists—my tribe. But along with grief came thoughts about the nature of some of *Charlie Hebdo*'s satire. Though tweaking the noses of Muslims might be as permissible as it is now believed to be dangerous, it has never struck me as anything other than a vapid way to use the pen." Sacco then allows himself to play the same game, drawing a black man with a banana in his hand, falling out of a tree, and a Jew "counting his money in the entrails of the working class," only to ask whether such caricatures are a substitute for thinking "about why the world is the way it is." Sacco then conjures an image of a prisoner, Ali Shallal al-Qaisi, being tortured by CIA operatives in Abu Ghraib prison, Iraq, before proposing the choice we must make between revengeful actions and "sorting out how we fit into each other's world."[20]

Sacco's invocation of Abu Ghraib is made singularly compelling because in a court deposition in 2007, Chérif Kouachi, the younger of the brothers affiliated with al-Qaida who shot the *Charlie Hebdo* journalists, said, "I got this idea when I saw the injustices shown by television on what was going on over there. I am speaking about the torture that the Americans have inflicted on the Iraqis." Although understanding why a person is moved to violence does not condone it, in the absence of any attempt at understanding we easily fall prey to the kind of stereotypical and self-serving thought that has always provided those who have recourse to violence with their slogans and rationales. Rabbi Michael Lerner, editor of the progressive and interfaith magazine *Tikkun*, also questioned the media coverage of the Paris massacre, arguing that our exclusive focus on this particular outrage effectively blots out our awareness of "the equally despicable acts of systematic murder and torture that Western countries have been involved in." Lerner castigates the self-righteousness of newspapers that evoke freedom of the press as their justification for publishing cartoons of the Prophet yet express indignation when their own sacred cows are slandered. "Media was outraged at the attempt by some North Korean allied group to scare people away from watching a movie ridiculing and then planning to assassinate the current (immoral) ruler of Korea," Lerner writes, but the question was not broached as to how we'd respond if a similar movie had been made ridiculing and planning the assassination of an American president. In the same vein, Lerner goes on, "the media has refused to even consider what it would mean to a French Muslim, living among Muslims who are economically marginalized and portrayed as nothing but terrorists, their religious garb banned in public, their religion demeaned, to encounter a humor magazine that ridiculed the one thing that gives them some sense of community and higher purpose, namely Mohammed and the religion he founded."[21]

We all tend to make our own small lifeworlds the measure of all things. It is not only jihadists who are blind to the humanity of those they kill in the name of Allah. We are all afflicted by tunnel vision to some extent, even those of us who are curious or brave enough to travel beyond the borders of our own familiar world and trust that perfect strangers will extend us hospitality and treat us as though we are potential friends rather than enemies. But as every traveler knows, and every honest ethnographer will attest, the stresses and anxieties of living outside one's comfort zone can occasionally undermine the sense of common humanity that one has come to espouse. After months of isolation in an unfamiliar environment, separated from family and friends, struggling with a difficult language and foreign customs, one can all too easily feel vulnerable and paranoid. That so many anthropologists expressed dismay or disenchantment when Malinowski's field diaries were published posthumously in 1967 may be taken as evidence of how assiduously anthropologists have worked to hide the feelings of self-doubt, loneliness, homesickness, sexual frustration, and exasperation that are inevitable concomitants of fieldwork.[22] Rather than deny such "weaknesses" we should learn to process them, not in secret, lest this mar our professional façade of being in total control of ourselves and possessing a total comprehension of the other, but in public, as a way of exploring the universal human dilemma of how to strike a balance between a sense of our difference and sameness from others, neither condemning them for not being in the least like us nor romanticizing them as being our brothers or sisters. Only in this way can one hope to achieve the goal of anthropology, which is not to presume an understanding of others as they understand themselves, or even to understand ourselves in a new way, but to discover to what extent we can find common ground with them, interacting in tolerant solidarity rather than radical opposition. "Sorting out," as Joe Sacco put it, "how we fit in each other's world."

Resignation

Understanding how we fit in each other's world is more challenging today than it ever was. A century ago, most of humankind lived in small communities. Events beyond the immediate horizon came to one's notice in small doses and could be readily assimilated into one's extant worldview or dismissed. But the tsunami of information now overwhelming our consciousness is hard to process or build psychic defenses against. The media that overdoses us with this welter of information—news of terrorist outrages, dire warnings against carcinogens and lethal viruses, statistics on the number of refugees now clamoring for asylum, or predictions of impending climate-related catastrophes—also offers us a palliative by providing simplistic and formulaic responses to these potential threats. Terrorism is evil, and we are good. Climate change is a serious issue, but we can adapt. Ebola is being brought under control. Science continues to make breakthroughs in combating cancer. But there remain threats we cannot protect ourselves from, anxieties that cannot be dispelled, problems that admit of no solution, pain that cannot be alleviated, questions for which we have no answers. These are, generally speaking, the existential aporias that have defined the human condition for many millennia—the struggle to find meaning in a life that is destined to come to an end, to be treated fairly in a world in which the resources of a worthwhile life are scarce and unequally distributed, to feel that one matters and is recognized for what one is worth. But though these issues are existential, they are often articulated in the languages of religion and politics, begging the question whether those vocabularies render the issues more tractable, or our responses to them less vexed.

On November 13, 2015, a day after suicide bombings in Beirut, Paris suffered its second terrorist attack, and intellectuals once again found themselves struggling to position their responses between the calls to arms and the calls for better knowledge of why such atrocities should occur. How can we come to terms with such events—the blind rage, rationalized by religion, or the self-righteous conviction that one has a right to redress a wrong by slaughtering innocents? Can the cycle of violence that began with America's response to 9/11, the colonial partition of Africa or the Middle East, or the slave trade ever be reversed, or is history, as Walter Benjamin wrote, a wind we sow and a whirlwind we reap, its debris piling up generation after generation as we are blown backward into the future? There are times when one reaches the limits of what can be thought or spoken, when even to evoke the unthinkable becomes a defense against the impossibility of thought. Is our only option to retreat into our little local worlds, drawing the shades against the explosive lights on the far horizon in the hope that the battlefront won't come any closer? One may survive this way, but at what cost?

In an interview with Theodor Adorno that appeared in *Der Spiegel* three months before the philosopher's death in 1969, the interviewer begins by saying, "Professor Adorno, two weeks ago, the world still seemed in order," only for Adorno to quickly interrupt and say, "Not to me."[23] Adorno is alluding to an episode two weeks before, when his lecture in a course on dialectical thought before an audience of nearly one thousand students at the University of Frankfurt was disrupted by female students rushing the podium, exposing their breasts, and trying to kiss him while male students delivered a barrage of verbal insults. Vilified for his refusal to engage in street interventions and other forms of political activism, harassed for his "quietism," and deeply depressed, Adorno turned, in his interview, to the question of resignation. When asked how one might change society without individual action, Adorno replied, "This is asking too much of me. In response to the question, 'What is to be done' I usually can only answer 'I do not know.' I can only analyze relentlessly what is." As for the despair, pessimism, and negativity into which people are sometimes plunged, Adorno observed that such feelings were understandable. But, he continued, "Those who compulsively shout down their objective despair with the noisy optimism of immediate action in order to lighten their psychological burden are much more deluded." To avoid being "terrorized into action," especially violent action, is not simply to recognize the danger of an "eternal circle of using violence to fight violence"; it is to valorize critical thought and to remind oneself that new ways of thinking have, historically, not only changed our ways of seeing the world but also changed the world itself.[24] Critical thought refuses to pretend that the task of thinking is to deliver judgments. Nor does it serve as a rationale for rushing in where angels fear to tread, as if action were always preferable to inaction. "Thinking is not the intellectual reproduction of what already exists. . . . Open thinking points beyond itself," writes Adorno.[25] This is the challenge of philosophical anthropology.

3. Relations and Relata

It seems as if the elementary psychic fact were not *thought* or *this thought* or *that thought*, but *my thought*, every thought being *owned*. . . . The universal conscious fact is not "feelings and thoughts exist," but "I think" and "I feel."

—WILLIAM JAMES, *THE STREAM OF THOUGHT*

A recurring problem in the social sciences is how we can grasp what William James called the "unsharable feeling which each of us has of the pinch of his individual destiny as he privately feels it rolling out on fortune's wheel,"[1] when our investigations are framed by a priori, abstract, and transpersonal terms such as "the social," "the cultural," or even *Dasein*. Martin Heidegger dismissed the "personalistic" tendencies in the philosophical anthropology of Wilhelm Dilthey, Max Scheler, and Henri Bergson on the grounds that the question of Being (*Dasein*) does not necessarily implicate questions of personal being or philosophies of life.[2] But how can one avoid what A. N. Whitehead called the fallacy of misplaced concreteness—treating analytical constructs as though they were lived realities and, as a corollary, treating lived realities as though they were a veil camouflaging unconscious forces that required scientific expertise to uncover and arcane coinages to describe? James writes against both reification and obfuscation, and his *Principles of Psychology* remains one of the most compelling demonstrations that our human being-in-the-world is irreducible to the ways in which existence is characterized, explained, rationalized, and represented.

Radical Empiricism

In his *Essays in Radical Empiricism*, first published in 1904, James characterizes "the philosophic atmosphere" of his times in promising, even prophetic, terms. Celebrating "a loosening of old landmarks, a softening of oppositions, a mutual borrowing from one another on the part of systems anciently closed, and an interest in new suggestions, however vague, as if the one thing sure were the inadequacy of the extant school-solutions," James gives the impression of being ahead of his times.[3] But for many academics nowadays, James's vision is idealistic or passé. In arguing against this dismissive attitude, I ask why we have not witnessed the realization of what James envisaged. But I want to do more than simply pay lip service to his view that our discursive conventions and mind-sets may have become "too abstract" and that we urgently need to introduce into our work a sense of the "confused and superabundant" character of life, "even tho it were at some cost of logical rigor and of formal purity."[4] I want to underscore the value of his radically empirical method for exploring philosophical problems through psychology and introspection and to indicate how it is also productive to explore philosophical issues through ethnography and biography.

Specifically, in this chapter I seek to do two things. First, to make a case for doing exactly what James advocated 110 years ago. Second, to show, through empirical examples, why his radical empiricism and his psychology of consciousness are by no means irrelevant to understanding the complexities of our contemporary world.

Let me begin by trying to capture the spirit of James's philosophical psychology by calling to mind its emphasis on relations over relata, on experience as encompassing both the experiencing subject and the object of his or her experience, and on the ever-changing character of consciousness and the multiplicity of self-states. These three themes are mutually entailed; all refuse to ground understandings of life processes in the conceptual or material products that human beings create in the course of living.

For James, it is never a question of whether reality is *either* intransitive *or* transitive (to use one of his own metaphors, a bird's lived reality constantly oscillates between perching and flying) any more than substantives are more significant in a language than the conjunctions, prepositions, adverbial phrases, and inflections of voice that "express some shading or other of *relation* which we at such moment actually feel to exist *between* the larger objects of our thought."[5] James would have undoubtedly embraced Merleau-Ponty's argument against polarizing the objective and the subjective, not only because the world without and the world within are always in dynamic relation to each other but also because what is methodologically crucial is holding both perspectives in balance—a process he compares to the way we move around in an art gallery so that we neither view a painting from so close that it becomes a blur or from so far away that it loses its detail and allure. This emphasis on striking a balance between "an inner and outer horizon" resonates with James's description of "experience" as double-barrelled.[6] By this, James means that experience admits of no absolute division between the experiencing subject and the object of his or her experience.[7] Experience denotes the farm as well as the farmer, the farmer's anxieties about the weather as well as the weather itself, his hope of a good harvest as well as the market forces that will determine the price he gets for his crop. When we bring the concept of experience to the social field, the same ambiguity exists, as I am always in relation to another, regardless of whether that other is momentarily absent, dead, or imaginary, as well as whether that other is a person, a common language, a community, a state, an economic system, an object, an animal, or a collective representation. Accordingly, human beings are never wholly constituted by their class, culture, or history, and every person's lived experience overflows, goes beyond, and is more complex than the terms with which we conventionally categorize it.

In keeping with James's insistence that life is always *more* than can be contained or covered in abstract concepts—that it possesses a fluidity and mutability that renders absurd our efforts to grasp and systematize all that is experientially the case—I begin with the most basic mode of consciousness of which one may be aware. While William James referred to this mode of consciousness as "irresponsible thinking" and compared it to "spontaneous revery,"[8] Carl Jung regarded this relatively aimless, arbitrary, associative mode of thought as so similar to dreaming that he called it "dream thinking."[9] In this allegedly "pure state," there is no sense of a knowing subject that is separate from an object to be known.[10] But consciousness is seldom settled in this state. The random shuffle of sounds, images, emotions, and incipient ideas becomes directed and organized in words and through objects. We begin "thinking with directed attention," talking to ourselves, making connections with past experience, entertaining ideas, sketching a picture, expressing ourselves *outwardly*.[11]

This relationship between inwardness and the expressive forms of language, gesture, or art remains mysterious. One never knows whether the outward form mirrors one's original intention or betrays it. And one can never predict what people will make of what we say or do. As the Latin adage *bis faciunt idem, non est idem* reminds us, though people *act* in the same way, this does not mean that they *are* the same. There is, moreover, always a discrepancy between subjective realities and objective appearances that makes it difficult to infer inner feelings from outward behavior or to know what is going on in the minds of others. Indeed, it is hard enough to know one's own mind.

Although we cannot understand inner realities except through the words and actions that render those realities visible, audible, and graspable, and therefore sharable, we are aware that there is always more to a person than meets the eye or finds expression in what he or she says and does. It is this *indeterminate* relationship between the processes and products of consciousness—whether in art, religion, or everyday social life—that fascinates me.

Let me begin with Patañjali's approach to this relationship. In Patañjali's exposition of yoga (*yogānushāsanam*), yoga is conceptualized as a techne for quelling (*nirodha*) the fluctuations and flux of the phenomenal mind (*chittam*) and for not confusing *who* one is with *what* goes on in one's head. Although Patañjali describes, at great length, both the nature of consciousness and the ethical, physical, respiratory, and mental disciplines for transforming it, the yoga sutras are informed by idealistic assumptions about enlightened understanding and correct behavior that not every yoga practitioner may share. For example, the state of consciousness known as *samadhi*—union of consciousness of the self and consciousness of the divine—is, to my mind, no more or less interesting than states of consciousness deemed to be discursive, digressive, dissociated, or undisciplined. All these may produce positive or negative effects.

My own inclination, therefore, is neither to follow Sankhya metaphysics by conflating certain forms of consciousness with purity or enlightenment, nor presuppose that intentionality is "a defining characteristic of consciousness." Edmund Husserl notes that "moods such as depression or euphoria are not always 'of' or 'about' something . . . and sensations such as pain or dizziness are not obviously representational or directed toward some object."[12] Moreover, as William James observed, consciousness is more like a stream than a train or chain; sometimes slow-moving, sometimes in flood, and continually disrupted by eddies, snags, and counter-currents, and there are times when consciousness is "one great blooming, buzzing confusion."[13] For these reasons it is impossible to endorse Immanuel Kant's transcendentalist view of the person, or the substantialist view preferred by Aristotle, René Descartes, and John Locke or the Humean view of the person as a stream of sensations, since our sense of self is constantly shifting among these modalities as our circumstances change.[14] In other words, it would be fallacious to make any one of these modes of consciousness the basis for a universal theory of mind.

One thing we can say: human consciousness is seldom stable. At one extreme, our thoughts are idle, arbitrary, distracted, and diffuse; at the other extreme, we become conceptually fixated, obsessed, and single-minded. We can be lost to the world one moment and the next wholly engaged in a task. Randomly, it seems, a shift of mood, a snatch of music, a fugitive memory, an inchoate idea passes through the mind like flashes in our field of vision. Fantastical or fragmentary images flit through our subconscious. One's concentration is broken by a text message or phone call or the sudden realization that one is late for a meeting. We flit in an instant from confidence and calm to doubt and uncertainty. Our moods swing, our emotions change, our thoughts wander.

Given this fluidity and complexity of consciousness, how is it possible to access other minds or even monitor the inner workings of our own thoughts without singling out certain elements and ignoring others?

In the following episode from *Ulysses* (1922), James Joyce begins by describing the world from afar. Three girl friends have come down to Sandymount shore to enjoy the evening air, "which was fresh but not too chilly," and to "discuss matters feminine." One of the girls, Gerty MacDowell, is described as "beautiful by all who knew her," her crowning glory a wealth of dark brown, naturally wavy hair. As Gerty by turns lapses into romantic reverie and chats with her friends, she notices a man observing her, whose "gaze there, in the twilight, wan and strangely drawn, seemed to her the saddest she had ever seen." Her heart goes out to him, and she responds to his probing, passionate gaze by exposing her legs and knickers. The man is sexually aroused. His hand slips into his pocket. As fireworks explode over Sandymount Green, it becomes clear to Gerty that the man who has been gazing at her so intently is masturbating. Not long after he has come, Gerty walks past him with quiet dignity. It is only now that Leopold Bloom realizes she is lame.

At this moment, Joyce shifts from a view from afar to the most intimate point of view of view possible, and we are borne away in the Humean stream of Bloom's consciousness.

Poor girl! That's why she's left on the shelf and the others did a sprint. Thought something was wrong by the cut of her jib. Might have a moustache, superfluous hair. Jilted beauty. A defect is ten times worse in a woman. But makes them polite. Glad I didn't know it when she was on show. Hot little devil all the same. I wouldn't mind. Curiosity. Like a nun or a negress or a girl with glasses. That squinty one is delicate. Near her monthlies I expect. Makes them feel ticklish. I have such a bad headache today. Where did I put the letter? Yes, all right. All kinds of crazy longings. Licking pennies. Girl is Tranquilla Convent that nun told me liked to smell rock oil. Virgins go mad in the end I suppose. Sister? How many women in Dublin have it today? Martha, she. Something in the air. That's the moon. But then why don't all women menstruate at the same time, with the same moon I mean? Depends on the time they were born I suppose. Or all start scratch then get out of step. Sometimes Molly and Milly together. Anyhow I got the best of that. Damned glad I didn't do it in the bath this morning over her silly I will punish you letter.[15]

There are moments in this passage when Bloom's associations seem quite random; at other times his consciousness resembles interior monologue, a soliloquy, or a kind of intuitive commentary on external events.[16] But unlike the initial description of the girls on the rocks of Sandymount Strand, Joyce's account of Bloom's mood, mind, and emotions is solipsistic. In effect, no other perspective than Bloom's exists.

There is, however, a third perspective in *Ulysses* that resembles the substantialist view espoused by Aristotle and Locke and is characteristic of the scientific standpoint. This perspective does not set the scene or enter the scene; it goes behind the scene. And it implies not a theory of consciousness but of the unconscious—of a reality that is implicit and invisible to all but the specialist scholar or scientist. This is the perspective that enables one to connect this episode in *Ulysses* to the episode in Homer's *Odyssey* when Odysseus, shipwrecked on the fairy-tale island of Scheria, fantasizes about making love to the alluring Nausicaä.

Joyce's *Ulysses* involves multiple perspectives—from Bloom's personal perspective to Joyce's narrative perspective to detached scholarly perspectives that Bloom would not have understood and Joyce may have balked at. Each discloses a different truth—from the experience-near to the experience-distant. None is entirely compatible with the others. But *Ulysses* not only chronicles multiple modes of consciousness; it also disrupts the conventional view that we possess singular personalities and stable identities. In the course of the novel, Joyce's characters "continually change their costumes, shapes, or identities."[17] The assumption of gender identity subverted, and the anthropocentric view that humans and animals are essentially unalike is shown to be an artificial construct. In "Circe," for instance, animals and their human counterparts shapeshift with the dramatic alacrity of characters in an African folktale so that not only are humans likened to animals (with vulture talons, weasel teeth, a parrot beak, turkey wattles, a horning claw), but they also are given different animals' voices.[18]

That it is possible to *imagine* consciousness so readily transgressing the boundaries between what we conventionally think of as categorically and essentially different forms of life—between humans and animals, mortals and gods, subjects and objects—suggests that the self itself is capable of dissociation and fragmentation without necessarily becoming dysfunctional. Indeed, as William James observed, though philosophers have tended to theorize the self from substantialist (Aristotelian), associationist (Humean), or transcendentalist (Kantian) perspectives, *all* these modes of selfhood find expression in our lives, and it would be foolish to define selfhood from the standpoint of one of these perspectives alone.[19] Abstracting a single mode of experience from the everchanging stream of experience and then pressing it into a fixed conceptual mold falsifies the phenomenological complexity of consciousness; moreover, it may entrench social prejudices. For example, many essays in social psychology draw a contrast between an allegedly Western mode of egocentric conscious and an allegedly sociocentric mode of Eastern consciousness, failing entirely to see that existence everywhere entails continual oscillations between our relationships with others and our relationships with ourselves.[20] Consider the figure of Proteus, the shapeshifting son of Poseidon, who presides over the opening sections of *Ulysses*. As Stephen Dedalus picks his way across Sandymount Strand, a variety of things catch his eye—seawrack, the incoming tide, squeaking pebbles, razorshells, a porter bottle—and each triggers its own train of thought. Then, as Stephens opens and closes his eyes, his thoughts drift from abstract associations to concrete realities, such as a dog running up to him only to be summoned, by a whistle, back to the couple walking it. Stephen's mind wanders from past to present and shifts from inward thought to external events, and at every turn these drifts and divagations suggest that *he inhabits different self-states*. This theme is returned to in the next section, Calypso, when Molly asks Bloom to tell her "in plain words" what metempsychosis means. Again we are drawn back to Greece, as Bloom explains that the ancient Greeks "used to believe you could be changed into an animal or a tree."[21]

Rather than make any one perspective—collective or individual, human or extrahuman—foundational to a general theory of knowledge or of the self, I want to explore the impermanence of self-states and the conditions under which different perspectives make their appearance in the lives of actual people. How does this interplay of inward-looking and outward-looking modes of consciousness help make a person's life viable in unpredictable and distressing situations?

Migrant Consciousness and the Multiple Self

For several years now I have been researching and recording the life stories of African migrants in three European cities—London, Amsterdam, and Copenhagen. Migrant narratives are, in many ways, allegories of human existence, in which the hope that our lives may be made more abundant, for ourselves and those we love, constantly comes up against the limits of what we may achieve and the despair into which we may be plunged when we find ourselves unable to achieve that state of well-being and flourishing that Aristotle called *eudaimonia*. Our lives oscillate between transitive and intransitive extremes. Whether planned or accidental, desired or dreaded, the passage from one place to another, one life stage to another, or one state or status to another often figures centrally in the stories we tell about our lives and who we are. Though we may hanker after hard and fast differences between self and other, human and animal, man and machine, or male and female, these boundaries get blurred, transgressed, and redrawn. We morph and migrate in and out of our bodies, in reality and in our imaginations. Along with all living things, *we move through life*. By this I mean not only that we are all bound to die (it is only a question of when) but also that we were all once migrants (again, it is only a question of when). These sweeping statements indicate the existential perspective from which I view migration. Rather than treat the migrant as a singular figure—an interloper, anomaly, or alien in our midst—the migrant exemplifies a universal aspect of human existence. Either we are moving or the world is moving— about, under, or above us. To cite the phrase so often seen on vehicles in West Africa, "No Condition Is Permanent."

When anthropologists and social theorists write about migration they often invoke binaries, speaking of divided selves and double-binds, of halfies, hybrids, and being in-between. Subjective conflicts are said to mirror social crises, also described in binary terms and suggesting radical breaks between autocratic and democratic regimes, political and occult economies, an orientation toward the past and an orientation toward the future.[22] But to describe the self "as torn between self-interest and collective good, struggling over desire and responsibility, negotiating contradictory emotions,"[23] may all too easily give the impression that human beings find little satisfaction in their mutability and prefer the illusion of a unitary and stable sense of self. Rather than imply that people necessarily find fulfillment in being settled in one place or possessing a single core identity, I consider it imperative that we complement this view of a stable self with descriptions of human improvisation, experimentation, opportunism, and existential mobility, showing that individuals often struggle not so much to align their lives with given moral or legal norms as to find ways of negotiating *the ethical space* between external constraints and personal imperatives. This capacity for strategic shape-shifting, both imaginative and actual, defines our very humanity.

I find it ironic, therefore, that most writers who invoke images of psychological division and historical discontinuity would *not* wish to make a case either for static, one-dimensional personalities or monocultural *societies* in which nothing and no one changed. Why, then, should we not embrace the view that "a pluralistic universe" applies equally to both polis and persons, to states and to selves?[24]

Recent psychoanalytical work on the self challenges the concept of the person as a seamless, stable, skin-encapsulated monad.[25] Rather than being constant, we constantly change, like chameleons, according to our surroundings, and we possess an extraordinary "capacity to feel like one self while being many."[26] Indeed, our ability to shift and adjust our self-state in response to whom we are with, to what circumstance demands, and to what our well-being seems to require is more than adaptive; our lives would be impossible without it.[27]

This conception of the self as several rather than singular has a long history. In 1580, Michel de Montaigne observed that

> anyone who turns his prime attention on to himself will hardly find himself in the same state twice. . . . Every sort of contradiction can be found in me, depending on some twist or attribute. . . . There is nothing I can say about myself as a whole simply and completely, without intermingling and admixture. . . . We are fashioned out of oddments put together. . . . We are entirely made up of bits and pieces, woven together so diversely and so shapelessly that each one of them pulls its own way at every moment. And there is as much difference between us and ourselves as there is between us and other people.[28]

In 1857, Herman Melville wrote in a similar vein against the "fiction" of an independent, unique self that remains stable over time. "A consistent character is a *rara avis*," he says, and a work of fiction "where every character can, by reason of its consistency, be comprehended at a glance, either exhibits but sections of character, making them appear for wholes, or else is very untrue to reality; while on the other hand, that author who draws a character, even though to common view incongruous in its parts, as the flying-squirrel, and, at different periods, as much at variance with itself as the caterpillar is with the butterfly into which it changes, may yet, in so doing, be not false but faithful to facts."[29]

In 1928, Virginia Woolf touched on the same theme, observing that the selves "of which we are built up, one on top of another, as plates are piled on a waiter's hand, have . . . little constitutions and rights of their own. . . . One will only come if it is raining, another [will emerge only] in a room with green curtains, another when Mrs. Jones is not there, another if you can promise it a glass of wine—and so on. . . . [E]verybody can multiply from his own experience the different terms which his different selves have made with him—and some are too wildly ridiculous to be mentioned in print at all."[30] It is not impossible that at the same time Virginia Woolf composed these lines, the heteronymous Fernando Pessoa was writing, "Each of us is several, is many, is a profusion of selves. . . . In the vast colony of our being there are many species of people who think and feel in different ways."[31]

William James also emphasized the multiplicity of the self, noting in 1890, "*A man has as many selves as there are individuals who recognize him* and carry an image of him in their mind." A man's self "*is the sum total of all that he CAN call his*, not only his body and his psychic powers, but his clothes, and his house, his wife and children, his ancestors and friends, his reputation and works, his lands and horses, and yacht and bank account." Furthermore, a person's own well-being is intimately tied to the well-being of these significant others, objects, or qualities. "To wound any one of these images is to wound him."[32]

All these writers touch on what I have elsewhere called "the migrant imaginary," our human capacity for calling forth or bringing to the forefront of consciousness hitherto backgrounded aspects of ourselves in dealing with changing situations.[33] Psychological multiplicity or plasticity is not, therefore, a problem that requires therapy, returning us to a one-dimensional, stable state that is continuous and consistent over time and in all situations; it is the creative and adaptive expression of sociality itself.

Let us consider three closely related aspects of this adaptability: adapting to other people, adapting to other societies or forms of life, and adapting to changes in our life course. While the first aspect involves being affectively moved in relation to other selves, the second involves movement from place to place, and the third covers the critical transitions that mark our passage through life.

Our capacity for becoming other in relation to other selves is the basis for mutual recognition and empathy. It is the suppressed aspects of ourselves, seldom fully acknowledged and often actively abhorred, that enable us to find common ground with people who initially appear so radically different from us that we sometimes hesitate to call them human. This capacity to see others in the light of normally occluded aspects of ourselves may, under certain circumstances, help us recognize animals and objects as sharing in the being we ordinarily attribute solely to ourselves. Thus, recent researchers have identified the symptoms of post–traumatic stress disorder in African elephants whose herds have been decimated by culls, illegal poaching, and habitat loss. Calves that have witnessed the killing of their mothers and female caretakers or have lacked male socialization show abnormal startle responses, depression, unpredictable asocial behavior, and hyper-aggression.[34]

The psychoanalytic anthropologist George Devereux has argued for the psychic unity of humankind in just these terms—that every individual contains the potential of Everyman, creative as well as destructive—and that what is foregrounded in one person or made normative in one society will exist in a subdominant, repressed, or potential form in another person or another society.[35] Our capacity for becoming other in relation to other selves also explains the persistence with which human beings, from time immemorial, have moved, migrated, and mutated, adjusting to radically new circumstances *despite the risks involved, the losses incurred, and the suffering undergone.*

One of the commonest experiences of encountering a complete stranger or moving from a familiar to an unfamiliar environment or passing from one phase of one's life to another is disorientation. This cognitive bewilderment is variously and viscerally experienced as vertigo, nausea, nostalgia, and exhaustion. "I'm the empty stage where various actors act out various plays, living the lives of various people—both on the outside, seeing them, and on the inside, feeling them," writes Fernando Pessoa, who appears to have lost all sense of any core self.[36]

In this dissociated state, selves that were previously foregrounded are no longer affirmed by others as normal, or even as natural, or they no longer serve one's immediate interests. The person you once reviled may now be the person on whom you depend for recognition and succor. You may have become an adult, but the child in you cries out for comfort. You have arrived in Rome and are trying to do as the Romans do, but you crave, if only for a moment, to be able to eat your own food, in your own home, with your own kith and kin. No shift in self-states is straightforward. To be in transition is to be in doubt and adrift and to experience dissociation—to suddenly discover that one has become a stranger to oneself. As Ibrahim Ouédraego—a friend from Burkina Faso—put it, reflecting on his first bewildered days in Amsterdam, "You cannot do everything you want to do. There are always rules that will stop you crossing borders, stop you going where you want to go, stop you finding an easier path. It's papers that count, not words. No one trusts anything you say. You can't talk to people directly. You've got to have papers. Even if the papers are false, they will count more than your words. There is no more truth in words." Sierra Leonean friends in London confessed similar consternation as they struggled to negotiate the labyrinth of a bureaucratic state. In West Africa one's destiny was determined by a network of face-to-face relationships with people to whom you were obliged or who were under obligation to you, people whom in local parlance you could "beg" or from whom you could borrow money or expect a meal or a roof over your head. But in Europe, one quickly discovers that one has passed from a patrimonial to a bureaucratic regime in which power resides less in people to whom one can appeal than in an impersonal force field that finds expression in a stranger's stare, a policeman's orders, a supervisor's demands, or the letter of the law. In this inscrutable and Kafkaesque world of bureaucratic protocols, indecipherable documents, abstract rules, and official forms of validation, one comes up against what Michael Herzfeld has called "the social production of indifference."[37] The "living spirit" of community has given ground to the "dead letter" of a system that recognizes no one because it is nobody.[38]

This is not a matter of being between two worlds, but of being *dismembered*, no longer being fully integrated into a familiar community. And so the migrant is obliged to *re-member* himself, to assemble, like a bricoleur, from the various aspects of his past and present selves, a new *assemblage*.[39] Thus, Ibrahim oscillates between a concern for his father's expectations, his mother's wishes, his wife and daughter in Holland,

and his personal ambition to become better educated—moving continually between these self-states, each of which is associated with a different country, a different period in his life, a different kind of loyalty, and a different person. In London, my friend Sewa found alcohol use problematic. As a Muslim, and out of respect for his beloved father, Sewa preferred not to drink, even though this seriously compromised his English social life. How could he drink beer with friends in his apartment if his father's photograph on the wall was a stern reminder of his lack of filial respect?

> There's one thing [my father] never wants any of his kids to do, and that is drink alcohol. If I went out and drank alcohol, as soon as I came home and stepped into my room and saw that picture, I would have to run out of the room again. I would want to go and take the picture and put it away, like in my cupboard or box. But if I had alcohol in my system I would not be able to touch the picture. I'd have to wait for days, days, to take that picture and put it somewhere, so I can walk into my room and not see it straight away. I know it's just a picture, but it's like it's him seeing me, what I'm doing, you know. You see, I've got all these beliefs. And when I stop drinking, pray to him, ask him for forgiveness, I know that's the only thing I'm doing that my dad's unhappy about.

It was Sewa's English girlfriend that suggested that he hang the photo of his father in the living room, then bare except for a small lacquered plywood map of Sierra Leone on which different seeds—sesame, millet, mustard, chili, and several species of rice—had been glued to mark the different provinces.

> "But I don't like pictures in the sitting room. I couldn't sit there, holding a beer, drinking, if my dad's picture was looking at me. So that's what's stopping me putting the picture up. I can't live in a house where friends will come and want to drink, and my dad is seeing me, I just can't do that. I feel I'm doing the wrong thing, that he doesn't want me to do, even though he's not alive in the real world, I just don't want to do that."
>
> "But you have made so many changes in your life, since coming to England," I said. "Big changes."
>
> "It's true, Mr. Michael. Sometimes I can't believe myself."

Despite the anguish Sewa often felt as he tried to work out new configurations and compromises in his lifestyle, he did not "fall apart." This is because, as Philip Bromberg points out, a multiple self is not incompatible with normal mental functioning because "a person can access simultaneously a range of discrete self-states that, despite their contrasting and even opposing perspectives on personal reality, are able to engage in internal dialogue. It is this capacity that permits oppositional aspects of self to coexist in consciousness as potentially resolvable intrapsychic conflict."[40] There are echoes here of James's view that "experience is trained by *both* association and dissociation, and . . . psychology must be writ *both* in synthetic and in analytic terms."[41]

Perhaps it would be more accurate to speak of multitasking rather than multiple selves, as the possession of a repertoire of potential social or practical *skills* does not necessarily mean that we are composed of several discrete *identitie*s.[42] In other words, the limit is not simply where things disintegrate and the perennial possibility arises of being born again.[43] It is where we are driven to intense experimentation, searching for a strategy or skill, object or ally, that will help us overcome an obstacle, regain a sense of agency, or perform a seemingly impossible task.

The migrant exemplifies, therefore, a vital aspect of every person's passage through life—an ability to change with changing situations, conjuring multiple mind-sets and calling on multiple means for addressing different challenges. "This view of self as multiple and discontinuous," writes Stephen Mitchell, "is grounded in a temporal rather than spatial metaphor: Selves are what people do and experience over time rather than something that exists someplace."[44] Thus, despite his encounters with racism in Denmark, a Ugandan friend, Emmanuel Mulamila, made a conscious choice not to see *himself* as African but to redouble his efforts to apply for work on the strength of his academic qualifications and personal qualities. My fieldwork among migrants also brought me into contact with a Mexican student at Harvard who had "converted" to Pentecostalism as he crossed the border into the United States, only to be picked up and deported before attempting the crossing again. But as Roberto Franco shared his story with me, I noticed that his recourse to religion occurred at those *moments* when he found himself at the limits of what he could endure—thrown into a prison cell among drunks and derelicts or facing another day of thankless labor in the fields. Though the police or field bosses treated him like dirt because he was "Mexican," Roberto negotiated his situation *in his own terms*, as a Christian, though at other times without any reference to God at all.

A contrast may be drawn here between agonistic and submissive attitudes. The agonistic attitude involves active resistance. We seize the initiative, determined to contest and change our situation. The submissive mode suggests passive resistance. We withdraw to lick our wounds, to figure out some way of enduring the situation, suffering and surviving it rather than willfully confronting it. In the modern West, we tend to extol the agonistic mode, deeming it heroic or noble. When someone dies of cancer, we speak of him or her as having lost a battle with the disease, as if fighting were ethically superior to submission. We wage "war" against cancer, terrorism, drugs, crime, and poverty and even speak of individuals as being at war with themselves. At the same time we disparage the submissive mode by calling it defeatist or fatalist, and this has long been one of the ways that men distinguish themselves from women or the West has contrasted itself with the East; while we supposedly take active responsibility for ourselves, people east of the Bosporus and south of the Sahara allegedly blame others for their misfortunes before they blame themselves, and they shift personal responsibility to God or fate, resigned to their lot rather than determining their own destinies. An empirically more accurate view of life in the global North and the global South reveals a constant shifting between these modes of activity and passivity. Except in extreme cases, no individual and no culture, Western or otherwise, is permanently stuck in one mode to the exclusion of the other. Human beings move constantly between activity and passivity, engagement and retreat, ego-centered and other-centered modes of being-in-the-world, depending on circumstance.[45] Even when a person abstains from action and appears to have relinquished agency, doing nothing—as we say—or placing his or her hope, trust, or faith in others or in higher powers—he or she may be actively imagining or thinking a great deal. Accordingly, behavioral passivity does not mean that the mind has ceased to seek out ways of coming to grips with the problem that has brought the body to a standstill. Indeed, it may be more useful to speak of an oscillation between being physically still and mentally active rather than an oscillation between passivity and activity, for in all but exceptional cases—such as when a person attains a mystical state of absolute physical and mental calmness—we are constantly moving between different modes of consciousness and engaging in different modes of acting. Human existence implies continual readjustment and revision, in our memories and imaginations as well as in our lived relationships with others and our environments. Roberto suppresses his Mexican past to better focus on the exigencies of his present American situation. Emmanuel, in order to meet the needs of his daughter, represses the anger that still boils up in him when he thinks of the abuse he suffered as a child. In many ways, this mobility and mutability of self-awareness is both phylogenetically and ontogenetically crucial to what we call adaptability. "To live is to be other," wrote Fernando Pessoa. "What moves lives."[46] No wonder, then, that I found in the experiences of the migrants I met in Europe and America dramatic analogues of my experience as an ethnographer where an ability to improvise and play with new possibilities of action and thought, experimenting with alternative modes of consciousness, not only defines the condition of the possibility of knowing others but also, perhaps more pertinently, offers a key to achieving viable coexistence in what William James called a pluralistic universe.

Coda

At the beginning of this chapter I noted that William James outlined an approach to the philosophy, psychology, and social science that he seemed confident would be the shape of things to come. But 114 years later, we have still to realize the full import of James's emphasis on relations over relata, his insistence that the "egotistic elements of experience" should not be suppressed, his argument that "our fields of experience have no more definite boundaries than have out fields of view," and his view that the flux and oscillations of lived experience are more significant than the theories we construct in an attempt to grasp it.[47] Perhaps our ambivalence toward James has something to do with the way his philosophy challenges any kind of established truth and, by extension, any kind of institutionalized learning. If truth is "what happens to an idea" when it serves us well in resolving some existential quandary, and not some a priori or inviolable wisdom that holds true for all people and for all time, then we may be wary of Harvard University's watchword of *Veritas* and find ourselves aligned with thinkers like William James, John Dewey, Hannah Arendt, and Theodor Adorno who repudiated "yardsticks by which to measure, and rules under which to subsume the particular."[48]

Realistically, though, we have to reckon with the fact that in the face of life's confusions and complexities we cling to substantives as drowning men cling to anything that promises buoyancy. Would any academy stay afloat if it fully embraced the intellectual tradition I have alluded to here? Would it emblazon on its gates "Abandon *veritas* all ye who enter here"? Paying lip service to absolute certainty is more conducive to asserting and establishing one's authority than a provisional, skeptical, ironic, or relativist worldview. And though skepticism may inspire us to seek authenticity, it is not going to inspire confidence in us should we seek high office. Poets are not good legislators of mankind. And would William James have been invited to preside over a great university when he held the opinion that all our thoughts and theories were "instrumental, are mental modes of *adaptation* to reality, rather than revelations or gnostic answers to some divinely instituted world-enigma"?[49] Ironically, something close to this actually happened, and the following story may serve to remind us that in life nothing is certain.

Within months of the founding of the American Philosophical Association in 1901, James was invited to become a member. He was in poor health at the time and declined the invitation, saying that he could not possibly join anything, adding, "I don't foresee much good from a philosophical society. Philosophical discussion proper only succeeds between intimates who have learned how to converse by months of weary trial and failure. The philosopher is a lone beast dwelling in his individual burrow.—Count me *out!*"[50]

Yet when his health improved, James changed his mind, joined the association, and became its president in 1904. It may seem contradictory that in that same year James published his *Essays in Radical Empiricism,* with its last page claiming that professional philosophy "seems too buttoned-up and white-chokered and clean-shaven a thing to speak for the vast slow-breathing unconscious Kosmos with its dread abysses and its unknown tides."[51] Yet changing one's mind, censoring one's thoughts, hiding one's true feelings, and acting a role do not imply ethical inconsistency or self-serving opportunism. Our social lives would not be viable unless we could shape-shift in these ways. Much as we extol the value of consistency in our views, constancy in our relations, and logical coherence in our thinking, we sometimes need to be reminded that our survival depends on our ability to change as circumstances change, to go with the flow, and to draw on a diversity of past experiences in response to who we are with and the situations in which we find ourselves.

4. Matters of Life and Death

Even though we have lost yardsticks by which to measure, and rules
under which to subsume the particular, a being whose essence is a
beginning may have enough of origin within himself to understand
without preconceived categories and to judge without the set of
customary rules which is morality.

—HANNAH ARENDT, *UNDERSTANDING AND POLITICS*

In *Negative Dialectics*, Theodor Adorno prepares us for a philosophy
that no longer has the infinite at its disposal and must do without the
consolation that the truth cannot be lost.[1] This "changed philosophy,"
disenchanted with the "conceptual shells that were to house the whole,"
insisting that no concept can adequately cover, contain, exhaust, or explain the wealth of lived experience, and declaring that "we cannot say
any more that the immutable is truth, and that the mobile, transitory is
appearance" was born in the shadows of Auschwitz.[2] There, the concept of God collapsed in the face of unspeakable suffering. In this "gray
zone,"[3] hope died, moral norms lost their force, and cultural codes were
eclipsed by desperate struggles to simply survive.

Though some might argue that the Holocaust has no precedent in the
history of man's inhumanity to man, examples come readily to my mind
of human life reduced to a state in which norms no longer hold true—
the plight of the Ik, the traumatic suffering of millions of Africans torn
from their homelands and shipped into slavery, the catastrophic loss of
lives and livelihoods that indigenous peoples endured under colonial regimes, and in our own time the *vita nuda* of countless refugees from
warfare and want, living in limbo with little prospect of ever returning
home. In his compelling account of the Harkis—Algerians who sided

with the French during the war of independence and in the postwar period found themselves "like figures in Greek tragedy, betraying (perhaps) and betrayed, abandoned, ostracized, and exiled to an alien land where they would remain strangers"—Vincent Crapanzano speaks of the individuals he came to know as both confirming and denying our traditional modes of understanding. He asks, what is it to be apart in a society, suffering "a condition that is constantly undermined by the reality of being among a people who would prefer you were not there and never had been there as they have to accept you or at least give you a place that is yet a no place?" What psychological and social price do the Harkis and their progeny pay for electing to forget the past, retreating into themselves and into silence? What is "the wound that never heals"?[4]

In a celebrated essay, Edward Said speaks similarly of exile as "the unhealable rift forced between a human being and a native place, between the self and its true home."[5] This rift has both existential and epistemological implications. Though anthropologists have documented, with compassionate thoroughness, the trauma of displacement, they have been less successful in responding to Adorno's call to rethink the conceptual apparatus of academic life—the substantive, supersensual terms like culture, religion, ethnicity, identity, and morality that belie the mobility, multiplicity, and mutability of lived experience, particularly in extremis, when abstractions are the last things on people's minds. To what extent do such abstractions, fetishized and made foundational for academic discourse, reflect the intellectual's settled and complacent situation rather than the lifeworlds that provide grist for the academic mill? How willing are we to take our interpretive cues from those whose lives we share in the course of fieldwork, allowing their thoughts to guide the way we think and their feelings to influence what we feel? As Crapanzano puts it, how can anthropologists reconcile their intellectual perspectives with the moral-existential perspectives of those they study—perspectives that are "at times so disquieting as to be nearly obliterated in our sheltering ourselves from them in the discipline's scientific goals."[6] Is it not the proper task of thought to challenge the concepts we have inadvertently ontologized, and from the standpoint of lived experience question if not actively subvert "all established criteria, values, measurements . . . customs and rules of conduct we treat of in morals and ethics?"[7] The challenge for anthropology remains the same challenge that Nietzsche issued to philosophy in *Thus Spake Zarathustra*: "O my brothers, is not everything in flux now? Have not all railings and bridges fallen into the water?"[8] In her phrase "thinking without a banister" (*denken ohne geländer*), Arendt urges us to take up Nietzsche's call to break our habit of seeking a transcendent grounding in supersensual categories of thought or, even worse, treating such forms of thought as if they were forms of life so that we become more attentive to what others say and do when at the limits of their reason, their language, or their endurance.

If this *is* our task, then the thinker is naturally aligned with those whose lifeworlds have been devastated and whose languages have been lost, who in the death camps demanded that God answer for His absence and indifference, and who, in searching for a life beyond the place where they were born, experience little continuity between what once was and what now is. In this regard, one exemplary work deserves to be cited. Ironically, it is by a philosopher, not an anthropologist, though it concerns a people who have been subject to anthropological study for more than a hundred years.

Jonathan Lear's *Radical Hope* begins with an arresting comment by the Crow (Apsáalooke) Indian chief Plenty Coups, in an interview with Frank Bird Lindeman in the late 1920s, when Plenty Coups was nearing the end of his life. Looking back on the era before the coming of the whites, Plenty Coups laments the passing of the buffalo and the impossibility of other traditional pursuits like war and horse stealing. "When the buffalo went away the hearts of my people fell to the ground, and they could not lift them up again. After this nothing happened. There was little singing anywhere."[9] Lear's book is a systematic exploration of what Plenty Coups meant by the phrase *After this nothing happened*— a phrase that suggests time brought to a standstill, hope abandoned, and unutterable sorrow. "Humans are by nature cultural animals," Lear writes, "we necessarily inhabit a way of life that is expressed in a culture. But our way of life—whatever it is—is vulnerable in various ways. And we, as participants in that way of life, thereby inherit a vulnerability." He goes on to say "that if our way of life collapsed, things would cease to happen," and he claims that we, in fact, are living in a vulnerable time "of terrorist attacks, violent social upheavals, and even natural catastrophes," collectively experiencing grave doubts about our future.[10]

Lear's implication is that while some people are fortunate enough to live in times and societies where the conventional wisdom of the tribe—its core values, customs, and cosmologies—is largely taken for granted, many other people do not know what it means to take the world for granted, as if yesterday, today, and tomorrow lay along a guaranteed continuum. There may be individuals, and perhaps there have existed entire societies, where nothing untoward ever calls the prevailing logos into question unless it is a personal tragedy—which, like a rite of passage, is only a momentary hiatus in the continuity of social existence. But for many peoples, including the Apsáalooke, historical and natural calamities have rendered even the most long-standing moral truths redundant and irrelevant. The rift between before and after is absolute. Though one may fantasize recovering the past or reinventing tradition, one faces a future that one simply does know how to negotiate.

In a recent essay, "On the Danger of Peace Work," the Israeli activist Yakir Englander evokes a story from the Talmud concerning Rabbi Yohanan ben-Zakkai, a prominent leader of the Jewish community during the Jewish revolt against the Roman Empire in the first century CE. Rabbi Yohanan's dilemma echoes that of Plenty Coups and, by extension, the ethical quandary we all face when we act in the certainty that our actions will do more good than harm. "During the Roman siege of Jerusalem, Rabbi Yohanan refused to be passive. He risked his life by surrendering to the Romans. He became complicit in the destruction of Jerusalem and of the dream for Jewish political sovereignty. In return, he was granted the ability to create a new Jewish community, in which Jewish life could continue, but under foreign and idolatrous rule. In the last hours of his life, his disciples asked: "'Rabbi, what do you see?' To their astonishment he replied: 'There are two roads open to me, one to heaven and one to hell, and I still do not know which way I will be led.'" As Yakir Englander points out, "Rabbi Yohanan's attempt to save Jewish lives, even in his last hours, was characterized by a profound 'unknowing' regarding the right way to walk in the conflict. Even the enormous criticism from his friends did not prevent him from acting and making painful decisions, possibly even incorrect ones. The Talmud's description indicates, in my opinion, that Rabbi Yohanan's peace work did not enable him to speak in absolute terms of true and false or right and wrong. He acted with self-awareness, with tears in his eyes, knowing the road to hell was open to him at every moment."[11]

Despite our "unknowing," life goes on, even as the generations of man pass away. As the Maori proverb puts it, *Whatu ngarongaro he tangata, toitu he whenua* (Man perishes, but the land remains). Significantly, *whenua* means both "land" and "placenta." Not only is the placenta buried in the land of one's birth, but also the land itself is regarded as the womb of the world from which all life springs eternal. However, such thoughts may offer little consolation to those who survive the passing of a loved one or the erasure of a way of life, though in the *longue durée* life is a process of transformation, with something new occurring even when all appears lost.

During fieldwork on southeast Cape York in the 1990s, my wife and I met an elderly Kuku-Yalanji man called Peter Fischer who had moved away from the former mission settlement of Wujal Wujal to create a clearing in the rain forest and plant a garden on which to subsist. Peter's biological father was a part-Aboriginal man called Dick Fischer, the son of a German immigrant, who mined tin for a while at a place called China Camp. Peter never met his father because when his mother became pregnant she was sent away. When Peter was a very small boy, the police came to his mother's camp looking for "half-castes." He hid in the bush, but his friend and age-mate Oglevie was caught and taken to the Mission Station at Yarrabah, south of Cairns, where he died two months later, Peter said, "of homesickness and a broken heart." As for Peter, his mother disappeared when he was seven, leaving him in the care of his maternal grandmother. "My granny was very good to me. She looked after me better than my own mother. When I was starving, she fed me wild yams. She is buried near here. That is why I came here to live and to die. I have had this place in mind all my life. I wanted to be close to her."

Peter made us mugs of tea, and we shared the food we had brought, even though Peter's garden contained enough food to feed a small community. Francine explained to Peter that we had visited the falls on our way up. "Kijanka," Peter said, using the *bama* (Aboriginal) word for the locality (lit. "moon place"). "You have to be careful when you approach the falls," he warned. They had the power to draw a person over the edge. He also mentioned a rock at the top of the falls that could move to the bottom and back to the top of its own accord. But when white miners began blasting with gelignite at China Camp, they killed the stone, which now lies immobile at the foot of the walls, bereft of life. "Same thing happened at Daintree," Peter said. "There was a stone. No matter how many times *bama* rolled it to the bottom of the waterfall, it would find its way back to the top. But you know how pig-headed Europeans can be? Well, some policemen wanted to roll the stone down to the bottom. *Bama* said, 'No, don't touch it, don't go near it.' But they rolled it anyway. After that it stayed there at the bottom, dead."

I thought: *When stone was in the hands of* bama, *it was not stone, it was an enchanted thing, animated by the respect it was given, the songs that perennially brought it back to life. When it was taken from them, it lost its meaning and died, like the alienated land itself, now untended and untraveled. And as one's connection with the ancestral world atrophied, so time stood still as if turned to stone.*[12]

If I am moved to cite these examples of what it means for a way of life to come to an end, what it means for one's innermost conception of a life worth living to suffer eclipse and for time no longer to unfold, it is because I want to bear witness to the way that catastrophe involves both discontinuity and continuity. Even though Plenty Coups suffered the tragedy of the life that was coming to an end, he saw that throwing in his lot with the whites might lead to salvaging something for his people—maybe even to a renaissance of what appeared to be passing away forever.

The history of the Apsáalooke is a turbulent one. As recently as the 1950s, the Apsáalooke were coerced into selling their traditional rights to much of the Bighorn Canyon so that a multipurpose dam could be constructed. People continue to struggle with high unemployment, poverty, poor health, alcoholism, and racial prejudice. But in often unexpected ways, life goes on.

The Tin Shed

In 1974 the American anthropologist Rodney Frey began a lifelong association with the Apsáalooke (Crow) of Montana. Early in Frey's fieldwork, an elderly man interrupted the young man's incessant questioning and pointed to a highway department building some fifty yards to the north. "You see that tin shed? It's like my culture. You can sit back here, ask questions, and describe it. But it's not 'til you get inside, 'til you see what's inside and feel it, that you *really know* what the tin shed is about. You can't stand outside; you've got to go inside." It turned out that the world inside the tin shed involved "an immense clan and kin network, participated in by the Buffalo and the Little People; the Sun Dance, with its sacrificial offerings, journeys to other worlds, and healings by medicine men; and an oral literature rich in heroes and tricksters." Frey also describes the interior of the tin shed in terms of the Apsáalooke image of a wagon wheel that both encompasses all peoples and all religions *and* accepts the diversity of and distinctiveness of each culture and each person. Thus, difference is not necessarily seen as deviance, and innovation is not always construed as a threat to tradition. Just as different Apsáalooke clans are compared to entangled mounds of driftwood washed up at various points along the Little Bighorn River, subject to continual scattering and reformation as the seasons change and the river floods and falls, so the world itself is constantly changing as turbulent currents and adversarial eddies are met at every turn.[13]

It is also true that one can never predict when and from what source some kind of reparation will occur. Not long ago, my friend Davíd Carrasco recounted how he had undergone a sweat bath ceremony— a ritual to alleviate the suffering of a loved one or cleanse oneself. An Apsáalooke elder, Tom Yellowtail, met Davíd and several other men in the Rockies near Boulder, Colorado, where the sweat bath was conducted in a small, domed structure made of saplings covered with blankets that substituted for the traditional buffalo hides no longer available.

I can see it now, in the season of the quaking aspen, yellow with leaf and yellower leaves when the sun blazed through, the Crow lodge by a modest mountain stream where very cold water from a glacier flowed. Burning the rocks, carefully moving them into the hole in the dark lodge, stripping down, crawling into the small circular dome made of willow branches and heavy blankets, sitting in the darkness and hearing the rocks singing! Your eyes adjust to the red glow in the darkness and before water is poured (four pours, four times, if I remember correctly) the rocks make a constant noise and I was told they were singing. Then the pourings which are carefully announced and done with noisy bursts of steam up to the dome of the enclosure and then rebounding slowly down on our heads, shoulders and entire bodies as we sat in a lotus position, slowly bending toward the ground as the hot steam seemed to thicken. Tom Yellowtail sang a song and offered prayers. The Crow know that a spirit resides in the sweat lodge, named "Little Old Man." Some claimed to see him hovering at the top of the lodge.

The single most powerful moment, physically, takes place after one crawls out of the lodge and into the sunlight and the brisk, very brisk, mountain air. A pail of water from the mountain stream is lifted by each person and poured in a single pouring over the steaming body, and I felt a sharp ecstasy as if my body exploded from just below my skin.[14]

It is often such minor modes of being, such unexpected transformations or sudden glimpses into a calmer world beyond the troubled, eddying, and often overwhelming stream of our everyday experience, that make all the difference between feeling that we are losing our hold on life or restored to it. The Danish ethicist Knud Løgstrup speaks of such moments as "sovereign expressions of life"—spontaneous acts of courage, compassion, or understanding that "precede the will" and are only partially motivated by moral principles or reflective of social norms.[15] Arendt speaks of such moments in terms of natality because they initiate something new "against the overwhelming odds of statistical laws and their probability. The new therefore always appears in the guise of a miracle."[16]

The Ebb and Flow of Life

In the winter of 1990, my wife and I were living in the Warlpiri settlement of Lajamanu in the northern Tanami Desert of central Australia. Our caravan was parked under a ghost gum behind the Wulaign Outstation Resource Center—a prefabricated, aluminum-sided shed and center of operations for the Central Land Council, under whose aegis Francine and I were doing our fieldwork. Wulaign's veranda offered shade, and I would sometimes sit there with older Warlpiri men, clumped together on the concrete as if a single body. One afternoon we were joined by Barnaby Japaljarri, a thickset, middle-aged man with a penchant for *pama* ("sweet things," including alcohol) but whose grumpy and taciturn manner suggested complete indifference to our desultory talk of Dreamings and related matters. Suddenly, Japaljarri toppled over. I thought he might be drunk and had passed out. But the other men did not stop to think. Moving as one, they reached out to him, pressing the palms of their hands against his body and his head. A few minutes passed and Japaljarri revived. Not a word was said as he sat up, resuming his place among us.

What prompted the men to act as they had? If a person loses consciousness, as Japaljarri had, it meant that his life force (*pirlirrpa*) had momentarily deserted him. To prevent this loss of life, this draining away of the *pirlirrpa*, one placed one's hands on the body of the afflicted individual, holding him together, so to speak, containing him.

Let me turn to an equally critical moment in a very different part of the world—the invasion of the Kuranko village of Kondembaia, Sierra Leone, by Revolutionary United Front soldiers in 1999.

Sporadic gunfire signaled the arrival of the rebels. People were seized at random and assembled under one of the great cotton trees in the center of the village. There, drug-addled rebels used one of the tree's buttressing roots as a butcher's block to sever the limbs of their victims. Forty men, women and children were murdered that day, and three years later survivors would recall the event in a series of disconnected phrases—*Yuge bi nala* (Badness has come), was the first terrified cry. Then, as word spread of what was happening, *Ma faga yo* (We are being murdered), *A bi na faga* (They are killing us), *Ma bin na faga* (We are all dead). And finally, *Allah ma ma dembe* (God help us), *Kele na l bama* (The world is coming to an end). It was if the event unfolded outside of people's ability to process it—"an unbearable sequence of sheer happenings."[17]

These events are critical events—matters of life and death. They were experienced limbically, as it were, rather than cerebrally. For as long as the event lasted, one's experience was neither thinkable nor narratable.

If overwhelming emotions such as terror, panic, and bereavement can momentarily obliterate our conceptual awareness, what are we to make of Alain Badiou's assertion, in an obituary for Gilles Deleuze, that for Deleuze thinking was "a component of life."[18] Is it not empirically more accurate to say that life often confounds, interrupts, disturbs and outstrips our conception of what life means? And is it not the case that our concepts are often playing catch-up—which is to say that they are deployed retrospectively in order to make sense of experiences and events that defied reason, confounded our expectations, and called all our assumptions into question?

If this is so, then the burning question is not one of dissolving the distinction between life and concept, as Badiou suggests, or even claiming that concepts are *implicit* in experience, but of exploring the oscillations in human consciousness between modes of experience that appear to occlude or obliterate conceptual thought and modes of experience that rationalize and reorganize lived experience in ways that make it bearable and intelligible.

Rather than ask what concepts might help us elucidate the events described above without diminishing or erasing their immediate impact, let us ask what *images* do justice to those events.

Let me begin with an indigenous exegesis. In the Warlpiri view, a person contains, holds, or is filled with life, but this life essence (*pirlirrpa*) derives from and is sustained by one's *relationship* with a greater existential matrix comprising the eternal and encompassing field of the Dreaming (*jukurrpa*) as well as the significant others on whom one's life depends in the here and now—kinsmen, affines, and countrymen. Despite the value placed on rugged individualism, Warlpiri stress the importance of *jinamardarni*—of looking after or caring for others as well as the land and the rituals that sustain a vital relationship with the land.

The Warlpiri concept of "being held" is directly comparable with the Pintupi concept of *kanyininpa*, which may be used to refer to the possession of physical objects ("I have two spears"), to the protective and nurturing relationship of parent to child ("My mother's breast milk nourished me"; "My father held me and grew me up"), and to rights over Dreaming rituals, songs and designs. Thus, the significations of *kanyininpa* "derive from the basic idea of an intimate and active relationship between a 'holder' and that which is 'held,' as suggested in the primary meaning of physical grasp."[19] The conflation of *having* rights to use an object without asking and of *being* held or taken care of by a significant other is also demonstrated by the complementary term, *wantininpa*, which means "leaving" or "losing" something or someone that sustains one's life.

Although there is a great cultural and geographical distance separating central Australia and West Africa, Kuranko concepts of being-in-the-world bear an uncanny resemblance to those of the Warlpiri and Pintupi. When Kondembaia was overrun by rebels in 1999, villagers felt utterly defenseless and vulnerable. The cries *A bi na faga* (They are killing us) and *Ma bin na faga* (We are all dead) articulated an individual *and* collective sense that life itself was over: *Kele na l bama* (The world is coming to an end).

Not only did people lose their lives that fateful day; the village itself was pillaged and burned to the ground. This metaphorical fusion of persons and possessions implies a concept of reciprocity that operates at the level of being *and* of having. What one *has* objectifies who one *is*. The Kuranko notion of *miran* makes this clear. *Mirannu* (pl.) can be both material possessions—particularly those that contain and protect, such as a house, clothing, water vessels, and cooking pots—and personal attributes that give one a sense of self-possession, presence, and substantiality of being—such as forceful speech, physical skill, and social adroitness. But *miran*, in both senses of the term—material possession and personal disposition—is never a fixed property or attribute. In practice, a person's *miran* may be bolstered by fetishes that symbolically enclose, contain, and protect the vital spaces that define his or her being—body, house, village, chiefdom—in exactly the same way that in a consumer society material possessions bolster and define a person's sense of well-being, substantiality, and standing. For Kuranko, the notion of a full container is a common metaphor for anyone who is in command of himself and working his utmost to do what is expected of him, to do his duty. But self-possession and morale may be undermined, sapped, or lost. Just as a person's property can be stolen, a pot broken, or a house fall into disrepair, so a person can lose self-possession and confidence, as when his or her *miran* is "taken away" by more powerful others (such as autocratic parents, forceful public speakers, and powerful bush spirits) whose voice and power "press down" with great weight, diminishing the *miran* of those in their presence. Then it is said that "the container has tipped over and its contents spilled out"—a metaphor for loss of self-control or for a state of laziness or despair when one has "let oneself go" (*nyere bila*). In the case under discussion, the superior force and military might of the rebels left people feeling like shattered vessels or ruined houses, their defenses breached, their autonomy lost, the life drained from them.

Although I have explored two events in which life itself was at stake, quotidian life is generally not a literal matter of being *either* alive *or* dead; rather, it is a struggle to get an edge on those forces that threaten to sap one's energies, wear one down, and make life unfulfilling, dispiriting, and scarcely worth living. In his *Ethics*, Baruch Spinoza proposes that life and death are never absolute poles of being and nothingness but matters of being more or less alive, as every life-form "endeavors to persist in its own being" (3.6), seeking whatever augments and amplifies its existence while avoiding all that imperils or reduces it.

Spinoza's *Ethics* resonate with non-Western thought. Maori posit a dialectical movement between *tupu*—the unfolding or efflorescence of life—and *mate*—the fading or withering away of life. This dialectic of *tupu* and *mate* is likened to the waxing and waning of the moon, the rise and fall of tides, the lighting and dying of a fire, or a tree that is growing and a tree that has been felled. But whether *tupu* or *mate* triumph depends on human action. Thus, while an insult reduces or weakens one's honor, avenging the insult restores it.

This dialectic is echoed in the Warlpiri notions of patency (*palka*) and latency (*lawa*). *Palka* means embodied in present time (*jalanguju palkalku*). *Lawa* means just the opposite. The words apply equally to the perpetual coming and going in Warlpiri social life and to the flux of things. Anything that has "body" is *palka*—a rock hole or river with water in it, the trunk of a tree, a person whose belly is full, country where game is plentiful, a person who is present. But if a rock hole is dry, a stomach is empty, tracks are erased, or a person faints, falls asleep, goes away, or dies, then there is *lawa*, absence. *Palka* is that which is existent, whether persons or possessions. By contrast, *lawa* connotes the loss of the persons and things that sustain one's life. However, just as persons disperse then gradually come together again (*pina yani*), so human ritual action can bring the ancestral order back into being, fleshing it out in the painting, song, and mimetic dance of the living. Giving birth to a child, singing up the country, and dancing the Dreaming into life are all modes of "bringing forth being" (*palka jarrimi*). And the passage from absence to presence is like the passage from night to day.

These ethnographic observations from West Africa, Polynesia, and Aboriginal Australia not only complement Spinoza's view that life and death are relative matters but also direct our attention to the fact that the wherewithal of life is always scarce and must be struggled for. This struggle unfolds in our relations with others, with the gods we worship and the scarce resources, both within ourselves and without, on which we draw in sustaining our lives. Existence is never simply a Darwinian struggle for survival, for what is at stake for human beings are existential imperatives like striking a balance between our commitment to others and our duty to ourselves or transforming the world into which we are thrown into a world we have a hand in making—so that we are actors and not merely acted upon. Life is never simply bare survival but realizing one's humanity in relation to others, and death is never physical extinction but rather the nullification of the relations that sustain one's life among others.

That being is precarious and unstable is obvious from the ontological metaphors with which we typically describe it. Quotidian existence is marked by ups (being high, feeling on top of things) and downs (being blue, snowed under, depressed)—and often compared, in popular thought, to changes in the weather or market oscillations between profit and loss. Allusions are also made to fullness (being full of life) or emptiness (being drained), or the contrast between activity (being on the move, being creative, making something of oneself, going places) and stasis, which is often synonymous with nothingness (being stuck, being trapped, getting nowhere). That one's sense of well-being is susceptible to constant change is shown by the way an affectionate glance, a gesture of recognition or concern, the company of close friends, or an unexpected gift can make one's day while a cutting remark, a snub, ill health, the loss of a job, or a falling out with a friend can cast a pall over everything. Although these minutiae of everyday life suggest recurring symbolic motifs—the need to be recognized, healthy, loved, happy, or free; to have security, wealth, an identity, a fulfilling job, a family, and friends; and to do well in life—it is important to note that being is never an "either/or" thing but a "more or less" question. Being is always what Karl Jaspers calls "potential being."[20]

The Social Life of Concepts

It is sometimes assumed that concepts are a product of rational contemplation—of pure reason. One deliberately forms a plan of action then implements it, or one retrospectively reviews one's experience and discovers an order within it (induction) or brings an order to it (deduction). Rather than preserve the traditional antinomies of concrete/abstract, sensible/intelligible, percept/concept that inform both inductive and deductive methods, I seek to identify the prototypes of these forms of thought in everyday consciousness. It may be the case that we sometimes experience ourselves as disinterested beings to whom life simply happens, or we feel that the world impresses itself on our consciousness, disclosing hitherto invisible or underlying causes, motives, rules, or ordering principles. It may also be the case that we sometimes experience ourselves as viewing our lives from afar, as if our existence had become an object of contemplation. But neither of these modes of experience *necessarily* entails scientific methods or philosophical truths. They are simply alternating forms of consciousness, both of which may provide a fleeting and consoling sense that we may comprehend our relationship to the world. They echo a distinction that precedes the development of modern science and is recognized in all human societies—that we are creatures who suffer an existence we have not chosen, fated to exercise patience in the hope that we may in the fullness of time or by the grace of God be indemnified for our pains *and* that we are creators of our own lives, responsible for our actions and capable of knowing and controlling with increasingly higher degrees of certainty the world in which we move.

Phenomenology and radical empiricism refuse to ontologize percept and concept, sensibility and intelligibility. These terms are false antinomies. They do not denote *real* differences between "pure experience" and "explanatory concepts" but convey a sense that our experience is constantly oscillating between a mode in which we act without much conscious thought and another mode in which we consciously think about or reflect on our actions. That our experience of our being-in-the-world continually and imperceptibly moves between these extremes does not imply that unreflective or habitual action is less significant than actions that are premeditated or reflected on; it urges us to focus on the interplay *between* experiences that slip from the mind's grasp, as it were, resisting language, *and* experiences that are formed as thoughts we can readily put into words. Phenomenology is not concerned with prereflective or pretheoretical life per se but with this *indeterminate relation,* this perpetual tension and slippage *between* modes of apprehending reality that we typically characterize in either-or terms as feeling versus thought, percept versus concept, and so on. As such, our focus is on those concepts that retain some sense of what precipitated them in consciousness, even as they anticipate the more reified character they often come to assume.

This focus on the transitive, on the in-between, has led phenomenologists to focus on poetic imagery, vernacular idioms, proverbial sayings, and mundane metaphors, for in these incipient, immanent, inchoate forms of expression are disclosed the amorphous forms of consciousness as well as the abstract figures of thought we call "concepts" or "ideas." These rudimentary modes of expression are not to be disparaged because they are less "objective" than, or give us less purchase on, the world of "subjectivity"; rather, they are to be explored as offering our best access to the elusive field of subjective experience. Moreover, because human differences are customarily couched in substantive terms, such as ethnicity, religion, and gender, any attempt to write a comparative anthropology of the human must develop methods for apprehending what forms of consciousness may be common to all before they find expression in a particular cultural, conceptual, or concrete form.

The Dialectic of Container-Contained

Let me return to the vernacular images of container-contained that emerged from my discussion of Warlpiri and Kuranko conceptions of intersubjective life. Just as a sense of reciprocal exchange—of expressions, gestures, and objects—underlies a child's earliest experiences of being-in-the-world, so the dialectic of holding and being held, of being a container and being contained, seems to be one of the most ontological primitive ways in which we apprehend our relation to others and our environment. In other words, the connection between Warlpiri and Kuranko concepts is ontogenetic, and the similar ontological metaphors found in these very disparate societies disclose something so fundamental about our nature that some might call them preconceptual or protocultural.

The model of container-contained was central to the psychoanalytic work of Wilfred Bion, who postulated that we can only process, comprehend, and accept overwhelming life experiences (Beta elements) by working them through with a caring other—someone who can contain or safely hold us and on whom we can rely in constructing life-affirming rather than life-negating responses to unbearable experiences.[21] In the more recent work of Peter Fonagy and Mary Target, this process of "working through" is construed as a form of play.[22] With others, we play with reality, oscillating between a "pretend mode," in which images and ideas are allowed to take on a life of their own, and a mode of "psychic equivalence," in which ideas are made to stand for some external reality. For both Bion and Fonagy, concepts are equated with other things that help a child objectify and vicariously control its relationship with the world, such as mother's milk, food, toys, blocks, paints, and found objects. Conceptual thought, in this view, is a means to manage one's life in relation with others, a way that we contain and control the life experiences that threaten to engulf, undermine, or nullify us.

However, to be contained is not simply to be held securely, for being held may also be experienced as constricting, confining, and claustrophobic. The struggle to balance our need to be contained against the equally powerful imperative to open ourselves up to the world—including to experiences that may take us the very limit of what can be contained, processed, or endured—is perhaps nowhere more vexed than at the transitional periods of our lives and in the lives of migrants.

Life Within Limits

For more than forty years, my fieldwork among the Kuranko of northeast Sierra Leone has provided me with culturally specific examples of how freedom is never limitless but instead exercised within limits, contained rather than unconfined. While one's social identity is determined patrilineally (and one's physiological essence stems solely from one's father's semen), one's destiny may depend as much on one's mother and mother's brother as on one's father and his brothers. This counterpoint between a space dominated by rules and a space of greater informality, affection, and playfulness finds expression in the contrast between one's father's place (*fa ware*)—the place where one was born and raised—and one's mother's place (*na ware*)—the home of one's mother's brothers. This tension between the patriarchal law of the father and the loving care of the mother informs the intersubjective life of the family and finds expression in images of the polis, since rulers, whether local or national, are expected to embody the power to administer the law of the land as well as the power to protect and care for their subjects.[23] When Kuranko say they are "in the hands of" a chief or power holder, the metaphor is double-edged, as they are at once subject to his whims, under his thumb, at his mercy, and in his debt.

Among the Kuranko, the dialectic of obligation and choice is evident in the interplay between village and bush, for while the village is often associated—particularly by the youth of today—with oppressive limitations, "the bush" signifies an encompassing, dangerous, yet potentially liberating space in which social norms are placed in abeyance, social boundaries are transgressed, and miraculous transformations happen. The bush is an imagined elsewhere, a transitional space, in which the socio-moral ties of the town can be loosened and a person experience his relations with others in transcendental terms, mediated by music, palm wine, money, friendship, spirit possession, laughter, love, magical mobility, and even the promise of eternity. But just as the achievement of independence carries the responsibility to provide for those who brought one into the world, so any gains won in the wilderness must be shared with the community from which one originally set forth.

This ethical ambiguity informs all the migrant narratives I have collected. One can agree with Ernst Bloch that "something is missing" in a person's life, making him or her feel empty, dissatisfied, unfulfilled, and incomplete, but exactly *what* will satisfy this inchoate need is seldom clear to the person who experiences it.[24] Inchoate, amorphous, and volatile, one's will-to-exist fastens or focuses opportunistically on various objects, some actually at hand, some absent, some wholly fantastic, in a search to objectify or consummate oneself in the world. But unlike reality testing, the imagination always goes beyond what the world actually is or any person can actually be. Money begins, Philippe Rospabé argues, as "a substitute for life."[25] But many other things beside money can give momentary form to the vague sense of what will make good the lack in one's life. When a migrant speaks of a quest for a better life, we cannot presume to know what this "life" may be. Utopia, need we remind ourselves, means no-place (*ou-topos*). Migrant narratives bring into sharp relief the variety of things that have been lost, gone missing, or not yet been found and without which one's life is profoundly impaired—an absent parent, a lost home, or a lack of food, money, mobility, or companionship—while at the same time suggesting that dreams are seldom realized. This view that the world as given is not enough, or is too confining, and its corollary—that one must chose another world for oneself, cultivating one's own garden rather than working on one's father's farm—entails a double bind that every migrant experiences in some measure yet speaks to us all, caught as we inevitably are between the circumstances that shape our lives and the lives we project and struggle to shape for ourselves.

5. Ourselves and Others

Natural species are chosen not because they are "good to eat" but because they are "good to think."

—CLAUDE LÉVI-STRAUSS, *TOTEMISM*

In *The View of Life* (1918), Georg Simmel observes that what is so striking about human existence is that in acting to preserve, enhance, and expand our life, we generate "objectified forms" such as languages, religious doctrines, moral codes, political ideologies, and philosophies that constitute "more-than-life." Though born of the life process, these objectified forms take on a life of their own, coming to have such a hold over us that "life often wounds itself upon the structures it has externalized from itself as strictly objective."[1] There are echoes here of Karl Marx's thesis that regardless of historical circumstances and independent of its location in the private or public realm, labor power (*arbeitskraft*) possesses a "productivity" of its own. This productivity, comments Hannah Arendt, "does not lie in any of labor's products but in the human 'power,' whose strength is not exhausted when it has produced the means of its own subsistence and survival but is capable of producing a 'surplus,' that is, more than is necessary for its own 'reproduction.'"[2] Psychoanalytically, Simmel's "objectified forms" and Marx's "reified products" function as intrapsychic defenses and may be compared with established social norms and discursive conventions that also tend to deaden our awareness and prevent us from "living openly."[3]

These observations suggest that reified ideas both determine *and are determined by* our existential situations and that there is always both continuity and discontinuity in the relationship between life as lived and life as we come to understand it. This is also true of relationships between what Ludwig Wittgenstein called different "forms of life,"[4] though I gloss this expression to cover *both* what Simmel calls forms of "more-than-life" *and* what biologists refer to as life-forms (species, genera, etc.). This is because we are sustained in life not only by the culture we acquire but also by the life-forms, mega and microbial, that coexist with and within us. Moreover, our fulfillment in life depends on so many things—food, drink, work, leisure, sleep, wakefulness, thought, action, speech, silence, love, hate, peace, war—that every person's life course involves perpetual oscillations from one form of life to another, each move motivated by a search for well-being that a myriad of trivial or imperative things may, at least potentially and momentarily, provide. Even at the end of life, when these existential potentialities become severely diminished, a person may review and evaluate his or her options as if the most imperative issue is, as D. W. Winnicott put it, to be alive when I die.[5]

At eighty-one and diagnosed with multiple metastases in the liver, Oliver Sacks posted an op-ed in the *New York Times* in which he wrote:

> Over the last few days, I have been able to see my life as from a great altitude, as a sort of landscape, and with a deepening sense of the connection of all its parts. This does not mean I am finished with life. On the contrary, I feel intensely alive, and I want and hope in the time that remains to deepen my friendships, to say farewell to those I love, to write more, to travel if I have the strength, to achieve new levels of understanding and insight. This will involve audacity, clarity and plain speaking; trying to straighten my accounts with the world. But there will be time, too, for some fun (and even some silliness, as well).[6]

Life Itself

Just as we are continually moving about in our environments, experimenting with different ways of finding fulfillment, we are *changing our environments* by bringing life from where it abounds to where it is felt to be scarce. Both in thought and in deed, we import, purchase, purloin, borrow, or otherwise acquire *from elsewhere or from others* the things that sustain us. In this process we ourselves are changed. A book may provide food for thought, just as a meal may nourish our bodies. A companion animal may give us the recognition and love we once found in a close friend. It is as if *life itself* moved through all things, organic and inorganic, human and extrahuman, divine and mundane, effectively blurring the lines we often draw between these realms.

Yet we are haunted by the thought that the life we enjoy comes at the cost of another life destroyed.

One of the tragedies that mercantile capitalism, colonialism, and industrialization brought in their wake was the extinction of entire populations, societies, languages, and craft traditions. Extinction ceased to be an issue for individuals alone, or even for families decimated by disease or warfare; extinction increasingly became a specter for entire species and, imminently, for the very species that had created the conditions under which so many others had perished. As Thom van Dooren observes, the question of extinction is never simply a question of the death of any one life-form, for all life on earth is woven into "relationships of coevolution and ecological dependency."[7] John Donne wrote that no man is an island. Were he writing today, he might well say not only that "I am involved in Mankinde" and that "any man's death diminishes me" but that our species and our society are involved in life itself and that the death of any species or society diminishes all.

For van Dooren, one response to this sense of being involved in a planetary life crisis is to recount extinction stories that bring home to us the complex entanglements that connect all life-forms. Such narratives are ethically necessary, even though they may not change the way things are or the way things are going.[8] Mourning extinction, whether the death of a single person or the last passenger pigeon that passed away in 1914, is a way of choosing life over death since to mourn is to keep alive a sense of what it means to be alive, to be among the living. It is an act of witnessing and of solidarity.

This eco-philosophical way of appreciating the felt interconnectedness of all life-forms bears a family resemblance to the existential model of reality as consisting of *eigenwelt* (one's own world), *mitwelt* (the world of other people), and *umwelt* (the surrounding or wider world, which includes the natural environment as well as entities we call things, animals, and aliens—sometimes speaking of them in derogatory ways, sometimes reverently and with awe, as such beings include both demons and divinities). Although these spheres are often thought of as separate domains, they are just as often considered to be interconnected. Thus we liken the wider world to our own world, imagining that divinities share certain attributes with us, assuming that certain animals experience us as we experience them, and acting as if certain material objects possessed consciousness and will—were, indeed, subjects. Though most human beings conventionally distinguish between "persons" and "things"—subjects and objects—or humans and animals, these category boundaries are notoriously unstable.

In a remarkable ethnography entitled *How Forests Think*, based on fieldwork in Ecuador's Upper Amazonia, Eduardo Kohn takes us into a world where certain animals are thought to see us in the same way that we in our society see them. Kohn begins his book with an anecdote.

> Settling down to sleep under our hunting camp's thatch lean-to in the foothills of Sumaco Volcano, Juanicu warned me, "Sleep faceup! If a jaguar comes he'll see you can look back at him and he won't bother you. If you sleep facedown he'll think you're *aicha* (prey; lit., 'meat' in Quichua) and he'll attack." . . . If, Juanicu was saying, a jaguar sees you as a being capable of looking back—a self like himself, a *you*—he'll leave you alone. But if he should come to see you as prey—an *it*—you may well become dead meat.

Such ethnographic aperçus force us to consider that *our* notion of the human is by no means universal and that "seeing, representing, and perhaps knowing, even thinking, are not exclusively human affairs."[9]

Rather than make a case for multiple ontologies in which no single human society is permitted to have the last word on the nature of reality or the definition of the human, I want to explore the conditions under which people in any society might imagine that properties conventionally associated with being human—particularly conceptual thought and speech—might be assumed to be properties of other life-forms as well, and even of material objects.

My focus is on human-animal relationships—the ways the loss of one implicates the loss of another, the ways that the life of one passes into another, and the ways each makes the other thinkable. After showing how this interchange of being is understood in various societies, I propose an existential theory of ritual that explores the proposition that many myths and rites are informed by an urge to redistribute *life itself*, which always tends to be perceived as scarce and unequally distributed.

Life-forms are, therefore, constantly moving, both physically and imaginatively, from where life is scarce to where it is abundant, and these life-forms are also in constant competition with one another for the scarcest of all goods, life itself. These actual or virtual redistributions of life are typically justified by moral dogmas that determine which life-forms are more deserving of life (including eternal life) and which have less urgent claims on the right to exist. For if life is to be taken from one person, creature, or place and incorporated into another, then some kind of moral discrimination will be needed to justify why one being's right to life is greater than another's.

Living with Otherness

In the process of their interaction, the essence of any one form of life—be it a book, a person, a plant, an animal, an image—will tend to bleed into and transform the essence of others.[10] An industrial laborer may feel that his work is soul-destroying, as if the inertia of the things on which he toils degrades his own being. A scholar may feel that his favorite authors are alive and speak to him. A hunter may imagine that his prey participates in his own will and consciousness. And a prized possession may be thought to embody the spirit of the person who made it or gave it to another person as a gift. Though Marx and Marcel Mauss pioneered our understanding of such phenomena, they have recently been subject to new interpretations under such rubrics as the "social life of things," "cosmological perspectivism," "actor-network theory," and "the new materialism."[11] All these intellectual projects begin with a fascination with the emotional and conceptual effects of coexisting with divinities, significant others, material things, animals, forests, urban spaces, prosthetic devices, and implanted organs. But rather than invoke the phenomenological epoche to bracket out conventional distinctions between appearance and reality (or subject and object) in order to engage the lived experience of individuals in real life situations, selected aspects (often shamanic or fantastic) of these experiences are sometimes made the basis for epistemological generalizations that effectively conflate being with thought. Anthropologists are, of course, not alone in confusing ontology with epistemology. This is what all human beings often do. But this interpretive move can make it difficult to see whether, and in

Ourselves and Others

what ways and on what occasions, the informants in question vary or change their points of view, bringing some ideas to the fore and pushing others into the background as they judge how best to negotiate a given situation. To put it succinctly, a focus on worldviews can easily obscure what Simmel calls "the life process"—the constant changes that occur in human consciousness as a person steers a course between different forms of life, including extant beliefs, critical events, social roles, and personal interests.

For this reason, I consider it imperative that we assume that experience and episteme are seldom congruent or completely overlapping. Given this assumption, our analytical task becomes one of exploring the conditions under which animals are interacted with *as though* they were or were not human or objects are handled as if they did or did not possess agency.

Of Dogs and Men

In *Train Dreams*, the fiction writer Denis Johnson recounts stories from the Idaho panhandle in which dogs behave like people. One goes for help and saves the life of a lone prospector who has injured himself badly trying to thaw out frozen dynamite on a stove. Another dog shoots his master after getting wind that the man was going to shoot it. "Much that was astonishing was told of dogs in the Panhandle," Johnson writes, "and along the Kootenai Rover, tales, rescues, tricks, feats of super-canine intelligence and humanlike understanding."[12]

In such stories, a relationship of reciprocity is assumed to exist between animal and human such that each is felt to owe its life to the other. Since each is morally constrained to sustain the life of the other through a relationship of exchange, it is logically possible that one may actually change into the other or take the place of the other. Thus, a Kuranko man whose clan totem was the elephant ontologized this relationship and became convinced that he could actually change into an elephant at will.[13] Lucien Lévy-Bruhl refers to such shape-shifting as "participation mystique," and Rane Willerslev speaks of the phenomenon as "mimetic empathy."[14] Consider these examples:

On Kabak Koyu beach in southwestern Turkey, a woman is throwing a ball for her cocker spaniel. She is so focused on the dog that she does not realize that her small child is crawling toward the ocean. But the spaniel sees the danger and races to the edge of the sea, where it blocks the child's path to the water. "Let's face it," one commenter wrote after watching a video of this event on YouTube, "Dogs are better than humans."[15]

In the death camps of the Third Reich, humanity is in the hands of those who have no humanity while those who suffer, and are all too human, are stripped of everything that would suggest to their tormentors any kinship, any common ground. Though the prisoners are compared to animals, it is not ordinary animals that the SS have in mind—for these are useful and even loveable—but a degraded and useless species or collection of things—*figuren* or *stücke*, dolls, woods, merchandise, rags. "Move faster, you filthy dogs," the SS bellow. People are herded into cattle trucks. Police dogs tear a man apart. Those who survive become like animals, scavenging for a crust of bread, a scrap of cloth, a pair of shoes. Sometimes it is only an animal that is capable of recognizing the humanity of these degraded beings, as Emmanuel Levinas recalls, describing how, for a few short weeks during his long captivity, a stray dog entered the lives of the Jewish prisoners of war among whom he numbered. On their way to work in the forest each morning, the prisoners would be observed by German civilians, in whose eyes, writes Levinas, "we were subhuman, a gang of apes . . . no longer part of the world." And then, one day, this cur that lived in some wild patch near the camp came to meet the pitiable rabble as it returned under guard from the forest. This happened many times, the dog greeting the prisoners at their dawn assembly and on their return from work, jumping up and down and barking with delight. "For him, there was no doubt that we were men."[16]

The Kuranko Yaran and Kamara clans recount a legend that explains how they became close, "like brothers and sisters," and do not intermarry. The wives of the first Yaran and Kamara gave birth to their children in the same house on the same day. While the mothers were away from the house, a fire broke out. The family dog picked up the infants, took them from the burning house, and placed them under a banana tree. When the mothers came home they began to cry, thinking their babies were dead. They did not notice the dog, running hither and thither between them and the banana tree. When someone alerted them to what the dog was trying to tell them, the mothers found their babies but could not tell them apart. Because neither mother would ever know which baby was hers, the two clans became effectively one.[17]

Stories in which animals and human beings give life to each another, either by providing help or succor in a time of peril or by sacrificing their own lives so that the other may live, are legion. All these tales are predicated on a distributive theory of being. For example, among the Kuranko it is axiomatic that will and consciousness are not limited to human beings but distributed beyond the world of persons and potentially found in totemic animals, fetishes, and even plants. The attributes of moral personhood (*morgoye*) may become manifest in the behavior of totemic animals and divinities while antisocial people may lose their personhood entirely, becoming like broken vessels or ruined houses. In other words, *being* is not necessarily limited to *human being*. Indeed, in Kuranko totemic myths, an animal saves the life of the clan ancestor who then decrees that his descendants must respect the animal as if it were a kinsman for it exemplified the magnanimous qualities of *morgoye*.

The source of the life of any species, whether animal, plant, or human, is understood to be life itself, which is distributed unequally and unevenly throughout the world. It may, however, be ritually, imaginatively, and magically redistributed, increased, subtracted, or exchanged. Thus, among the Kuranko, bush animals are "fair game" and hunted for meat while every effort is made to respect and preserve the life of a totemic animal and the lives of "village" animals (goats, sheep, cows) are only taken when offering a sacrifice to one's ancestors. Even hunting is highly regulated, however, for a life can only be taken on condition that something equivalent is given in return, which is why hunters offer blood sacrifices to the first hunter, Mande FaBori, just as villagers offer sacrifices to their forebears. The same logic obtains among the Warlpiri of central Australia, for the life of the plants and animals on which human life depends requires periodic rituals of increase.

Typically, these ritualized transfers of life across species boundaries imply a reciprocity of perspectives in which *one is thought of in terms of the other or seen as itself in other circumstances.* This was vividly brought home to me when observing mimetic performances of mythological events by older Warlpiri men who had grown up in the desert as hunters and gatherers and knew the habits of their totemic animals by heart.

A Slice of Life

In the course of our fieldwork, my wife and I visited a Warlpiri Dreaming site associated with the travels of two mythical kangaroos. We were accompanied by Paddy Nelson Jupurrurla, his brother-in-law Japanangka, and an elderly Jakamarra whose hand signals guided us across spinifex and saplings, around ant hills, ghost gums, and mulga brakes, to a wide floodout and sandy creek bed where we left our vehicle and walked the remaining half mile to a broad expanse of red rock and a large pool of still water. There, Paddy showed me the kidney-shaped depressions in the rock where the kangaroos had camped in the Dreaming. The two kangaroos rested at Yirntardamururu for two or three weeks, Paddy said, before traveling south. But he revealed no further details, and I did not press him to do so. All he would say was that this was an important initiation site and that many people used to camp here when he was a boy. My imagination was stretched as much as by the lack of detail in Paddy's remarks as by my difficulty in picturing the two kangaroos who seemed to be simultaneously animals and human beings.

"Were they like kangaroos to look at?" I asked Paddy.

"*Yuwayi* [yes]."

"Were they half men, half kangaroos?"

"No."

"But they acted like *yapa* [Aboriginal people]?"

"*Yuwayi*. They were very powerful."

Later I would learn more about the travels of the two kangaroos, but it was only when Zack Jakamarra actually *performed* an episode from the myth that I was able to fully appreciate it. As Zack had told me many times, abstract knowledge meant nothing; you had to see things with your own eyes, experiencing them bodily, sensibly, and directly.

The incident took place before the two kangaroos reached Yirntardamururu. Following a cloudburst, the country was flooded, and as the kangaroos searched for higher ground, one became bogged down in the mud and drowned before his companion could rescue him. Though grieving his loss, the surviving kangaroo journeyed on alone, and at a place called Wulyuwulyu (Western chestnut mouse) he discovered a marsupial mouse cowering in the spinifex. He decided to transform the mouse into a kangaroo, "a new mate."

Ourselves and Others

"He bin grab 'im now," said Zack, already animated by the story. "He bin carry 'im along Mulyu [nose/snout], teach 'im there like in school. Big camp there. He make that little one really kangaroo now . . ."

Zack placed his forefingers alongside his ears to show me how the ears got bigger. He pulled at his nose, drawing it out into an imaginary snout. He stretched his legs . . . the long, sinewy hind legs of a kangaroo. He tapped its genitals and tail, giving the kangaroo the features of an initiated male.

I laughed.

Zack narrowed his eyes and cocked his head. He looked paternally on his protégé as it hopped around, getting accustomed to its new body.

Zack said, "That kangaroo bin ask 'im: 'Can you eat grass?' Go around now, look for tucker, good tucker there. That little rat bin look around. Come back. 'How are you? You all right?' He bin ask 'im, 'Can you scratch?' Teach 'im, you see. Teach 'im about those things . . . lie down, get up, look around country. Learn 'im all that. Really make a kangaroo out of 'im now."

Zack repeated his antics, mimicking the little kangaroo as it took its first tentative steps, nibbling at the grass, venturing out on its own. "Growing 'im up, you know?"

Of course, Zack was in a sense "growing me up" too, as well as re-vealing to me, albeit obliquely, that the two kangaroo Dreaming was intimately connected with initiation and that ritual acts of subincision and increase occurred at almost every place the kangaroos camped in the Dreaming. Zack was also making it clear to me that knowledge was both mimetic and eidetic.[18] He could not have embodied his Dreaming without possessing a keen firsthand knowledge of the behavior of these desert marsupials, and this knowledge had been acquired mimetically in his youth, hunting with older men.

Such deep familiarity with the habits of desert fauna gave Warlpiri a practical edge over the animals they hunted. But there is a subtle and im-portant distinction between mimicking an animal and identifying with it. The hunter may be skilled in reading the spoor of an animal and divining how best to track and hunt it, and this skill may suggest that he knows the animal as well as he knows himself, but at no moment is the line between self and animal so completely erased that the hunter no longer knows himself and no longer acts as a separate being.

Consider the following commentaries on this phenomenon by a philosopher and by an ethnographer.

When I find again the actual world such as it is, under my hands, under my eyes, up against my body, I find much more than an object: a being of which my vision is a part, a visibility older than my operations or my acts. *But this does not mean that there was a fusion or coinciding of me with it*: on the contrary, this occurs because a sort of dehiscence opens my body in two, and because between my body looked at and my body looking, my body touched and my body touching, there is overlapping or encroachment, so that we must say that things pass into us as well as we into things. Our intuition, said Bergson, is a reflection, and he was right, though "the truth of the matter is that the experience of a coincidence can be, as Bergson often says, only a 'partial coincidence.'"[19]

Rane Willerslev sums up his understanding of Yukaghir hunters in similar terms.

It is this borderland where self and other are both identical and different, alike yet not the same, that I have tried to capture using phrases such as "analogous identification," "the double perspective," and "not animal, not *not* animal." What I mean to suggest by this is that if we are to take animism seriously, we must abandon the idea of total coincidence (the Heideggerian tradition) or total separation (the Cartesian tradition) and account for the mode of being that puts us into contact with the world and yet separates us from it. And there is, of course, such a mode of being, a mode that is grounded in mimesis.[20]

That we may imitate life, theatrically and sympathetically, and draw analogies between different life-forms does not mean that we completely lose ourselves in the other or assume a single invariant mode of selfhood. Moreover, a distinction must be made between "strong" and "weak" versions of the human-animal, human-object, or humanity-divinity interfaces since, in "traditional" societies and "modern" Euro-American societies alike, folktales are performed and art created in which animal characters act *as if* they were human and human beings behave like animals without, however, an absolute fusion of categories. Indeed, the copresence of two forms of life may sharpen our awareness of their difference rather than result in our seeing them as one.

In illustrating this "law of dissociation by varying concomitants," William James takes a concrete example from the work of Harriet Martineau. A red ball is removed from a billiard table and replaced by a white ball. This makes us notice the *color* contrast between the balls. If the white billiard ball is now replaced by a white egg, we will become aware of the *form* of the object.[21] Victor Turner invoked this law in explaining how the "grotesque" combinations of normally separated objects and images in Ndembu masks (animal-human, male-female, bush-town) inspire neophytes to bring into focus the key elements of their culture. "The monstrosity of the configuration throws its elements into relief. Put a man's head on a lion's body and you think about the human head in the abstract."[22]

It may be true that dissociation fosters mutual recognition, yet this should not be romanticized, as mutual recognition may find expression in actions that *appear* to be altruistic yet involve an implicit ethical demand that something be given in return. In Kuranko hunting stories, a recurring theme concerns an animal that changes itself into a seductive female in order to take revenge on a hunter who has killed many of "her" own family, thus redressing a moral balance between the human and animal worlds.[23] In a similar vein, Willerslev quotes a story told to him by an elderly Yukaghir woman whose husband enjoyed extraordinary good luck in hunting. But the hunter failed to notice that his son's health declined as his success in hunting increased. It is not that the taking of life requires the giving of a life in return; rather, there is a constant ambivalence between hunters and animals, for while the animal master-spirits are seen as "generous parents who are obliged to feed their hungry children" (i.e., the Yukaghir), the spirits may at any time be preparing to switch roles and force the "children" to feed them, in which event the hunter becomes the prey.[24]

In her "Notes on the Deer Dance," Leslie Marmon Silko describes how, in the fall of each year, Laguna Pueblo hunters go into the hills and mountains to find deer. "The people think of the deer as coming to give themselves to the hunters," she writes, "so that the people will have meat through the winter. Late in the winter the deer dance is performed to honor and pay thanks to the deer spirits who've come home with the hunters that year. Only when this has been properly done will the spirits be able to return to the mountain and be reborn into more deer who will, remembering the reverence and appreciation of the people, once more come home with the hunters."[25]

This theme is echoed in Patricia Vinnecombe's compelling analysis of San art in southern Africa. In *People of the Eland*, Vinnecombe argues that the naturalistic polychrome representations left by San hunters on rock shelters in the Drakensberg Range may be symbolic compensations for the killing of animals essential to San life—animals with whom people felt a close kinship, particularly the eland (in the south) and gemsbok (in the north). According to myths among Khoisan-speaking peoples, the ancestral shape-shifter Kaggen created and reared the first eland. When younger members of Kaggen's family killed his "child," Kaggen felt deep sorrow and bade the killer ritually atone for what he had done. This atonement involved "a ceremony *which brought the eland back to life*" so that now, whenever eland are killed it is vital that the blood and heart fat from the eland are mixed with the pulverized ochers used to paint the eland's image on a rock face. "It . . . seems to be not improbable," Vinnecombe continues, "that many of the eland paintings, particularly those associated with over-painting and re-painting, are connected with an act of reconciliation and of reparation to atone for killing. By this means, dead eland would have been symbolically re-created in order to replace the life which had been taken, and thus to ensure their continued existence."[26]

These examples invite us to reconsider Kant's categorical imperative: that we should never act in such a way that we treat humanity (or non-human species that we regard as sharing "human" features) as a means only but always as an end in itself. Yet it is difficult to imagine (or find) a society in which such a view is completely realized, though lip service may be paid to the idea. Lambs are sometimes loved, sometimes eaten; dogs are man's best friend yet often cruelly treated; we campaign for the human rights of some but not others. Among the Runa of Ecuador's Upper Amazonia, hunters and their dogs "partake in a shared constellation of attributes and dispositions" that Eduardo Kohn calls a "transspecies ecology of selves."[27] Yet, though dogs and humans possess souls and share the same subjectivity, dogs and people *live* in independent worlds. "Dogs are often ignored and are not even always fed, and dogs seem to largely ignore people." This is reminiscent of the way that Warlpiri (and other Aboriginal people) give skin names to their dogs, thereby assimilating the dogs into their social world, yet treat dogs with an indifference and harshness that stands in complete contrast with how they treat their kinsmen. Among the Yarralin, a distinction is made between camp dogs, which are dependent, like children, and dingoes, which are independent of humans and wild. To be fully human "is to be neither totally dependent nor totally wild," which is why socialization involves learning how to live and forage as an autonomous person in the bush.[28]

What is true of human relations with animals is equally true of human relations with other people and with objects. Though sameness *and* difference are *potentialities* of all these relationships, we must be careful to describe the contexts and interests that determine which one of these potentialities is realized.

The Ritualized Redistribution of Life

I suggested earlier that whenever exchange takes place, whether between people or between humans and animals, the logic of reciprocity is engaged, for if the gift of life in any of its forms—respect, care, shelter, security, food—is taken from one being and bestowed on another, the question invariably arises whether the gift has been deserved or, in the case of a life being taken from one being to improve the life chances of another, whether the death can be justified. In other words, a rationale must always be found, either in the conventional wisdom of the community or in individual fantasies that offer moral legitimacy for the giving and taking of life.

In her memoir, *The Mistress's Daughter*, A. M. Homes captures the moral anguish of the adopted child who, having been "given up for adoption," asks herself endlessly what compensation is now due to her and what form it could possibly take. "Every year I cannot help but think of the woman who gave me away. I find myself missing someone I never knew, wondering, Does she miss me? Does she shop for the things I buy myself? Does my father know I exist? Do I have siblings? Does anybody know who I am? I spend weeks grieving."[29]

This single paragraph touches on the existential interplay between *being* and *having*. Not knowing your parentage implies not knowing who you really are, while not being given the things parents normally give their children implies that you lack true love. Not knowing one's origins implies that your life story can never really be told.

This metaphorical bond between who we are and what we have is consummated in the act of giving, which, as Mauss pointed out, always combines material and spiritual values.[30] This is not the logic of logicians, although it involves a similar process of inference and, like mathematics, involves addition, subtraction, and division. It is, however, an *existential* logic—the logic of the gift—-based on the exchange of life itself and formalized in the threefold obligations to give, to receive, and to return what has been given. In the following pages I explore this existential logic in the contexts of Kuranko sacrifices to the ancestors, witchcraft confessions, and migration.

Sacrifice (*saraké*, from the Arabic *sadaqa*) denotes any form of life or any life-affirming object—cows, goats, sheep, or chicken; cloth or clothing; rice flour or kola—that is ritually given to the ancestors, to God, or to the spirits of the wild (djinn). As a general principle, there is a direct correlation between the value of what is given and the gravity of the situation that occasions the sacrifice. While cows are the most materially valuable possessions (one cow is equivalent to fifty pans of rice or two hundred spans of cloth), rice flour and kola nuts have great symbolic value; rice is the "staff of life" and kola the "first food in the world." Thus, when a chief dies and an entire chiefdom is momentarily without leadership or protection, or when a man from a ruling house passes away, many cows will be offered in sacrifice to the ancestors. But when only the well-being of a single household is at stake, rice flour and kola will be offered, for though these things have great spiritual value they cost little. When the well-being of an individual is at stake, cloth (usually white) is often all that is given.

That the value of what is given is a function of the significance of the *relationship* between the giver and the receiver is well nigh universal. So too is the assumption that all sacrifice is essentially self-sacrifice. Something of oneself must be given up if something of the other is to be given in return. Moreover, not only do all gifts incorporate something of the giver; giving something one *has* symbolizes *vita pro vita*, the gift of one's own *being*. Accordingly, the value of any gift is measured both by what it costs the giver and what it offers the receiver. And the more imperiled a polity (or person), the greater the sacrifice needed to protect it. Human sacrifices at Aztec temple complexes increased significantly when the empire was under threat.[31] As food resources dwindled on Easter Island, the scale of human sacrifice increased, as did the expenditure of human labor on making and erecting the great volcanic stone *moai*. Sacrifice is thus a strategy for countering entropy in the human world by channeling energy into the world of the gods who, it is hoped, will reciprocate by reinvigorating the waning world of mortal men. The greater the threat to the human order, the higher the value of what will be given to the powers-that-be, which may explain why virgin girls are often chosen to be sacrificed since their life-giving potential has not yet been diminished by the bearing of children. Thus, in the past, Kuranko chiefs leaving their country to attend festivals or funerals in other chiefdoms might order the sacrifice of a pale-complexioned virgin girl for the safety of the country, burying her alive in a pit at the chiefdom boundary, her mouth filled with gold and her head covered by a copper container.[32] The logic of this practice is reminiscent of the large-scale sacrifices of young men in Western wars for the defense of an imperiled state, or Aztec sacrifice where the lives of women, captives, and children were ritually fed to the sun, their "vital energy transferred" to the cosmos as a kind of "debt payment to the hungry gods" for the expected regeneration of life on earth.[33]

But whether we are speaking of life-giving resources freely given, gratefully received, or vengefully reclaimed, what is at stake is life itself. Not the life of any particular person but the life of a lineage, a community, a people, a global ecosystem. What augments life in the broad sense of the word is right, what diminishes it is wrong—sentiments, if not principles, we too espouse when in the face of personal loss we declare, "Life must go on," or speak of "life everlasting."

The opposite of sacrifice is witchcraft. The logic of sacrifice is that the more one gives of oneself or the more one is prepared to give up or give to the ancestors or the gods, the more one stands to gain, if only because one's self-sacrifice places an obligation on the ancestors or the gods to provide something in return. According to the logic of witchcraft, however, one is not obliged to give anything up; on the contrary, one has the right to take life from others without offering them anything in return.

The Kuranko word *suwage* (witch, lit. "night owner") suggests some-one who acts surreptitiously, under cover of darkness, using powers that are invisible to ordinary eyes—witch weapons, witch medicines, witch gowns, witch animals, and even witch airplanes. A witch's "life" (*nie*) supposedly leaves her sleeping body at night and moves abroad, often in the form of an animal familiar. As her "life goes out" (*a nie ara ta*), her body may be shaken by convulsions and her breathing cease. In this state of suspended animation, the body is vulnerable; if it is turned around, then the witch's spirit will not be able to reenter it and she will die. A witch will also perish if the dawn finds out of her own body. Witches are predatory and cannibalistic, but they do not attack a victim's *nie* directly; they consume some vital organ (usually the liver, heart, or intes-tines) or drain away the victim's blood or break his backbone by tapping him on the nape of the neck.[34]

It is said that witches work in covens and that the greatest threat of witchcraft attack lies within the extended family. Witchcraft works through blackmail. A witch will somehow open the door of her own house by nullifying the protective medicines that the household head has placed over the lintel. Then another witch from her coven steals into the house and "eats" one of the occupants, usually a child because children are less likely to be protected by personal medicines. The aggressor is obliged to discharge her debt at some later time by making it possible for her co-witch to claim a victim from her house.

Witchcraft is the inverse of sacrifice. While both involve a ritualized or fantasized movement of life itself from one person or place to another, sacrifice is a matter of giving up something of value in order to increase the well-being of one's social group whereas witchcraft is a matter of taking something of value from one's social group for personal gain. If sacrifice is based on the logic of generalized reciprocity (giving without demanding that something will be given in return), witchcraft is based on negative reciprocity (taking without giving anything in return).

In the course of fieldwork, I collected some fifteen hearsay accounts by self-confessed witches in which they named their victims and explained why they had killed them. In every case, the fantasized attack on the life of the victim was in retaliation for a slight, a withholding of favors, or a failure to fulfill an obligation (e.g., a brother's failure to assist a sister in need, a husband's refusal to provide his wife with the wherewithal to live, a co-wife's bullying). In other words, witchcraft was motivated by a sense of grievance. One had the right to take back something that had been wrongly taken from one.

Consider, for example, an anecdote shared with me by Kaimah Marah in 2008. As a child, Kaimah had traveled with his parents to his mother's natal village in Temneland. On their first night in the village, Kaimah fell ill. He was so weak he could not even get out of bed. After much discussion, it was decided that Kaimah was bewitched. A local woman with shape-shifting powers had transformed herself into a night owl. She had perched on the roof of the house where Kaimah was sleeping and consumed his blood. But on the second night, the villagers caught the owl and beat it to death. The witch, now weakened and seriously ill, confessed to her crime and explained how she had assumed the form of an owl in order to attack Kaimah. Perhaps she bore some grudge toward Kaimah's mother, Yebu. Her exact motive was never known, for she died soon after confessing.

If witchcraft and sacrifice exemplify two opposing forms of reciprocity—the first vengeful and self-serving, the second affirming the mutual interdependence of everyone occupying the same lifeworld—it is not surprising to find that animals figure symbolically in both cases.

The animals most closely associated with witches sum up the traits of witchcraft: predatory (leopard), scavenging (hyena, vulture), underground (snake), or nocturnal (bat, owl). Moreover, these are all wild animals. By contrast, the animals associated with sacrifice are domestic animals, and the body of the animal symbolizes the social body in whose name the offering is made to the ancestors and, through them, to God. Following the consecration and killing of the animal, portions of the butchered meat are carefully laid out on banana leaves before being distributed according to custom among the different groups present at the sacrifice—the upper foreleg to the town chief, the lower foreleg to the household head, the rump to the lineage sisters, the neck to the sisters' sons, the heart and liver to a respected person (on several occasions I was the honored recipient), the hide to the leather workers, the hooves to the genealogists and xylophonists, the stomach (in days gone by) to the slaves, and the remaining meat to the household and lineage.

What Godfrey Lienhardt observes for the Dinka holds true for the Kuranko. "Sacrifice includes a re-creation of the basis of local corporate life, in the full sense of those words . . . the whole victim corresponds to the unitary solidarity of human beings in their common relationship to the divine, while the division of the flesh corresponds to the social differentiation of the persons and groups taking part." In the words of one Dinka informant, "The people are put together, as a bull is put together."[35] In exactly the same way, Kuranko make the body of the consecrated animal a surrogate for the social body. Partaking of its flesh is an expression of social solidarity. By contrast, to quote a Kuranko informant, "Witchcraft is eating alone."

Being a Part of and Being Apart from the World

If sacrifice and witchcraft signify the polar opposites of participating in the world or setting oneself outside it—between sociality and selfishness—then these terms might also be read in the light of philosophical anthropology's perennial dilemma of trying to strike a balance between deep immersion in the life of the world and disciplined withdrawal into the life of one's own mind. While worldly engagement provides us with a wealth of experience, detachment is also necessary if we are to process those experiences.

A comparison may be drawn, therefore, between a Kuranko migrant's struggle to sustain links with his family and homeland while breaking free of traditional constraints in seeking a better life for himself and the intellectual's struggle to describe life as lived even as he or she works to produce some coherent narrative or explanatory model that answers his or her need to feel that life can be translated into words. Wilhelm Dilthey argues against the view that the laws of thought can mirror the laws of life and that it is possible to "subordinate the whole of reality to a metaphysical system." Hence his emphasis on inner experience and his caustic comment that "no real blood flows in the veins of the knowing subject constructed by Locke, Hume and Kant, but rather the diluted extract of reason as a mere activity of thought."[36] But if one cannot reify thought, then one cannot reify lived experience either, if only because thoughts are integral facts *of* our experience and as forms of "more-than-life" are as vital to our well-being as "life itself."

One cannot fault philosophers and anthropologists for attempting to render existence comprehensible. Their only errors are in mistaking what Simmel called forms of "more-than-life" *for* life itself, using them as magical means for escaping the complexities of life-as-lived, and refusing to see that their thoughts are neither better nor worse, epistemologically or practically, than the ways that so-called tribal peoples make their own local moral worlds coherent and viable.

6. Belief and Experience

There are times in the life of an anthropologist when one is asked to
believe impossible things, when one's credulity is taxed to the limit and
skepticism undermines one's commitment to respect the beliefs of others. A reindeer voluntarily sacrifices its life to a hunter so that he and his
kinsmen will have meat to sustain their lives. A monitor lizard comes
upon a man near death in the wilderness and altruistically goes out of its
way to show the man where to find food and water. A woman confesses
to being able to leave her body at night, assume the form of a predatory
animal, and sap the life from a kinsman who has offended her. A man
whose self worth and well-being have been eroded by circumstances beyond his control re-empowers himself by transforming himself into an
elephant, the totem of his clan.

Philosophy and theology also ask us to accept impossible beliefs. Car-
tesianism postulates a separation of body and mind before proposing
baroque explanations for how *res cogitans* and *res extensa* nevertheless
operate coincidentally or in harmony.[1] Or we are invited to accept a well-
argued case for the existence of God and take on trust the assertion that
His son was crucified then, after three days in a tomb, was raised from
the dead so that those who believe in him will be redeemed of their sins
and have eternal life. Nor is anthropology immune to building models

of human life that defy common sense, such as the structural-functional model of a social system of roles and regulations in which individuals are socialized and through which they pass like zombies or sheep, their sense of their own identity utterly absorbed into the ancestral protocols of the tribe.

Hardly a day passes that we hear stories, have experiences, or confront events that beggar belief and leave one lost for words. I write these lines only twelve hours after a twenty-one-year old man entered the Emanuel African Methodist Episcopal Church in Charleston, South Carolina, convinced that "blacks were taking over the world [and] someone needed to do something about it for the white race." Wanting a return to racial segregation and hoping to ignite another civil war, Dylann Storm Roof, spent an hour with the congregation before taking out a .45 caliber handgun and murdering nine worshippers. "I have to do it," he explained as he stood over one of his victims. "You rape our women and you're taking over our country. And you have to go."[2]

For all the consternation and incredulity one experiences in the face of alien beliefs and practices, the question emerges as to whether espoused beliefs determine behavior or simply serve to rationalize behaviors whose sources are too complex and elusive to sum up in a single phrase. A corollary of this question is whether any *belief* fully encompasses or summarizes a person's *being* and under what conditions a person is so in thrall to his or her belief that he or she is not free to see the world in any other way. Does calling Roof a racist cover all the facts of this case? Does calling a woman a Christian simply because she embraces a belief in the Christian God say everything there is to say about her? Does characterizing a society as animist or totemic do justice to the experience of every individual in that society? Does labeling a person "bipolar" or "autistic" not only capture conclusively *who* a person is and *what* is wrong with them but *how* best to medicate them and make them "normal" (as if normality can also be confidently defined)? Empirically, we know that beliefs tend to be held with different degrees of commitment or faith, varying in intensity depending on context, and that doubt and inconstancy are part and parcel of even the most fervent believer's life. No human being exemplifies a belief, espouses a philosophy, or possesses a personality with the kind of constancy and pervasiveness we often assume to be the case when we identify people solely in terms of their culture, religion, class, gender, or ethnicity. In other words, belief and being are nonidentical. This means that we must be careful not to conflate *epistemological* assertions regarding what a person knows or believes with *ontological* conclusions regarding who that person is. There is always an indeterminate relationship between normative ideas and lived experiences, and it is this indeterminacy that good philosophy and good anthropology must disclose. Occasionally, for instance, a Kuranko woman will confess to being a witch, and most Kuranko will cautiously admit that they believe in witchcraft, but it would be simplistic to conclude that Kuranko "believe in witchcraft," as everyone has his or her own opinion on this matter and many people are reluctant to expatiate on it lest they incriminate themselves. Even confessed witches only partially confirm the stereotype. As my own fieldwork revealed, witchcraft beliefs are not only highly variable but ordinarily lie dormant and unrealized until a crisis, such as epidemic illness or moral danger, precipitates a frenzied search for explanation and for a scapegoat. Yet even in such critical situations, interrogating a self-confessed witch to see what is in her heart or to prove what was on her mind is far less important than concerted action to rid the body politic of the evil that appears to have penetrated its defenses.[3] Something similar is true of Islamization in northern Sierra Leone. Although most Kuranko now pay lip service to Islam, one cannot infer that they have become Muslims or ceased to be *sunike* (pagan or agnostic); some incorporate Islamic practices into their lives, but most simply "go along," following what others do for purely social reasons but without the depth of commitment, thought, and faith that we in the West associate with religious "sincerity" or "authenticity." That is to say, people act in a subjunctive mode, *as if* they believed.

The Life of the Mind and the Life of Action

In drawing her famous distinction between the *vita contemplativa* and the *vita activa*, Hannah Arendt is at pains not to disparage reflective thought (*theōria*) but to question its classical association with eternal verities and relocate it firmly within the world of everyday existence—a world of ever-changing social relations, in which people struggle to make a living and cope with difficulty and disaster. Methodologically, this perspective may require us to suspend our desire to know the causes or culmination of events in order to describe the situations in which life unfolds. Whether we are doing philosophy or anthropology, our work begins, therefore, in medias res, and where it carries us is not for forethought to determine but for life itself to decide.

It is early summer 2015. My wife and I are saying farewell to our house in Lexington, Massachusetts, for the last time. Our children have left the nest, and tomorrow we fly to Denmark for three weeks before returning to the United States and a new home in Arlington. As if attuned to our mixed emotions in leaving our family home, nature conspires to make us witnesses to a minor crisis of its own. A robin's nest has fallen from its precarious niche on top of a downpipe, and a fledgling is haplessly struggling on the path, trying to follow its mother's distressed cheeping from a nearby hickory tree. My wife fetches a ladder and attempts to restore the nest to its place under the eaves. When this proves dangerous because of overhead power lines, she climbs down the ladder and picks up the fledgling in her gloved hands, hoping to place it and its nest on the ground under the tree. But the bird refuses to stay put. Fearing it will fall prey to a cat or raccoon, she finally builds a screen of branches around the stranded bird. But we are due at our attorney's office at noon for closing and have to leave the fledgling to its fate.

As we drive off, my concern for the distressed robin is suddenly eclipsed by an overwhelming memory of our dog Clover, whom we had to have put down two summers before, after she contracted an incurable neurological disease. I used to walk Clover in the nearby woods every day, and after her death I rarely went into the woods again. Now I felt as if I was abandoning her and that her shade was as much in need of care and attention as any living soul, including the fledgling robin.

This bereavement reaction is universal. It is difficult to overcome loss, even the loss of a dog or a wallet. We continue searching for a lost object long after we have persuaded ourselves that it has gone forever, whether taken by death or by a pickpocket. The belief that the object is still there, invisible to us, is stronger than the physical evidence that it has gone. Our beliefs lag behind our experience, and to some extent outrun empirical evidence, as if they possess a life of their own. While experience changes, often with every passing second, beliefs remain relatively stable and even resist change. This is why it is a mistake to infer a belief from experience, just as it is fallacious to think that experience confirms belief.

But the persistence of beliefs may be explained not through inertia or force of habit but through their potential to enable us renew our lives in the face of loss. Crucial to this process is the fact that beliefs are not simply matters of personal conviction but are widely shared. Nor do beliefs refer simply to what *is* the case (their explanatory power), for they offer us scripts or templates that enable us to act in concert with others (their instrumental power). To "believe" in ghosts, or in God, is to possess a collectively sanctioned compass for finding one's path through disorienting circumstances and to move beyond an impasse in which we did not know how to go on.

In Denmark, I shared my thoughts with a former colleague Tine Gammeltoft. Tine had lived in Hanoi, Vietnam, for several years, researching the experiences of pregnant women whose fetuses had been declared "abnormal" after ultrasonography and prenatal screening. Both state and individual preoccupations with fetal "normality" and "abnormality" reflect the high incidence of birth defects still caused by the chemical defoliants with which the American military saturated northern Vietnam, and they provide a telling example of how human subjectivities are shaped by human history. Hence the title of Tine's recent book, *Haunting Images*.[4]

One thing that mystified Tine, however, was that Vietnamese seldom allude to the wars that polluted their countryside and destroyed tens of thousands of lives, even though, forty years after the war's end, young parents remain terribly anxious that their children might be born deformed as a result of these historical atrocities. It was as if, Tine said, people had a capacity—one she did not have—for putting the past behind them so that traumatic events would not sink so deeply into their consciousness that their ability to live in the here and now was impaired.

What people choose to "believe" is conditioned by immediate existential needs rather than some abstract interest in the nature of the world, and this became very apparent to me in the wake of Sierra Leone's civil war. Instead of dwelling on trauma as an intrapsychic wound or personal insult that cried out for revenge or needed healing, people seemed to have an extraordinary ability to suppress such subjective clamor and focus entirely on the practical needs of the day—food for a family, school fees or medicine for a child, social meetings, or answering the summons of life itself.

Though anthropologists working in third world countries have often remarked on this capacity for enduring unspeakable suffering and loss, one must be careful with terms like resilience, stoicism, or acceptance. It is not that people take hardship in stride, as though impervious to the brutality of life; rather, they have a capacity for making a realistic assessment of where best to commit their limited energies. Turning one's back on the past or refusing to allow yesterday's tragedy to undermine the business of meeting the demands of life today is not so much a moral virtue as a practical necessity, something James Scott calls *mētis*, as its essence is "knowing how and when to apply the rules of thumb *in a concrete situation*," particularly situations "that are mutable, indeterminate (some facts are unknown), and particular."[5] Thus, in the immediate aftermath of war in Sierra Leone, people would speak of "forgiving and forgetting" or leaving it up to God to see that justice was done. Forgiving had little to do with absolving one's persecutor; it had everything to do with not wasting one's life on seeking justice or taking revenge. It was a declaration not to remain in thrall to those who had momentarily taken one's life out of one's own hands. But while one might forgive in order to move on with life, even living in the same village as those who destroyed one's livelihood or killed members of one's family, one would never forget what had occurred. But to remember would remain a personal matter; it would seek neither public recognition nor performance. More important than one's own peace of mind was keeping the peace within one's community, and this is precisely where suppression is different from repression.

Outward Appearances and Inward Feelings

The problem of knowing whether outward appearances reveal or belie inward feelings was exacerbated by the anachronisms I experienced returning to Denmark. Passing the apartment on the corner of Norre Allé and Ahornsgade where we had lived ten years prior, the whole neighborhood seemed so unchanged that I felt that if I entered the building and went up to the first floor I could walk in on my family just as we were a decade before. The morning after we arrived, I walked out of the house where my wife and I were staying with old friends. The sun was shining in a clear blue sky. Yet within minutes I was forced to take shelter in a doorway from torrential rain and hail. This sense of being assailed by anomalies and incongruities only intensified that evening when I boarded a bus to Brønshøj. As the bus passed the Assistens Cemetery, where Søren Kierkegaard is buried, and moved on into the depths of Nørrebro, I had an uncanny sense of having been miraculously transported from middle-class Copenhagen into a shabby Middle Eastern city, its street lined with shawarma, falafel, and kebab cafes, halal butchers, Punjabi greengrocers, currency exchanges, hair salons, and used-clothing stores. In fact, the street was locally known as "Little Arabia"; almost 30 percent of its population were immigrants from Pakistan, the former Yugoslavia, Turkey, Somalia, or the Middle East.

These incongruities presaged the events of the following evening, when my wife and I visited Emmanuel Mulamila; his wife, Nanna; and their daughter, Alice Maria, in their apartment in Søborg. I had become friends with Emmanuel when ghostwriting his story in 2011–2012. Now, as in the past, Emmanuel's experience of being a Ugandan in Denmark continued to be bedeviled by a lack of fit between inward feelings and outward appearances.

After Emmanuel had prepared a dinner of salmon and salad, we sat at the kitchen table, drank to one another's health, and listened as Emmanuel told us about his life since I had last seen him a year ago. Largely for Francine's sake, Emmanuel also rehearsed some of the grueling childhood experiences he had once shared with me, being harshly caned by teachers, bullied by older students, ostracized by his maternal kin. This led to an exchange of anecdotes about bullying.

"What Danes call bullying," Emmanuel said, "I would call teasing."

Nanna did not agree. "Psychological wounds can cut as deep and hurt as much as the cuts of a teacher's cane, perhaps even more."

But Emmanuel was determined to emphasize physical rather than psychological hurt. To him, bullying by mockery or humiliating language was child's play compared to what Ugandan first-year students have to endure—being electrocuted in their iron dorm-room beds, forced

Belief and Experience

to sleep on a bed of feces and then, unable to wash, having to eat with shit-stained hands.

Though Emmanuel harbored no hatred toward most of his childhood persecutors, he made an exception of one man—a certain teacher called Mr. Madobo. As a young man, Emmanuel nursed such vengeful feelings toward this man that he fantasized about killing him should he encounter him again. Almost inevitably, they did meet. At first Emmanuel did not recognize his old nemesis. The man had AIDS. The symptoms were all too clear. And it was also clear that this man did not have long to live. In a split second, Emmanuel's hatred turned into pity. He found it impossible to reconcile the sight of this emaciated, abject, and diseased individual with the person who had tormented him as a child. He was not looking at a bully but a victim. And yet it was indubitably the same man, Mr. Madobo.

As Emmanuel recounted his story I was thinking of an article I had read earlier in the day in which Lotte Buch Segal presents a searing account of the experiences of Palestinian women whose husbands are serving long, often life, sentences in Israeli jails. Lotte brings into painful relief the difficulty these women have, not only of keeping body, soul, and family together or coping with their inner longing to see and be with their husbands but of maintaining the façade that is expected of a loyal and patriotic wife—supporting others, extending hospitality to visitors, containing her feelings of loss and suffering, exemplifying a political and moral ideal.[6]

Emmanuel too had struggled, as a child, to take beatings without flinching, to put on a brave face, to suffer in silence. He learned how to turn himself to stone, dissociating himself from his pain. As a migrant he had also learned what to show and what to hide, how to feign and not give offense, his feelings hidden, his thoughts kept to himself.[7] To criticize such coping strategies in terms of a bourgeois code of sincerity, transparency, and honesty is absurd; for people without power, the skills of stealth, cunning, dissociation, two-facedness, and even trickery become means of survival—techniques of "building smoke," as Emmanuel put it; of "provocative impotence," to use Sartre's phrase; or what James Scott calls "weapons of the weak."[8] These are not symptomatic of moral collapse or of a failure to "get a life"; the powerless know only too well that those in power are masters of speaking with forked tongues.

Though Emmanuel knew the risks of being open to strangers, he nonetheless remained alert to every opportunity that came his way, though carefully assessing it lest it prove to be another trap, another dead end, another humiliation. When I asked him about the work he was doing a year ago, making and delivering Paradis ice cream, he said that the café had closed and that he was now acquiring an international truck driver's license. He had passed the Danish exams and would take the EU exam in a few days' time. He liked being in command of a powerful truck, seated high above the traffic, a master of his domain. And now that Alice Maria was growing up, it would not be hardship if he was away from home for several nights at a time. There was one obstacle, however, that he was still struggling to get around. A psychologist who worked for his driving school had become curious about him. Sensing that he was far better educated than any of the other trainee drivers, and fluent in Danish despite being a foreigner, she accompanied him on test drives, "prying" into his life and repeatedly asking him questions to which he was prepared to give only minimal answers. Given his experience of doors closed in his face when it was discovered he was African or "overqualified for the job" or educated at an Islamic University, Emmanuel also feared that if the psychologist learned details of his childhood she would diagnose him as suffering PTSD or suspect him of planning a terrorist attack. "I kept asking myself, what relevance did her questions have for driving a truck. Did she think I would load it up with explosives and destroy the Danish Parliament? Or was it simply a friendly interest?"

"I think it is a romantic interest," Nanna said.

Later that night, when going over the events of the evening with my wife, I asked her how she as a psychologist understood the driving school psychologist's probing questions. "Where do we draw the line between being interested in another person and invading their privacy?"

When Francine described the phenomenon of *opia*, "the ambiguous intensity of looking someone in the eye," which can make you feel vulnerable and invaded, I thought immediately of other African migrants whose stories I had researched and their preoccupation with the disconcerting effects of being stared at or subject to unsettling barrages of questions. Once, in London, my friend Sewa Koroma and I were leaving his house in Islington when I noticed his English neighbor and his son leaning on their gate and observing us intently. No words were exchanged, and it was only when we were out of earshot that Sewa asked irritably, "Why do they stare at us like that? Back home, I would confront them. I would tell them to stop. If they did not stop I would beat them. But here, you're in another man's land; they just stare at you like that, and you can do nothing about it." Sewa was alluding to a Kuranko form of witchcraft called *ya yugo mé* (lit. "evil eye"). To stare at a pregnant woman will cause her pain in childbirth or prolong her labor. And it was widely thought that staring could destroy a person's prosperity.

In Amsterdam, Ibrahim Ouédraogo found it equally difficult adjusting to the inordinate interest the Dutch had in one another's private thoughts and feelings.

"I could not understand why Dutch people were always talking," Ibrahim said one evening over dinner. "Talking on the phone, gossiping, talking about themselves, all the time. In Dutch they call it 'Having your heart on your tongue.'"

"And here I am, talking too much and making it impossible for you to eat!" I said.

Ibrahim smiled.

"In Burkina it's not good to be too direct," Ibrahim's wife Evelien interjected from across the table. "For example, when Ibrahim and I decided to get married we wanted to avoid any difficulties with the immigration authorities, so instead of filing for a civil marriage we explored the possibilities of a religious marriage. Ibrahim went to the imam of his mosque, and said, 'I know of an African guy who is thinking of marrying a Dutch woman.' And when Ibrahim visits my sister [Evelien's sister had recently been seriously ill in hospital], he sits with her, holding her hand. He doesn't get emotional with her and say everything that's on his mind."

"It is the same in Sierra Leone," I said, thinking of how long it took me to adjust to a form of sociality that required sitting with someone in amicable silence rather than busily baring one's soul, making small talk, or engaging in detailed conversations about abstract matters.

Evelien said, "Ibrahim will ask my friends, 'Are you well? How is your family?' and be amazed at all the personal details they give in response."

"People are always prying into your life," Ibrahim said. "Always asking me what jobs I am doing, whether I like them, how much I earn. It is too much, really."

The Inscrutability of the Other

It is not only the hidden depths of other people that perplex us; it is the world that lies about us, beyond our sensible grasp, outside our control. This is why a central question for philosophical anthropology is the question of how human beings imaginatively, ritually, and practically bridge the gap between their own immediate, known, and manageable worlds and the forces that impinge on them from within and without, throwing them into doubt, stopping them in their tracks, and threatening their very existence. Although the deep uncertainty that Freud called "the uncanny" (*unheimlich*, lit. "the unhomely") may be greater for people in limbo than for others, it is a constant of the human condition, for there is always more to life than meets the eye and a limit to what we can comprehend and control.

Emmanuel's struggle to prevent the psychologist penetrating his defenses and his unrelenting efforts to understand what he called "the Viking mentality" weighed on my mind as I wandered, several days after seeing him, through the dimly lit Moesgaard Museum in Jutland.

Suddenly, I found myself in the thick of a digitalized Iron Age battle between two opposing armies, equipped with large shields, javelins, swords, and bows and arrows. Most overwhelming, however, was not the battle itself that raged about me or its immediate aftermath, when the bodies of the dead were left to carnivores or the processes of natural decay. It was what transpired on the steep shores of a dark lake, where women worked to bend and break the looted weapons of the vanquished army and their menfolk conveyed them in bundles out onto the lake, lowering them into the depths where, apparently, the mutilated bodies of the enemy were also cast. There was something archetypal in this scene. The surface of the peat-dark lake reflected the world you knew firsthand. You could see your face in it, framed by scraps of cloud, blue sky, and wind-stirred foliage, but you could not peer into it let alone divine what wights inhabited its depths. The lake's surface was like a porous membrane where one blurred into a world of otherness, where a familiar foreground suddenly became background and the clear distinction between self and wider self disappeared. The lake bore comparison, therefore, with the natural symbols of many religions, in which the depths of a forest or of the sky, the roots of a great tree or an underground cavern, mirrored one's familiar world, albeit inverted and in reverse. The imagination populates these impenetrable spaces with quasi-human beings that combine genders or fuse human and animal features in grotesque yet powerful forms. But in both these realms and between them—the first empirical, the second surmised—the rule of reciprocity applies. The reasoning is as follows: All threats to one's life and livelihood—violent storms, military invasion, epidemic illness, death—as well as the things that guarantee well-being—rain, sun, security, health—are beyond one's power to control. Since it is unthinkable that such forces are entirely arbitrary, they must be in the power of extrahuman agents to control. Despite the inscrutability and remoteness of these external powers, they resemble human beings, both in their physical appearance and their morality. Relations with them are, therefore, possible under the rule of reciprocity. And so the broken weapons and bodies of outsiders are delivered to their dark abodes as sacrificial gifts on the understanding that they, whether named or unnamed, will recognize an obligation, incur a debt, and return a favor.[9]

What We Owe Ourselves and Others

At the heart of all religion and all morality is the question of how far reciprocity reaches. It is not only a question of what the powers-that-be, whether secular or supernatural, owe us. It is a question of what we owe one another. When Cain slew Abel (Genesis 3), God asked Cain where his brother was, only for Cain to reply, "I know not. Am I my brother's keeper?" If we owe it to our kinsmen to protect and care for them, then do we owe the same benefit to strangers? Do we owe the wherewithal of life to other species or to the planet we share with them? For whom and what am I personally responsible? Is there a limit to what I owe those who suffer natural catastrophes or social injustices?

My visit to Denmark coincided with the worsening crisis in the Mediterranean, as thousands of desperate people, displaced by war in Syria and Africa, sought asylum in Europe. One moment captured the political and ethical impossibility of resolving this crisis. During a televised discussion entitled "Good Life in Germany," a young Palestinian called Reem told Angela Merkel in fluent German that she and her family, who had arrived in Rostock from a Lebanese refugee camp four years previously, faced the threat of deportation. "I have goals like anyone else. I want to study like them," Reem said. "It's very unpleasant to see how others can enjoy life, and I can't myself." The German chancellor responded by saying she understood but that "politics is sometimes hard. You're right in front of me now and you're an extremely nice person. But you also know in the Palestinian refugee camps in Lebanon are thousands and thousands, and if we were to say you can all come . . . we just can't manage it." As the chancellor went on to express the hope that quicker decisions would be made to determine which refugees could stay and which must return, she was interrupted by Reem's crying. "Oh, God," Merkel said, before stroking Reem's shoulder and telling her how eloquently she had presented her case.[10]

In the Moesgaard Museum one may quickly forget the outside world, the tranquil summer day, the evening news, the world's ongoing catastrophes. But one's escape is short-lived. Gazing on the compressed and leathery body of Grauballe Man in the Moesgaard Museum, it is easy to be drawn to him as one of us. His features, his toenails, the soles of his feet, his fingerprints are ours. As Seamus Heaney wrote, "Who will say 'corpse' to his vivid cast? / Who will say 'body' to his opaque repose?" Yet in the world beyond this reverential museum, the same violence done to this Iron Age man is still being done. Soldiers are sacrificed to secure our homeland. The poor are locked up to protect the rich. And though we are stirred to pity by this distant ancestor, whose throat was slit before he was laid naked in the preserving peat, are we equally moved by the victims of our contemporary state? Naming those killed by vigilantes and policemen in the United States during 2015, the writer Gary Younge comments, "The precise alchemy that makes one particular death politically totemic while others go unmourned beyond their families and communities is not quite clear."[11]

Perhaps it is a question of recognition rather than mourning, for how can one mourn someone whose humanity one has never experienced except as an abstraction? Recognition means remembering. It involves reminding oneself of whom we have to thank for who and what we are, not only our parents and intellectual predecessors but the peasants and slaves on whose broken backs our wealth was accumulated and the indigenous peoples whose land we had the temerity to claim as our own. It means never forgetting that their lives were the precondition of our own. We recount stories that were originally theirs. We think through their thoughts. We dance to their tunes. We play the music that they composed.

Consider Steven Feld's illuminating essay on the social life of a Ba-Benzélé musical composition from the Central African Republic, recorded and distributed on a 1966 ethnomusicological LP entitled *The Music of the Ba-Benzélé Pygmies*. The opening track on the LP alternates voice with the sound of a single-pitch papaya stem whistle (*hindewhu*). The track was "adapted," unacknowledged, by Herbie Hancock on his 1973 Columbia LP *Headhunters* and later by Madonna for her 1994 CD *Bedtime Stories*. In 1985, Feld asked Herbie Hancock "if he felt any legal or moral concern surrounding his *hindewhu* copy on *Headhunters*" and whether he felt that musicians "could side-step the music industry and copyright conventions to directly remunerate the sources of their inspiration." Hancock replied that blacks were brothers and all had suffered equally from oppression, so Feld's question was not relevant.[12]

If this issue *is* relevant, then it behooves us to ask whether anthropology's alternative rationales, of scientific authority or artistic authenticity, blind us to the practical exigencies of everyday life among marginalized peoples and give rise to the illusion that our preoccupation with the latest intellectual fashions and discursive styles trump all other concerns. Because many contemporary philosophers and anthropologists are products of bourgeois upbringings, how is it possible for them to resolve the contradiction between the values of the class to which they belong and the concerns of the classes or cultures from which they draw their raw material? Does making our discourse more literary help overcome this contradiction or exacerbate it? As for those whose origins are working class or third world, how can they overcome the guilt at having abandoned the people and places that formed them? In her compelling study and memoir of family and class in postindustrial Chicago, Christine Walley condenses this experience into her changing relationship with her father. "In the inner places of my psyche, I . . . wondered whether somehow [in becoming a middle-class university teacher and intellectual] I had betrayed him by choosing to lead a life he could not follow."[13]

The Embourgeoisement of the Humanities

A couple of years ago, on a return visit to my own country of origin, I looked up old friends who had been living on a remote commune for more than thirty years. I was immediately struck by how much of their energy and attention was absorbed by the tasks of day-to-day survival—fishing, gardening, cooking, repairing things that were broken. In the subdued light of their living room, it was easy to see them as pioneers. It wasn't only the surroundings that reinforced this impression—the wood-burning stove, the ironware, the tins of homemade bread, the bucket of local honey, the organic fruit from the commune orchard. It was their very appearance: their serviceable clothing from Kathmandu or Swanndri, their lack of cosmetic pretension, their ability to make do with basic amenities, their rough and ready language. You discussed fitting a wider diameter pipe to a stove, improvising a chimney cowl from a scrap of hammered tin, or replacing a worn wheel bearing on a truck with the same intensity and ingenuity with which a group of Harvard professors might debate the ethics of intervention in a foreign state. If you rarely touched on or inquired into the life of another mind or school of thought or the nature of experience, it was not because these things were irrelevant; rather, time did not permit such departures from the mundane and the never-ending struggle to make ends meet. As for social life, relationships were mediated more by doing things together than by sharing intimacies. All this strongly reminded me of my experiences of living in West African villages and brought home to me the difficulties of being an intellectual in societies or situations where the life of the mind is supererogatory, if not absurd.

Much of what we know as middle-class existence depends on having sufficient means to get the mundane tasks of life performed for us by a tradesman or a machine and of being cushioned from the primary work of production. Having bought time in the form of leisure, we can afford to cultivate manners (rather than crops), dwell on our own thoughts and emotions (rather than occupy ourselves with the demands of extended family), and contemplate nature as an aesthetic object (rather than as a resource whose exploitation exhausts us). Because we possess a surplus of time and money, we are free to devote our energies to décor, fashions, fine foods, and fads, none of which are, strictly speaking, necessary for our physical survival.[14] We create worlds centered on ourselves. In rituals of shopping, showing off, distracting ourselves, or taking costly holidays to "get away from it all," we magically conjure illusions of autonomy and of being "special." For the African migrants in Europe with whom I had worked, this pattern of immediate sensory gratification and personalized consumption stood in stark contrast with the traditional African emphasis on accepting hardship and awaiting one's due—a contrast between narcissism and stoicism. Indeed, the bourgeois cultivation of inwardness and "intravidualism" implies a set of symbolic contrasts for separating self from society.[15] Such contrasts draw invidious distinctions between the civilized middle classes and peasants, primitives, and underlings. The migrant's preoccupations with economizing—in what one spends money on, what one consumes, what one says, and what one does—reflect the value placed on conviviality as a measure of the worth of one's words and deeds. What one possesses accrues value in being given away and loses value in being kept solely for oneself. Gluttony and logorrhoea are both modes of self-gratifying overconsumption and have no social value. Language should be used to express rather than impress, to connect people rather than create hierarchies. Everything is measured against the standard of social, rather than merely personal, fulfilment.

I have often asked myself whether my philosophy of writing reflects these African values, and whether my years of living in one of the poorest societies in the world have made me more than ordinarily aware of the need to economize and minimalize, both in practical and literary matters. Perhaps this is why I have argued for a view of writing as techne rather than episteme—a "tool for conviviality," a means of bridging the gulf that lies between oneself and others, subsuming the singular in the plural.[16] Perhaps the notion of *mētis* is even more in keeping with this view, suggesting as it does departures from hard-and-fast rules—tricks of the trade, refusals to respect disciplinary boundaries, a responsiveness to whatever life throws up or throws together, an aversion for systematizing, and an acceptance of happenchance.

My conversations with African migrants continue to remind me of this historical tension between societies in which people struggle for bare life and those in which people's desires and preoccupations "sur-pass the material reproduction of existence."[17] In its fetishized concepts, its specialist jargons, its loquacity and intellectual excess, the academy exemplifies this "affirmative culture" of the bourgeoisie, and I some-times imagine the conventional academic essay as an overfurnished ba-roque drawing room, designed to impress but hermetically sealed off from the brute realities of the outside world.[18] Nevertheless, I do not want to exaggerate the differences between these worlds, making one the measure of the real and mocking the other for its artificiality and folly. Neither world guarantees complete well-being. And while the cult of inwardness and the "dissociation of sensibilities" that accompanied the rise of the urban bourgeoisie in eighteenth-century Europe did not preclude the possibility of community or nostalgia for the agrarian past, so-called primitive ontologies have never precluded the possibility of self-realization, reason, and critique.[19] What is common to all cultures is the quest for life. Though intellectuals tend to emphasize the "mean-ing" of life as a fundamental existential imperative, meaning is only one form that life assumes in the human imagination, and it is no more or less significant than mobility, love, family solidarity, health, wealth, en-ergy, or union with the divine—all of which figure as paths for attaining well-being.

7. Persons and Types

Begin with an individual, and before you know it you find that you have created a type; begin with a type, and you find you have created—nothing.

—F. SCOTT FITZGERALD, "THE RICH BOY"

F. Scott Fitzgerald's story "The Rich Boy" begins with the observation that "there are no types, no plurals," only individuals, and he warns against the literary tendency to begin with individuals only to create types, for types offer us "nothing."[1] Although Fitzgerald has in mind the stereotypes with which the poor depict the rich and the illusions the rich have about themselves, his comments apply equally to the glib contrasts we draw between men and women, good and evil, old and young, and modern and premodern. Not only do we all too readily believe that these category distinctions reflect empirical reality, but we also become convinced that one category is superior to the other and that we who deploy these antinomies with great aplomb are more rational and clear-sighted than those who occupy the inferior positions in our equations.

From the beginning of my life as a writer, I have dreamed of integrating the art of storytelling with the disciplines of philosophy and social science. Not surprisingly, this has meant wrestling with the question whether individuals and types are as antithetical as Fitzgerald suggests or whether these two ways of understanding the human condition are equally illuminating, depending on what a given situation calls for. Rather than see persons and categories as antithetical, the first being immediate and authentic, the second artificial and alienating, can we not see these frames of reference as mutually entailed?

The Case of Prime Evil

In 1997, the South African psychologist Pumla Gobodo-Madikizela secured an interview with Eugene de Kock, whose nickname, Prime Evil, summed up a widespread opinion of him as one of apartheid's most brutal covert killers. Incarcerated for life in the maximum-security wing of Pretoria's Central Prison, where so many of his victims had been tortured and murdered, de Kock was classified as one of its most dangerous inmates, so it was with considerable trepidation that Gobodo-Madikizela visited the prison to interview him.

A leading psychologist with the Truth and Reconciliation Commission (TRC), Pumla had become intrigued by de Kock's request, toward the end of his first appearance before the TRC, to meet with the widows of two young anti-apartheid activists whose murders he had planned and executed; he wanted to apologize to them, but in private. The meeting took place, and when Pumla interviewed the widows later, she was surprised to learn that they had been "profoundly touched" by de Kock's contrition. Pearl Faku confessed, "I couldn't control my tears. I could hear him, but I was overwhelmed by emotion, and I was just nodding, as a way of saying yes, I forgive you. I hope that when he sees our tears, he knows that they are not tears for our husbands, but tears for him as well . . . I would like to hold him by the hand, and show him that there is a future, and that he can still change."[2]

How might one understand this event?

Pumla said that she felt compelled to establish whether the widows were really forgiving Prime Evil or, rather, recovering through *his* grief the life *they* had lost, the humanity *they* had been denied and that de Kock had forfeited in become the willing servant of an evil regime.

I do not think I would have trusted this man's tears. Though stripped of his privileges and powers, de Kock remained someone so habituated to possessing the power to determine whether others lived or died and having the last word, perhaps even the last laugh, that he would find a way of manipulating the hearts and minds of others, even when shackled to a prison wall. Here was a man who had been fed a diet of Afrikaner nationalism and anticommunism from an early age, had joined the secretive Broederbond, and was convinced that if four million whites did not keep forty million blacks in line that they would lose their homeland and probably their lives. Now that the apartheid era was over and the apocalypse had not occurred, had he really changed his mind, or had he simply adopted the tactics necessary to survive and perhaps fight another day?

Answering these questions is not my goal. Rather, I want to inquire into the difference between individuals and types through Pumla's experience of coming face to face with an individual she had considered a type, indeed the worst type of person one could imagine: the embodiment of prime evil.

Her first impression of de Kock was that he was not the dangerous individual she had been warned about. Her second impression was that he was more complicated than she had bargained for. "When de Kock spoke about his past," she writes, "his recollections seemed to reflect some of the same factors that led others to reduce him to a label. . . . He had belonged to a world that created violence, I to a world that was the object of this violence: he belonged to a world where morality meant the same thing as hate, and I to a world that knew the difference. Our worlds were the black and white of lies and truth, and yet as de Kock spoke, the boundaries of our world did not always seem so clear."[3]

It isn't that Pumla came to see South Africa from an Afrikaner point of view or that she reaffirmed a black one; rather, she came to see that there were multiple perspectives, reflecting an infinite variety of social contexts and complex biographies, and that this variety of ways of seeing the world and acting within it could not be reduced to two monolithic categories, whether racial, cultural, or moral. That this changed perspective proved to be deeply unsettling is conveyed by Pumla's description of a critical moment during her first interview with de Kock, when she asks him to talk about his meeting with Pearl Faku and Doreen Mgoduka. De Kock is "visibly distressed." He tears up. Voice breaking, he says that he wishes he could do more than apologize, that there was some way of bringing the bodies back to life so he could say to the women, "Here are your husbands."

Despite the fact that de Kock may be manipulative and in bad faith, Pumla is moved to reach out and touch his shaking hand. She surprises herself in doing this, for, as she writes, "these same hands, this same voice" had "not too long ago" authorized and initiated "unspeakable acts of malice against people very much like myself." But she also says that she responded to him "in the only way one does in such human circumstances."[4]

As with the two widows, I am tempted to say that Pumla's humanity *trumps but does not necessarily forgive* the inhumanity of de Kock and that what these women actually give de Kock is recognition that he is not merely a type—a replica of all the others who killed in the name of keeping South Africa free of communists and terrorists—but a person who, on one level, is like them, a person who weeps, who suffers remorse, who cannot bear to be chained, and who fears death. That moment, she writes, "gave me a glimpse of what he could have been. Hard as the memory of having touched him was, the experience made me realize something I was probably not prepared for—that good and evil exist in our lives, and evil, like good, is always a possibility."[5] Yet Pumla continued to wrestle with the question of the extent to which she should open her mind and heart to de Kock and the extent to which she should follow the majority view that he was unworthy of dialogue, let alone sympathy—a view that Hannah Arendt came up against when she decided to engage the question why Adolf Eichmann was such an efficient and willing cog in the atrocious machinery of the Holocaust. What is there to understand? Such persons are pure evil; they are subhuman; they are incorrigible; they are not worth our pity.

In this matter, Michel de Montaigne is edifying. "The changes and contradictions seen in us are so flexible that some have imagined that we have two souls, others two angels who bear us company and trouble us each in his own way, one turning towards the good the other towards evil, since sudden changes cannot be accommodated to one single entity."[6] Pumla, however, is determined not to draw Manichean contrasts between the good and the evil but to acknowledge their copresence, even their dialectical necessity, in everyone, including herself.

It is all very well admitting, like Montaigne, that "every sort of contradiction can be found in me . . . depending on how I gyrate,"[7] but living as if this were the case is difficult, so we persist in the illusion that the self is a seamless whole, or should be, and that constancy can be achieved in our relationships over time, with others and within ourselves.

Not having recourse to type is as difficult as not saying the sun rises. After Copernicus, many of us know that the sun does not rise, just as, after Montaigne, some of us know that "we are entirely made up of bits

Persons and Types

and pieces, woven together so diversely and so shapelessly that each of them pulls its own way at every moment" and that "there is as much difference between us and ourselves as there is between us and other people."[8] But certain illusions persist because they make us less anxious. Typecasting helps us escape from complexity and find refuge in simplicity. And it gives us an excuse for not assuming responsibility for our actions, since stereotypes, like racial profiles, protect us from ever coming to terms with the individual humanity of the other. We can kill a terrorist, a towel-head, a nigger, or a filthy dog with impunity because the category term transforms the other into a foreign object. Insofar as the other is a nonentity, we are killing no one. But to kill another human being face to face is quite another matter, even when one has been prepared through military training or repeated stereotyping not to see the other as human.[9]

As Arendt and Gobodo-Madikizela both discovered, not only do we categorize murderers in ways that make them appear utterly unlike ourselves, but murderers may also hide *their* individuality behind the mask of being a type—someone whose entire being is at the service of a utopian ideal or collective goal, such as cleansing the body politic of danger, dirt, disease, deviance, or degeneracy and thereby creating a pure state, at once monocultural, monotone, and monolinguistic. Even though de Kock sought recognition as a person, he could not let go of his identification with his cause. He later tells Pumla, "That was my trigger hand you touched," and when he asks her, "Have I killed any of your friends and family?" he is, by implication, splitting off individuals he regrets killing from unnamed others—terrorists, communists, enemies of the state; in a word, types—for whom he feels no remorse.[10]

Writing against the disastrous effects of assimilating our individual humanity to a stereotype, Pumla states: "Philosophical questions can and should give way and be subsumed to human questions, for in the end we are a society of people and not of ideas, a fragile web of interdependent humans, not of stances."[11] But isn't there an unsettling similarity between our academic attachment to types and categories and the fascist mentality in which individuality is effaced in order to create a uniform mass? How seriously do we reflect on the distancing devices *we* deploy in order to artificially separate our discourse from the world of experience? And how might we come to terms with the discomfort to which Pumla alludes when we try to have it both ways—engaging in dialogues with the other that do not privilege or empower any one party while seeking the kind of neutrality or disengagement that satisfies our craving for types, and for a transcendent standpoint?

For me this question takes the form of a decision—when do I turn to fiction and when do I turn to social science; when do I turn from image to idea?

Distance Without Reification

In showing how difficult it is for us to remain faithful to and respectful of the individual or particular, while acknowledging the vital role that generalizing and typifying play in our lives, I hope to move beyond the either-or position of F. Scott Fitzgerald and explore the circumstances in which it is edifying to focus on types and those in which it is more edifying to focus on individuals. Neither discursive mode is *intrinsically* good or bad; ethics is essentially a matter of deciding which mode does justice to a given situation and which does not.

The ethical question is what, at any given moment, we are going to make the touchstone against which we measure the goodness or rightness of what we are doing, saying, or writing, or, for that matter, whom we are talking to. That every new situation demands a different touchstone is poignantly brought home by Pumla Gobodo-Madikizela's experience as part of the TRC and her meetings with Eugene de Kock. The apartheid period dictated one appropriate way of comporting oneself, the post-apartheid period demanded another, and Pumla found herself caught between two fires—vengeance or forgiveness, engagement or separation.[12]

This kind of ethical uncertainty informs our everyday lives. Upon the outbreak of war, does a pacifist revise or suspend his views because a stronger imperative now prevails—protecting the homeland, defeating fascism, defending democracy? If, following a tragic road accident, a loved one has suffered brain death and has been placed on life support, does one cling to the hope that a miraculous recovery may occur or does one let her go? And if one falls out of love with one's spouse and meets someone else, what touchstone now holds true—the one that approves the consummation of desire or one's duty to protect his children from the pain of betrayal and divorce? The moral dilemma is often a matter of deciding between individual good and a so-called higher good, reflecting traditional values, the national interest, or some quasi-Kantian categorical imperative. Human rights is such a general good, as it is alleged to hold true for all individuals, at all times, and to the same extent.

This brings me back to the contrast between individuals and types, and the question as to which perspective one will invoke in any particular life situation. If neither perspective is intrinsically better than the other, then we are led to the pragmatist question of deciding which perspective, in any given circumstance, will do the least harm or lead to the most edifying outcome. William James put it this way: "The truth of an idea is not a stagnant property inherent in it. Truth *happens* to an idea. It *becomes* true, is *made* true by events. Its verity *is* in fact an event, a process: the process namely of its verifying itself, its veri-*fication*."[13]

Kuranko storytelling events, and the process whereby stories speak usefully to the quandaries and difficulties of an individual life, can help elucidate James's thesis. In a sense, the Kuranko encompass two notions of truth—the intellectualist notion that James criticizes and the pragmatist one he defends. This difference finds expression in two clearly distinguished narrative genres that I call myths and folktales. Myths are known as *bimba kumenu* (ancestral words) or *kuma kore* (venerable speech). They are "charter myths" in Bronislaw Malinowski's sense of the term; they justify "by precedent" and supply a "retrospective pattern of moral values, sociological order, and magical belief."[14] Folktales (*tileinu*), by contrast, are make-believe. Their truth is not measured against some absolute, ancestral standard but in terms of their edifying potential, their ability to change a person's experience of his or her situation, and their utility in making a human life more bearable in the here and now. This may happen because the tales distract, entertain, or amuse or because they offer the prospect of magical escapes from untenable situations. But the tales may also answer moral questions or afford glimpses into the meaning of life. Whatever one finds in these stories, however, their truth is conditional upon what James calls their payoff, their usefulness, their expediency for the individuals who hear them.

Kuranko folktales create their effects not through depicting individuals in particular situations, as in the novel, but through types such as "the wife," "the husband," "the orphan," "the chief," or animal characters like Fasan (Mr. Hare) and Fasuluku (Mr. Hyena) that signify social roles (in this case younger versus elder sibling). Moreover, the tales always begin with a similar phrase—*wo lai yan* or *wule yan be la*—that situates the narrative in a place "far off" and a time "long ago." But while a story may unfold outside of the here and now and involve imaginary beings, stock characters, disguised voices, and miraculous events, it remains tied to an immediate lifeworld—a parable or allegory of quandaries in the lives of those who tell and attend to the tale. Accordingly, one Kuranko storyteller's tales of conjugal distrust and infidelity may obliquely express the circumstances of his own unhappy marriages while another's stories of a corrupt and autocratic ruler may allegorize his own unresolved relationship with an abusive father. The general is thus used analogically as a screen onto which are projected and reworked memories and emotions that are too close for comfort, too subjective to be grasped, too painful to be told.

In explaining this preference for types over individuals, George Devereux points out that when a narrative is stripped bare of idiosyncratic detail and real personalities and gets "ground down to its universally valid nucleus" it becomes more available to the listener, who can uninhibitedly flesh the story out in relation to his or her personal experience, making it, in effect, his or her own. Devereux calls this process "intrapsychic alibiing."[15] It enables a person to sustain a shared illusion that the story is make-believe, or merely for entertainment, while surreptitiously using it to work through deeply personal dilemmas—a junior wife oppressed by a senior wife, a younger sibling bullied by an elder sibling, a village ruled over by a tyrannical chief, an orphan child persecuted by its "stepmother," a man betrayed by his closest friend, a man cuckolded by his wife, a wife betrayed by her husband.

Far from showing that stereotypes are by their very nature dehumanizing and simplistic, Kuranko folktales suggest that stereotypes may mediate changes in our experience that are just as profound as those mediated by great novels. Though we like to think of folktales and novels as essentially different genres, writing the former off as childlike and celebrating the latter as more sophisticated, such pejorative distinctions ignore what these narrative forms have in common: they are both fictions, and they both reflect a human imperative that goes back to our earliest beginnings, namely the need to process our most intimate and entangled experiences *indirectly*, through outlandish idioms, objective images, and other existences.

Life Imitating Art

Whether de Kock was faking contrition, as a chameleon might improve its chances of survival by changing color in response to its changing surroundings, may never be resolved. But the issue of consistency remains as pressing in life as it is in art. No one likes a person who cannot be trusted, and transparency is a moral ideal in most human societies, even though one's survival may, in practice, depend on an ability to prevaricate and lie. What is storytelling but an art of pretending—what Samuel Taylor Coleridge called an art of suspending disbelief, in which a writer insinuates a "semblance of truth" into a fantastic story and the reader suspends judgment as to its veracity. In short, storytelling presents us with the paradox that a lie may reveal a truth.

Few writers have explored this paradox more compellingly than Herman Melville, for whom the storyteller is akin to the confidence man—a master of masquerade, of aliases, of duplicity. When Ralph Emerson espoused the lofty ideal that if you trusted someone, then the trust would be repaid, Melville's riposte was, "God help the poor fellow who squares his life according to this."[16] For Melville, we are all too willing to be conned or deceived, and the idea of a self that remains constant over time, immune to life's distractions, temptations, and false hopes is illusory. "A consistent character is a *rara avis*," he writes, by way of explaining that a work of fiction "where every character can, by reason of its consistency, be comprehended at a glance, either exhibits but sections of character, making them appear for wholes, or else is very untrue to reality; while on the other hand, that author who draws a character, even though to common view incongruous in its parts, as the flying-squirrel, and, at different periods, as much at variance with itself as the caterpillar is with the butterfly into which it changes, may yet, in so doing, be not false but faithful to facts."[17]

If identity is so mutable, so conditional on the masks we wear, then is there anything that remains constant, behind the masks?

The Story of Na Nyale

It was my immersion in the world of Kuranko storytelling, with its fabulous resolutions of everyday dilemmas, its economy of expression, and its brilliant theatricality that not only led me to explore, academically, the connections between storytelling and ethical inquiry, but to make the folktale a model for how I might write fiction. It wasn't that I shared Walter Benjamin's nostalgia for a mode of oral storytelling that "foregoes psychological shading" or his view that the twentieth century had become significantly "poorer in communicable experience."[18] Rather, I wanted to follow his example in writing *allegorically*, integrating documentary and imaginary modes of meaning making in the same text.

Many of the most compelling Kuranko folktales concern constancy in friendship and in love (the same word, *dianye*, connotes both). Staying loyal to a friend, in good times and bad, or showing resilience in the face of misfortune are stoic virtues, though the emphasis given to them is perhaps an indication of how rarely they are realized. It is also ironic that while women are often stereotyped and scapegoated as fickle and untrustworthy ("Never let a woman know your secrets"), it is often a woman whose emotional steadfastness exemplifies the ideal of constancy. Thus, in the following story, Na Nyale never doubts that she will be reunited with her lover, despite his death, dismemberment, and disappearance, and her faithfulness to his memory shores her up against the ruin of her life.

The story is told by Kenya Fina Koroma, in the village of Kondembaia. First, she sets the scene. Na Nyale's husband, the village chief, was jealous and possessive, and his wives had all taken lovers. Every day, the women left the village for their farm. Each woman carried a large raffia basket in which her lover was concealed. Upon their arrival at the farm they put down their baskets, then spent the day with their lovers. But Na Nyale's lover was too heavy for her to carry all the way to the farm, so one day she left him in the basket in the farmhouse. Unbeknown to the women, their husband had followed them to the farm, and while poking about in the farmhouse he noticed Na Nyale's basket. When he declared his intention of opening it, the basket began to shake, whereupon the chief took his machete and cut the basket open.

The chief said, "Who are you?"

"I am Fara Mara," said the man.

"What are you doing here?"

Fearing for his life, Fara Mara said, "Allah has destined that this should happen."

The chief said, "Well, Allah has indeed destined that something should happen between us today. Now get out so that I may kill you."

Fara Mara pleaded for his life. "Oh chief, why don't you simply fine me. Whatever the amount is, I will pay it."

The chief said, "No, I must kill you."

Fara Mara got out of the basket. The chief seized him, and placed one foot on Fara Mara's legs, and his other foot on Fara Mara's hands. Then he drew his knife and cut Fara Mara's throat.

Fara Mara's blood splashed onto the leaves of a cassava plant, and one leaf changed into a little Senegalese fire finch.[19] The fire finch flew to the part of the farm where the women were weeding, and began to sing.

Na Nyale, oh Na Nyale, Na Nyale, oh Na Nyale
Ni i wara sole to mansa, ni i wara sole to mansa
Wara kemine ye m'bi yo, oh Na Nyale

[Na Nyale, oh Na Nyale . . . If you left your basket,
the chief has discovered your lover today, oh Na Nyale]

After listening to the fire finch, Na Nyale told her companions that she could not go on weeding and would return to the farmhouse to see what had happened. Her companions gave her leave to go, and she hurried down the hill to the farmhouse. But what did she see? She saw the basket on the floor, the ropes around it severed. Then she saw the chief.

"What happened here?" she asked.

"Is this yours?" the chief replied.

"Yes. But you have nothing to fear. What did you do?"

The chief said, "Well, I have not left any man in my farmhouse. But if I found a man in the basket with the bones of a chicken and a pan with traces of palm oil on it, it means that the food he eats is sweeter than the food I eat,[20] so I killed him."

The woman said, "After you killed him, what did you do with him?"

"After I killed him, I burnt his body and threw the ashes in the river."

"What river?"

"The Seli."[21]

Na Nyale returned to the village for some money and vowed that she would never rest until she had found her lover. No matter what happened, she would find him.

She set off, following the river downstream. For two years she followed the river. She said she had to find her lover. Wherever she stopped she would find palm birds in their nests. She would tell the birds to be quiet, that love was in the air and on the ground and under the water. She would say, "I am searching for my lover."

> I ya l moina, Fara Mara, i ya l moina? Dondo
> I ya l moi dondo? I ya saya soron n'de le fe
> Dondooooo. Don.

> [Do you hear me, Fara Mara, do you hear me? All is quiet
> Do you hear how quiet it is? You died because of me
> All is quiettttt. Quiet.]

She heard nothing but the sound of her own voice and went on her way. Wherever she stopped by the riverside, she sang the same song. For two years she followed the river, searching for her lover.

Then all the living things of the river met together and said, "That man who was killed and burnt, and whose ashes were thrown in the river— whoever ate some of his ashes should bring it forth now. There is someone searching for him, someone so desperate she cannot rest. All those who ate the bones should spit them out. All those who ate the flesh should regurgitate it. Those who ate the eyes should give them up. We should put all these parts back together again and make the man as he was."

So everyone brought forth the different parts. All those who were able to reassemble the skeleton did so. All those who were able to put flesh on the bones did so. They put all the parts together again. Then they asked who had taken the life. The one who had taken it said, "I took the life." They said, "Well, go and get it." He went for the life. They told him to put the life back in the body. He did so.

Then they told the man that someone was looking for him, someone desperate to find him. At that moment, Na Nyale arrived at that spot. It was a place so fear-inspiring that no one ever ventured there. But so desperate was this woman that she cared nothing for her own safety. She stood there. There was dense forest all around. She heard the palm birds chattering. She scattered some coins in the forest and said, "All you djinn who live here, this is my gift to you. I am looking for someone, for the man who was killed on account of me. If I do not find him I prefer to die by this river. I cannot live without him." Then she scattered some coins along the riverbank and said, "All living things in the water and on the land, listen to me."

But silence surrounded her.

She stood and sang [as before].

Then the man sang in reply:

Ah, n'de Fara Mara; n'ya saya keni i le l le fe dondo
[Ah, I am Fara Mara; I preferred death because of you . . . all is quiet]

The woman leapt into the river—*gbogbon*. She said, "He is here. No one but Fara Mara knows my song. He must be here." Then she saw him.

The creatures that dwelt under the water now took care of them for two years. They were well fed and provided for. In the third year they were given a xylophonist.[22] A horse was given to the lover, and the woman was given two boxes of dresses. Then they were carried to the surface of the river. The water creatures said, "We must tell you that when you return you should immediately find the man who killed you and take your revenge. If you don't do this, we will kill you. Here is what you must do: when you return, ask for him, and spend a night lodged in his house. Next morning, tell him you want to dance. Invite him to dance with you. Sit on your horse and let him sit on his. Then, as you dance, take your sword and cut off his head, thus paying him back in his own coin.[23] By cutting off his head you will satisfy us." The man and the woman agreed and set off.

In every village they passed through, they asked: "Is that chief still there?"

People asked, "What chief?"

"That chief who killed a man some time ago, a man who was hidden in a raffia basket on a farm."

Then people said, "He is there."

Finally the couple reached the village where that chief lived. But they did not recognize his compound. Again they asked, "Is that chief still here?"

Again people asked, "What chief?"

"The chief that killed a man on his farm, a man who was having an affair with his wife."

They said, "Yes, he is here."

Then the man said, "Well, he raised me, so I have come to thank him. Can you show me the way to his compound?"

He was led right into the chief's house. Everyone stared at the two strangers. Then one of the chief's wives said, "Eh! This man's wife resembles Na Nyale, the one whose lover our husband killed. She looks like her."

The woman went and greeted Na Nyale. But Na Nyale said, "I am not Na Nyale." The other woman said, "Well, people can certainly look alike!" She went away. But then she said, "The man looks like Fara Mara." The talk went on, but the strangers said nothing.

Then the man took £15 and gave it to the chief, saying, "You raised me. You have forgotten, but you did." (The chief had no idea that a plot was being hatched against him, to make him do what the strangers wanted.) The woman then gave two lapas and two head ties to each of the chief's wives. Then they retired for the night.

In the morning the man told the chief that he was going to offer a sacrifice because it was a long time since he had done so. He said, "I did not know that I would find my big man here." Then the chief mounted his horse. The man mounted his. The old women crowded around them, clapping, and the *jeleba*s played their xylophones, singing the praises of the chief. The man scattered coins on the ground. People scrambled to get them. Even Fara Mara's mother did not recognize him. But he did not go to her place. The *jeleba*s were playing. Everyone was happy. But Fara Mara had a sword hidden under his gown. He put his hand under his gown and grasped the sword. He said, "Oh God, I did not start this. This man killed me. My body was burnt and my ashes strewn in the river. If this happened, may God help me take my revenge." As the chief passed him, he drew his sword and with one blow cut off the chief's head. His head fell there. His body fell there. There was a great commotion among the people. Everyone was crying. Fara Mara said, "Heh, everybody be quiet. Everyone will get a chance to tell me why he or she is crying." (A killer's word is always feared.) Then everyone fell silent.

Next day he sacrificed two cows, one for himself and the other for the dead chief. He became chief in that town. All the chief's wives became his wives. Therefore, be you a chief or a nobody,[24] if you find your wife with another man, fine him but do not kill him. To kill is not our custom. That is not what we have met."

Since these events occurred, a stop was put to killing. No one does it now.

There are several reasons why I never forgot this story. The first is connected to the Sierra Leone civil war of the 1990s, when Kenya Fina's village of Kondembaia was sacked by rebels, and forty men, women, and children were murdered while others suffered the amputation of their arms or hands. In the aftermath of such atrocities, the burning question is whether one pursues vengeance or seeks reconciliation, which was the question South Africans faced in the post-apartheid years. In the Kuranko story, Fara Mara has no hesitation about fulfilling his promise to the river spirits who had restored him to life. Declaring before God that he had done nothing to justify the violence of the chief, he gives himself the right to do to the chief what had been done to him. But the storyteller takes a different view—one that echoes Fara Mara's words when he pleaded with the chief for his life: adultery should not be punishable by death but by the payment of a fine. The second reason this story has remained so vividly in my memory is the devotion of Na Nyale to her lover. Not only her readiness to risk her life in finding him again but the impossibility, for her, of imagining a life without him. Although Kenya Fina typecasts her characters, referring to them as "the woman," "the chief," or "the husband," she nonetheless captures their personal qualities (the chief's possessiveness, Na Nyale's fidelity to Fara Mara) in ways that touch me deeply. This is not a world where people are assimilated to rules and roles; it is a world of personal passions and moral dilemmas in which constancy is a recurring question.

First, there is the vexed ethical issue of whether Na Nyale's marital infidelity can be forgiven because of the undying love she feels for her lover. Second, there is the contrast between the constancy of love and the constancy of hate, for while Na Nyale keeps love alive by seeking reunion with her lover, Fara Mara keeps hate alive and seeks to avenge his death. Finally, there is the compelling question of whether, despite devastating loss and irreversible change—symbolized by the dismembering and burning of Fara Mara's body, which is then swept away in a river—there is anything that may be called constant, and whether, in the face of the finitude of our individual lives, there are archetypal forms, existential quandaries, and historical repetitions that truly deserve to be called constants.

8. Being and Thought

Chance furnishes me what I need. I am like a man who stumbles along;
my foot strikes something, I bend over and it is exactly what I want.

—JAMES JOYCE TO HARRIET SHAW WEAVER

It is a common fault, found in all people and in all societies, to imagine that our thoughts and our words can cover and contain all that is the case, that there is no phenomenon, human or extra-human, that lies permanently outside the pale of what we may know and say and that human genius and ingenuity can ultimately capture in concepts and words the truth not only of one's own particular lifeworld but also of the world at large. Though I am convinced that this conflation of being and thought, or of being and language, is fallacious and involves an unwarranted extrapolation from phenomena we *can* grasp to phenomena that are beyond our ken, I am nevertheless struck by the hubris that attends these endeavors, whether in the name of religion, science, or art, and by the fierce competition among these different modes of apprehending reality and arriving at the truth. Thus, while psychoanalysis emphasizes the power of the unconscious to determine conscious thought processes or social science often reduces thought to social conditioning or peer-group influence (social proofing) and chronobiologists emphasize how our biological rhythms spontaneously synchronize with the rhythms of others or our environment (entrainment), I want to explore the *interplay* between factors we admit not to fully control or comprehend and factors we consider to be within our power to know, name, and manage. It is therefore in a skeptical spirit that I explore, in this chapter, the interplay of two modes of thinking—the first characterized by an active, disciplined, focused application of thought to being, the second characterized be a more passive, attentive, open-minded approach in which the thinker simply registers or channels thoughts that appear to come from elsewhere.

In critiquing any kind of ontologizing of cultural representations of self and other, or sweeping generalizations concerning intrinsic cognitive or epistemological differences between primitive irrationality and modern rationality, I want to focus not on fixed mind-sets or mentalities but on the existential conditions under which thinking is experienced either as a process undertaken consciously and intentionally or as a process that simply happens to people without their choosing. The alternation between these perspectives reflects one of the most vexing and enduring questions of human existence: whether truth is revealed to us or created by us. Insofar as the Enlightenment made man the measure of all things, it rendered redundant the idea of divine revelation. That this opposition between man-made truth and revealed truth persists in the opposition between nurture and nature, or between reason and intuition, may reflect our tendency to treat these modes of thought as modes of being. We thereby see them as competing epistemologies rather than focus on the conditions under which they appear and the work they do in human life.

Being Thought

Rather than make a philosophical case for either agency or patiency, free thinking or conditioned thinking, I prefer to see these alternative conceptions in relation to the critical or everyday situations in which they arise. My thesis is that they are ex post facto rationalizations of what, in given situations, has proved to be most conducive to a person's sense of existential viability. By existential viability I mean what Baruch Spinoza meant when he proposed that every life-form struggles to persist in its own being, experiencing an increase rather than degradation of its sense of being alive. This viability, I claim, is enhanced by our human capacity for switching between one constellation of brain processes that enables us to act willfully and intentionally and another constellation that enables us to suspend will and passively receive impressions—a state of mind that often gives rise to the conviction that one has been inspired by

Being and Thought

or gained a glimpse into some implicate reality to which we assign various names—history, God, muse, episteme, tradition.

When one examines specific instances of such passive, inductive, or idle thought, it becomes clear, however, that it is invariably preceded or followed by deliberate and purposeful thinking. One entails the other. Neither is a constant that would permit a person to identify one mode of thinking with science and instrumental rationality and the other with religion and art. It is their mutual necessity that explains why many significant scientific breakthroughs have come after conscious thought has been suspended and why many artistic breakthroughs have depended not solely on inspiration but dedicated work.

Whether indeliberate thinking is seen as a virtue, as in some meditation practices, or as symptomatic of an ill-disciplined mind, it is remarkable how often we speak of doing something without a second thought or of an idea occurring to us serendipitously, striking us, or springing to mind, as though its source lay beyond us and, on entering our thoughts, possessed a life of its own. The same is true of emotions, moods, and actions, for we are often inexplicably moved against our will, "falling" in love, becoming "possessed" or "inspired," or being "touched" by another person's pain, as if a force external to ourselves took us by surprise, overcame us, or blew us away. In the same vein, we sometimes speak in the middle (or mediopassive) voice in which the subject often cannot be categorized as either agent or patient but may have elements of both, as in the Maori *ka mahi te tangata* ("worked the man," i.e., the man worked) or in spirit possession where a person is paradoxically no longer in complete possession of herself yet clearly capable of returning to herself.

These phenomena of being-thought or being-moved are basic to Michel Foucault's concept of the episteme. Dismissing the thinking subject from his histories of punishment, the clinic gaze, and the human sciences, Foucault speaks of discourse as an anonymous, pervasive presence that finds expression in individual minds yet is not a product of these minds and undergoes radical and unpredictable changes without the conscious mediation of any particular thinker, much as the weather passes from sunshine to rain, precipitating human commentary but bypassing human agency. Such processes are in the nature of things; they are creations neither of the minds of men nor of an omniscient God.

Moreover, just as God ceased to be the center of the universe at the end of the eighteenth century, so man is now being erased, "like a face drawn in sand at the edge of the sea."[1]

Apart from the logical contradiction—that an individual, namely Michel Foucault, can pronounce on phenomena that allegedly lie beyond the ken or control of any one human being—this view is at odds with a recurring phenomenon, confirmed by both common sense and a cursory knowledge of history—that new ideas *do* occur to human beings, only to come up against the dominant episteme of the age, which declares those ideas to be heretical, subversive, or untrue. In other words, there is always an unresolved tension in human life between our sense of being in a world that shapes the ways in which we think and act, and being in a world we have a hand in shaping. This is as true of a philosopher like Michel Foucault as of a creative writer like Elizabeth Catton.

When asked if she had yet embarked on another writing project, in order to capitalize on her success with *The Luminaries* and create more work while her stock was high, Catton said, "It's important to respect the seasonal nature of creation. After the harvest you need a winter before you can plant anything again. I would draw a really sharp distinction between creating and producing," she continued. "I think that they're very different things. What I feel is that true creation happens when you're making something out of nothing—like it's divine, you know. Creation is a completely divine concept. You have to wait for the call."[2] The theme of waiting for inspiration rather than willfully searching for it is common to creative artists, mystics and lovers—a connection that explains why, in so much mystical poetry from the Song of Songs to the *Spiritual Canticle* (1584), one's relation to the divine is spoken of as a passionate if spiritual connubium. "Where have you hidden, beloved, and left me moaning?" asks the bride at the beginning of the canticle. "You fled like the stag after wounding me; I went out calling you, but you were gone." There is therefore an intimate connection between the mystic's dark night of the soul, yearning for connection with an elusive God, the lover's long wait for reunion with his or her beloved, and the writer's anguished search for words that will do justice to what he or she longs to say or share.

But, as Elizabeth Catton observes, it rare to find passivity without activity. In 2010, an interviewer asked singer Nora Marie Invie if her compositions were calculated or happened naturally. Invie replied, "It might be more of a surprise every time it happens, but usually when I'm writing songs magical things happen that I don't understand where they come from, and that's a part of it."[3] But this does not mean that Invie does not work on the material that comes to her unbidden, hammering it into shape, revising her ideas about how best it can be composed for her band, and performed. Tellingly, one of Invie's most moving and memorable songs is called "Daydreaming."

Among the Warlpiri of central Australia, individual dreams (particularly women's dreams) provide glimpses into the universal ground of all being, known as the Dreaming (*jukurrpa*). These dreamt glimpses into ancestral events are then made the basis for ritual enactments. But though the dream enters the dreamer's mind as she sleeps, the ritual performance requires painstaking work, conscious thought, fervent discussion, and close cooperation.

Thomas Edison once remarked that genius is (only) 1 percent inspiration and (mostly) 99 percent perspiration. And while we typically disparage the role of inspirational or revelatory experience in modern thought, often dismissing it as childlike, undisciplined, or primitive, it is complementary to deliberate labor in all human societies.

Picasso put it perfectly: "Inspiration exists, but she has to find you working."[4]

Inspiration, Divination, and Storytelling

Divination might appear to confirm the view that primitive people avoid or are incapable of independent, critical thought, favoring an acquiescent attitude to the powers-that-be, whether divine, ancestral, spiritual, or secular. This view prevailed in social anthropology for a long time. It was assumed that tribal peoples lacked individuality and autonomy; they filled roles, fulfilled duties, conformed to ancestral protocols, and repeated patterns, generation after generation, that the ancestors had established long ago.

If a person suffered some reversal of fortune or faced an unprecedented event—a journey into the unknown, a mysterious illness, a run of bad luck—he or she sought the advice of a diviner who could channel unseen and extrahuman powers of insight and foresight, usually associated with djinn, ancestors, or divinities. The diviner, however, simply received messages, heard voices, read signs, and supposedly played no active role in interpreting his clients' situations or deciding how they might avert misfortune. The diviner was a tabula rasa, much like the classical empiricist, on whom the world left impressions or through whom the invisible was brought to light. Yet, as Karl Popper observes in his critique of induction, such "bucket theories" of knowledge overlook the extent to which subjective bias, selective attention, and subconscious motives enter into the interpretive process.[5] As such, a "searchlight theory" of knowledge is more appropriate because it recognizes the active, interpretive aspect of mind that in divination and classical empiricism is either denied or written off as interference. What is missing, therefore, in many anthropological accounts of divination is adequate recognition of the relationship between an initial phase, in which the diviner assumes a passive, open attitude toward the unknown, and a second phase, in which the client is told what sacrifices he or she must offer in order to avert a bad prognosis or confirm a good one. In this second phase, a person's fate is no longer in the lap of the gods but in his or her own hands, for if the sacrifices are not made or are compromised in some way, then any ensuing misfortune will be attributed to the client's negligence rather than the diviner's sources of inspiration.

This interplay between patiency and agency is equally evident in storytelling. During the first two decades of my fieldwork among the Kuranko I spent many hours with a gifted storyteller called Keti Ferenke Koroma. Mostly, I was content to simply listen to his stories and record them, indifferent to whether they were his own creations or drawn from the canon. But there were times when I was curious to know where the germ of his stories came from and how he developed a core motif or key idea. It wasn't simply that these questions were ethnographically important; they were questions that had fascinated me for a long time, reading accounts of the creative process among European artists and intellectuals. Was this unlettered West African fabulist any different?

"It is Allah who endows a person with the ability to think and tell stories," Keti Ferenke told me. "It was my destiny to tell stories. When my father went to a diviner before I was born, the diviner told him that his next-born child would be very clever."

Keti Ferenke's remarks were consonant with the Kuranko idea that a storyteller simply "sets down" or "lays out" something that has been given to him or put into his mind; he is, therefore, a *til'sale*, "one who sets down *tileinu*" (stories). In this sense a storyteller is like a diviner. The diviner is "one who lays out pebbles," though it is God or a bush spirit who implants the idea of how to interpret the patterns in the diviner's mind.

"When you are told something," Keti Ferenke went on, "it is good if it stays in your mind. Ideas come into my head, just like that. I am not asleep. I am not in a dream. But when I think of them, I put them together as a story. I could never stop thinking of stories, though I could stop myself telling them." And he described how, as he worked on his farm or lounged in his hammock at home, he would try to develop a narrative that did justice to the idea that had been seeded in his mind, bringing it to life in an entertaining and edifying way. Not only did ideas come to him when he was relaxed and susceptible to "divine" (we might say "unconscious") inspiration; it soon became clear to me that his stories themselves were plotted, like folktales throughout the world, as a series of critical episodes or encounters, usually three in number, that interrupt the narrative flow, creating moments of impasse and heightened suspense that are preludes to a breakthrough, a surprising intervention, a novel perspective. In Kuranko stories, these moments of hiatus and tension usually occur at a socio-spatial threshold—a river's edge, a ford, a crossroads, a bridge, the outskirts of a village or chiefdom—or at the temporal borderland between the rainy and dry seasons or night and day. Spatial and seasonal boundaries thus provide Kuranko with concrete images of existential limits in the same way that images of the no-man's land between *ius humanum* and *ius divinum* or of a censoring ego that regulates traffic across the threshold between the unconscious and conscious provide the European social imaginary with its metaphors of border situations. But in both lifeworlds, it is quasi-human figures—djinn and fetishes, scapegoats, angels and gods—that demarcate and embody the ambiguous zone where we cease to be recognizable to ourselves yet may see ourselves more completely than at any other time.

Keti Ferenke's experiences echoed my own, and they helped me clarify my creative process, for though I write for two to three hours a day, I never know from one day to the next exactly what I will write, or whether it will be poetry, fiction, or academic prose. I plan nothing and expect nothing; it often seems that everything is given to me. This has been the case for as long as I can remember. I make myself available to thought in the knowledge that my day's quota of words, insights, and images will come to me unbidden, born of my dreams, of a walk in the woods, of a conversation with a friend, or a book I am reading, or in the course of cooking a meal or cleaning the house. Like Keti Ferenke, I need idleness in order to receive the ideas I will then hammer into shape, conscious of what I am doing and of what I might aim for—though even then I reach a point where this purposeful and focused work is no longer paying off; then another prolonged period away from the word processor is required before a way forward is once again revealed to me.

Such personal and ethnographic experiences have made me question the academic tendency to draw hard and fast distinctions between entire societies or historical epochs in which truth is arrived at *either* through systematic scientific experimentation *or* divine revelation. People constantly switch between purposive and aimless modes of thinking depending on the situation at hand and what is called forth by such situations.[6] As William James observed, "The whole function of philosophy ought to be to find out what definite difference it will make to you and me, *at definite instants of our life*, if this world-formula or that world-formula be the true one."[7]

Thinking in Crisis

Almost by definition, a crisis brings us to the limits of language and the limits of thought. In crisis we are so flooded by emotions of fear and panic that we are literally struck dumb and physically transfixed. Neurologically, limbic processes become dominant, occluding cerebral functions. Under such circumstances, when words fail us and we cannot move, we may nonetheless be moved to utter sounds, to act blindly, and to experience fragmented thoughts as if our minds and bodies were not our own.

Minor oscillations between the experience of being in conscious control and being lost to the world are, however, continually occurring in everyday life. Sometimes this oscillation is felt as a movement between experiencing oneself as part of and standing apart from one's common world.[8] At other times it will register as a difference between mindfulness and mindlessness. Doing fieldwork, writing an essay, or simply walking in the street, one may become so carried away by what is doing that one "forgets oneself" and the line between oneself and the other, or the task one is performing, becomes blurred. Yet there are just as many times when one is suddenly "brought back to one's senses" and becomes so mindful of one's own body, needs, feelings, or thoughts that the social field or physical environment in which one was, only seconds before, totally immersed or even lost, becomes a vague background against which the small drama of one's own consciousness resumes center stage.

The philosopher Gillian Rose was one of the world's most astute commentators on the German critical tradition, from Kant and Hegel to Adorno and Benjamin. In her early forties, Rose became gravely ill with ovarian cancer that failed to respond to chemotherapies and quickly metastasized. Her confrontation with imminent death was both an existential and philosophical challenge, and in the book she wrote during her dying days she interleaves meditations on both these issues. Philosophically, her book *Love's Work* is a defense of reason. That reason often fails us is no reason for abandoning it or making it a scapegoat for the ills of modernity; it is, rather, a cause for rededicating ourselves to the struggle to know and to grow. This is above all an ethical struggle, for the impossibility of arriving at certain knowledge, like the impossibility of exemplifying any moral ideal, is no reason to abandon the struggle, for that would be to fall back into the belief that truth is revealed, or to place all one's hopes in science or to embrace postmodern relativism. Philosophy for Gillian Rose is uncannily like ethnography for me. It is a "singular journey" involving aporias, not dogmas; difficulties, not consolations.[9] And it entails a constant shifting between two different conceptions of control. The first implies management and mastery, in which the world bends to our will, and our knowledge promises to light up the darkness, offering us greater certainty in our relationships with objects and others. The second is more elusive, but it is what enables one to live one's death. Rose writes

> of a sense which, nevertheless, saves my life and which, once achieved, may
> induce the relinquishing of "control" in the first sense—"control" means that

when something untoward happens, some trauma or damage, whether inflicted by the commissions or omissions of others, or some cosmic force, one
makes the initially unwelcome event one's own inner occupation. You work
to adopt the most loveless, forlorn, aggressive child as your own, and do not
leave her to develop into an even more vengeful monster, who constantly
wishes you ill. *In ill-health as in unhappy love, this is the hardest work: it requires taking in before letting be.*[10]

Something of this attitude finds expression in Jorge Semprún's account
of his experiences in Buchenwald concentration camp in 1943–1945.

Maurice Halbwachs, author of the classic monograph on memory, is
dying. Too weak even to speak, Halbwachs is lying in the middle level
of the three tiers of bunks, just chest high to Semprún, who takes him
in his arms and recites a poem by Baudelaire "the way one says a prayer
for the dying." Halbwachs, however, is "past all desire, even the desire to
die. He [has] clearly gone beyond all that, into the pestilential eternity of
his decomposing body."[11]

As Halbwachs is dying a Hungarian Jew is also dying, but unlike the
Frenchman this unnamed individual is able to say kaddish, and Semprún
holds this man as he had held Maurice Halbwachs. He tells stories "to
help him live," and he is able to get the dying man to the *Revier* (sick
bay), where a French doctor nurses him back to life. But it is not this
man's survival that moves me, nor is it Semprún's compassion; it is the
thought of a dying man singing kaddish, singing his own death. And I
think of Albert Camus, who observes in *The Myth of Sisyphus* that the
gritty surface of the stone Sisyphus shoved uphill each day (only to have
it tumble back to the foot of the hill each night) imparted to the toiler
a sense of living his own life, of life being literally in his own hands.
"His fate belongs to him. His rock is his thing. . . . Each atom of that
stone, each mineral flake of that night-filled mountain, in itself forms a
world."[12] His task was initially an accursed punishment by the gods; in
the end, however, the rock has become his rock.

Sol Reader observes that "we are culturally biased towards thinking
of persons as agents. We thus presume that people count, only when
they are agents, so if persons are passive, incapable, constrained or
dependent, society's duty is to help them back to agency and personhood."[13] Yet it would be a grave error to reduce individual experience,

in any society, to either patiency or agency, for our endurance of hardship sometimes depends on thought and action, sometimes on allowing
ourselves to be thought, or to be acted on. And in this matter no one can
predict what will make a life, or a death, livable.

Happenchance

In chapter 4 of E. M. Forster's novel *A Room with a View*, Lucy Honey-
church is crossing the Piazza Signoria in Florence when an altercation
between two young Italian men over a debt escalates into a fight in which
one man knifes the other. Fatally wounded, the victim falls so close to
Lucy that when he opens his mouth she feels that he is about to impart
a message to her. Then, at the very moment that the dying man is borne
away by the crowd and Lucy is about to faint, George Emerson appears
and carries her to the steps of the Uffizi Arcade, where she revives, only
to wonder how the dying man could have been so instantaneously replaced by George Emerson. Despite her faintness and bewilderment, she
assures her rescuer that she is perfectly well, wishes to be alone, and does
not need him to escort her back to her hotel. George accompanies her
anyway, and in the course of their conversation, he tosses into the Arno
some photographs that she had purchased and that he had retrieved
from the piazza when she fainted.

"I didn't know what to do with them," George says. "They were covered with blood."

For Forster these moments are freighted with significance. A young
Italian man dies, only to be replaced by a young Englishman whose voice
is one moment the "voice of an anxious boy" and the next the voice
of a man. "The boy verged into a man," Forster writes, and it is this
changed man that now declares to Lucy, "Something tremendous has
happened; I must face it without getting muddled. It isn't exactly that a
man has died."

As they walk on toward their pension in the gathering dusk, they stop
along the embankment just short of their destination.

Forster prompts us again. "It was not exactly that a man had died;
something had happened to the living: they had come to a situation
where character tells, and where childhood enters upon the branching
paths of Youth."

But if Lucy feels this, she will not admit it.

"Well, thank you so much," she repeated. "How quickly these accidents do happen, and then one returns to the old life!"

"I don't."

Anxiety moved her to question him.

His answer was puzzling: "I shall probably want to live."

"But why, Mr. Emerson? What do you mean?"

"I shall want to live, I say."

Leaning her elbows on the parapet, she contemplated the River Arno, whose roar was suggesting some unexpected melody to her ears.[14]

In these few pages, Forster captures the overwhelming suddenness of the most significant moments in our lives. Within minutes, two strangers have been intimate witnesses of an event that binds them. Almost instantaneously, they pass from childhood into adulthood—so quickly in fact that Lucy simply cannot comprehend what has occurred, and even George's thinking, though far less bound by convention, is "muddled."

We often compare falling in love with an accident or epiphany. In a trice, one's former life falls away like a shed skin. Icarus falling from the sky with melted wings; Saul falling to the ground when he hears the voice of God on the road to Damascus. Such moments leave us lost for words, though our lives have been changed forever. "Something tremendous has happened," George Emerson says. And Lucy also senses, despite her insistence that she is "perfectly well," that she, like the murdered Italian, has "crossed some spiritual boundary."[15]

When George Emerson reiterates his view to Lucy that something tremendous has happened and he means "to find out what it is," he says, "It has happened," as if it is something that has befallen them—an event they have neither willed nor even desired. These are the kinds of events that cause us to invoke fate or destiny, for if there is any agency involved, it is not our own but a force beyond our comprehension or control.

But we are always in the dark in such matters, which is why we may disagree, when we watch the 1985 movie of *A Room with a View*, directed by James Ivory, over the meaning of George Emerson's comment, "Something tremendous has happened." For some, there is no ambiguity: Lucy and George have fallen in love, and what transpired in the piazza was presaged in their first encounter, over dinner in the Bertolini Pension, when Lucy's cousin Charlotte complained that their room had no view. For others, fiction requires that the world be seen in this way, but real life is different. It is governed by contingency, not design, and nothing in reality is inevitable.

But surely both these views are true. The series of events that preceded the fateful meeting of Lucy and George was contingent. But once this meeting had occurred, necessity took over—in the form of love or desire or the sheer power of life itself to sweep us up into its arms and carry us away. It is like the difference between the moment of inspiration that moves one to write—when a random image or thought swims into one's consciousness—and the moments that follow, and may consume several years, when one works to transform that raw material into something that may be shared. Walter Benjamin speaks of a "vital connection" between the life and afterlife of a work of art. "Just as the manifestations of life are intimately connected with the phenomenon of life without being of importance to it, a translation issues from the original—not so such from its life as from its afterlife."[16]

Sometimes, then, we make things happen, we bring things about. At other times, things happen to us, and we are borne away by thoughts and feelings whose origins we cannot fathom and whose repercussions we cannot anticipate. This is as true of ourselves as it is of our relationships with others. In attempting to communicate our thoughts and feelings to others we sometimes feel like castaways on a desert island, putting messages into bottles that we toss into a sea whose tides and currents we can never be sure of, and never knowing whether or not our messages will ever be picked up. Yet the miracle of friendship and of love is that the other is always there for us, meeting us halfway. As we struggle to speak our minds, the other forestalls and assures us, "I hear you," "I know what you mean," "I have often felt the same way myself," "I love you too." None of these assurances may be empirically testable or true, but they absolve us of the need to be known by the other or to know the other, as we know the time by looking at a clock—or to be true to ourselves or to the other, as a good translation is true to the original. Without seeking to do so, we have allowed knowledge to be supplanted by a far more profound measure of truth, which is the unspoken pact between two people that they will be responsive to each other, that they will reach out to each other, affirming the other's existence as though it were their own.

When someone we love dies, we may be haunted by the thought that we did not know her or him, that we cannot provide a reckoning of who she or he was. But the question of knowledge is always a function of estrangement. The closer we come to another person, the more the question of knowing dissolves into a question of being—of *being with* the other, responsive to the other, and working on the shared project of making a life together. No longer is the relationship a matter of two people addressing each other across a crowded room, establishing some kind of knowledge of each other as a prelude to conversation or a prerequisite for interaction (much as a dating agency requires forms to be filled out in order to determine a perfect match). Falling in love cannot be referred back to some database that explains the attraction, nor, at the end of a life together, can a key be found to what made a marriage work, for it was composed of a myriad of a minor moments of shared happiness and sympathetic sorrow, of affection and disaffection, of coming together and moving apart, so that what emerged was not a synthesis to which one can assign a name or pin down as something one can know. As Byron put it:

> But grief should be the instructor of the wise;
> Sorrow is knowledge: they who know the most
> Must mourn the deepest o'er the fatal truth,
> The Tree of Knowledge is not that of Life.[17]

9. Fate and Freewill

1st Gent. Our deeds are fetters that we forge ourselves.
2nd Gent. Ay, truly: but I think it is the world
       That brings the iron.

—GEORGE ELIOT, *MIDDLEMARCH*

When I was in my twenties, few thinkers spoke more immediately to me about the vexed situations in which I found myself than Albert Camus and Jean-Paul Sartre. The more familiar I became with the racism and injustices that Aboriginal people endured in Australia or the plight of the homeless in England or the victims of Cold War power struggles and corporate greed in the Congo, the more urgently I asked myself to what extent, by dint of my color and class, was I complicit in this violence and social suffering and to what extent, given the force of social conditioning, any human being is free to resist the dominant discourse of his or her times? The incipient answer to my questions lay, of course, in the fact that I wrestled with such questions while many others did not and in the evidence I encountered almost every day of the diverse ways in which people thought about and acted toward each other. But did this diversity imply that people were exercising choice, or was the diversity merely a sign of random variation in some inscrutable force field over which human beings had no control?

In Sartre's view, lived experience (*le vécu*) is dialectically irreducible to the terms with which we typically explain it—cultural conditioning, adaptive advantage, structures of the mind, the hard wiring of the brain. We all reflect a unique interplay between what others make of us and what we make of what they have made of us. In the case of Jean Genet, a foundling who spent his early years in a reformatory before being placed with a foster family of Moravian peasants when he was seven, the child is one day denounced as a thief, and with this single stigmatizing word, his fate is sealed. But recalling this life-changing moment years later, Genet writes, "I decided to be what the crime made of me." Citing this phrase, Sartre says that as Genet "cannot escape fatality, he will be his own fatality; since they have made life unlivable for him, he will live this impossibility of living as if he had created it expressly for himself . . . he wills his destiny."[1] Elsewhere, Sartre speaks of "the small movement which makes a totally conditioned social being someone who does not render back completely what his conditioning has given him."[2]

Though this minimal sense of *dépassement*—of having gone beyond the conditions that shape one's life—may provide an illusory though necessary sense of significance to one's own singular existence, Sartre argues that we really *do* go beyond the situations into which we are thrown, both in practice and in our imaginations, and we are, therefore, both creatures and creators of our circumstances. The mystery remains, however, whether the manifestly unpredictable and surprising ways a life unfolds are evidence of conscious decisions or mere contingency (retrospectively glossed as motivated, willed, or intended).

Perhaps this is a false antinomy, and we would do well to desist from ontologizing these terms and treat them simply as rough and ready ways in which people attempt to articulate their *sense* of being either free or bound. In any event, seldom do we stand at some metaphorical crossroads, contemplating which direction to go, rationally appraising our situation then making a choice. Equally rarely are we blindly and haplessly moved through life by forces utterly outside our ken and control, mere puppets or playthings of fate. Fatalistic submission, the influence or advice of others, and careful calculation all enter, to some degree and in constantly varying ways, into our responses to critical situations. But however we construe these moments in retrospect, recounting stories in which we were victims or heroes, passive or active, we are always strategists in a game where winning is judged according to how successfully we find ways of responding to the situations we encounter and of enduring them—"to live and to create," as Camus puts it, "in the very midst of the desert."[3]

Sartre's notion of praxis as a purposeful surpassing of what is given is not an invitation to embrace the Enlightenment myth of the rational actor or the possessive individualist like Robinson Crusoe who, from his own resources, creates a world from scratch. Nor does it imply a romantic view of human agency and responsibility, exercised in a world no longer governed by gods, fates, or furies, since acceptance, anonymity, and abnegation are no less life choices than heroic projects of self-making or revolt. To speak of an existential imperative that transcends specific cultural values or worldviews is simply to testify to the extent to which being is never simply given or guaranteed, in genetic or cultural codes, by democracy or tyranny, by poverty or wealth. And though the source of our well-being may be variously said to lie in the hands of our parents or God, to depend on capital accumulation, or to reside in physical, intellectual, or spiritual talents, it remains a potential that can only be realized through activity, through praxis. This is why, as Sartre notes, our analytic method must be progressive-regressive—fully recognizing that while every event, every experience, is in one sense a new departure, it conserves the ancient, inert, and inescapable conditions that make each one of us a being who carries within himself or herself "the project of all possible being."[4]

In this chapter I explore the theme of fatality and freedom not as a philosophical problem but as a fact of experience—as something to be lived through rather than resolved though some kind of intellectual legerdemain.

Fate and Freedom in Colonial History

One can identify, in every period of Australia's post-settlement history, individuals who expressed the worst and the best of what was possible in their time. Aboriginal and non-Aboriginal individuals emerge from the archival record who went beyond or simply went along with the prevailing ethos. Of those who stretched the limits of what might have seemed possible at the time of first contact, Governor Arthur Phillip and Bennelong stand out.

Not long after the first fleet made landfall in Botany Bay in 1788, a twenty-five-year-old Eora man called Bennelong appeared on the scene, not only as a fearless fighter but as a man of unusual intelligence and insight who quickly saw the advantages that might be gained by consorting with the enemy. When he died, in 1813, he was remembered as being "as much responsible for the colony's affairs as [Governor] Phillip, and in their tango of strange intimacy, deceit and manipulation, they created a short-lived period of friendship and tolerance."[5] Marcia Langton speaks of this as a "tangled tale," for despite these glimmers of what might have been, its overwhelming context is horrifically and irredeemably dark.[6]

In the mid-nineteenth century, no individual did more violence in the state of Victoria than Angus McMillan, who initiated and led "one of the most vicious campaigns of wanton murder and destruction this violent country has ever seen."[7] That McMillan covered his tracks, making it impossible for historians to determine exactly how many Aborigines were murdered in his campaigns to alienate land for sale and settlement, suggests some self-awareness that he was exceeding the limits of what even conquest and colonization demanded. That Queen Victoria, like most of her subjects, turned a blind eye to the atrocities committed in her name only reinforces the urgency of the question some of us now ask ourselves: why were so few voices raised against this holocaust, and can such traumas ever be healed or such injustices ever redressed?

Consider, in this context, a letter written by Murrumwiller, an Aboriginal man who received an education at the Merri Creek School for Aboriginal children and then apprenticed himself to a Melbourne tailor. His sense of the injustices done to his people was only exacerbated by the abuse and derision he personally experienced among whites. Hoping he might return to his traditional land and farm, he wrote:

> I mean to write to the Queen and ask her to give me a piece of land . . . to build a house on; and I mean to ask her for 400 pounds . . . to build my house. You say one time the Queen a good woman. And yet she send white man out here, take black fellas's land, and drive them away, and shoot them, and build planty [sic] house and garden on my land; and when I say, I ask her to give me back a piece of my land and money to build a house, you say she think I not know better. I know better. This land, my land first of all. Four hundred pounds not much to the Queen, and she take plenty land from me.[8]

Yet some whites did "know better," among them the Presbyterian lay preacher John Green and his wife, Mary, who arrived in Victoria from

Scotland in 1858 and dedicated themselves to the Kulin people's struggle to reclaim land and win the right to determine their own destinies. After establishing the settlement of Coranderrk, where Kulin people could become autonomous gardeners and farmers, the Greens found an ally in a wealthy grazier, Anne Bon, whose regard for Aboriginal people had earned her the contempt of white squatters and government officials. Yet the dominant view that Aborigines were incapable of achieving true civilization, and ongoing bureaucratic warfare to undermine the settlement, gradually exhausted those who had fought so hard to make Coranderrk a success. It was sold in 1948 to provide land for soldier settlers after World War II, though no Aboriginal men who had served in the army received land grants on their home soil.

How might one explain the extraordinary character of Anne Bon or John and Mary Green? Can one invoke their burning resentment toward the English who had brutally cleared the Scottish Highlands, displacing thousands of farmers who had no option but to emigrate or stay on, scratching a living as crofters on untenured patches of land?[9] Or was it because of their Christian faith? That many others who shared their religious values and had been forced to leave their natal lands were prepared to violently displace the indigenous people of Australia suggests that no single explanation, circumstantial or moral, can be given for why people act as they do. This is why it is impossible to identify actions that are freely chosen or actions that reflect social conditioning, even though human beings typically invoke determinism in justifying their alleged powerlessness or, dismissing contingency altogether, sometimes boast that they have accomplished everything in their lives by virtue of their own willpower.

For these reasons, I am less interested in the philosophical issue of whether or to what extent we are free than in how we rationalize our actions in these terms. Feeling powerless or wanting to absolve oneself of all responsibility for one's actions, one may declare that one's fate was written in the stars, one's genes determined one's disposition, or one's early upbringing determined the course of one's later life. Alternatively, one can play up the hand one has in shaping one's own destiny. Hence Cassius's declaration that "the fault" (Caesar's ambition to be a god) "is not in our stars, but in ourselves," or Nietzsche's line *from the military school of life*—What does not kill me makes me stronger."[10]

Rendering an indisputable moral account of our actions is notoriously difficult. We cannot know the repercussions of what we do, even when we act in good faith. And we cannot ascertain all the factors that came together in disposing us to act one way rather than another. Yet rather than accept that we are playthings of fate and possess no capacity for deciding our own destinies, we often perversely reject responsibility for actions for which we were clearly responsible (the Eichmann plea) or just as perversely assume responsibility for actions for which we were not entirely to blame. Consider Sophocles's Oedipus story. Oedipus's father, Laius, abandoned his son soon after he was born and ordered that a spike be driven through the infant's ankles to prevent him walking. And Oedipus could not have been aware that the woman he came to marry was Laius's widow, his own mother. Is he to be held accountable or cursed for acts he did unknowingly? And why should the descendants of Laius be held responsible for Laius's rape of the young prince from a neighboring kingdom, an event that occurred before Oedipus was born? Though we may consider Oedipus to be innocent of patricide and incest, he assumes responsibility for these crimes as though he could have averted his fate and, after blinding himself with his tunic pin, wanders into the desert to die. It is as if he has construed fate as free will.

Whichever way we turn, extolling our freedom or accepting our fate, we cannot avoid this sense of being caught between Scylla and Charybdis, of never knowing for certain which current will prove strongest, taking our frail craft toward our chosen destination or sending it onto the rocks.

Negotiating this turbulent passage is the meaning of an ethics that is, in James Faubion's terms, paranomic (beside or parallel to the law)—less a matter of adjusting to or conforming to moral, legal, or customary formations than of bending rules without necessarily breaking them.[11] Virtue is thus a matter of virtuosity—skill in overcoming difficulties and living with unresolvable existential aporias.

Oedipus and Job in West African Thought

If I am drawn to West African thinking in this matter it is because it succeeds so well in treating questions of fate and freewill existentially, contextualizing them in lived situations that are familiar to everyone, and seeing them as dilemmas we wrestle with rather than problems we can solve. Arguments are not made for whether we are free or unfree. Rather, the issue is depicted as a site of struggle. In this sense, West African cosmologies echo the dramas of Euripides, Aeschylus, and Sophocles, which may explain why the great twentieth-century Nigerian writers Wole Soyinka and Chinua Achebe draw parallels between their own work and the classical Greek tragedians. What we experience as we witness these dramas is emotional catharsis rather than the intellectual satisfaction of seeing a logical problem solved.

Among the Tallensi, the tension between being an actor and being acted on finds expression in the dialectic between chosen and preordained destinies. "Life—symbolized for the Tallensi in the breath (novor)—is only the raw material for living," writes Meyer Fortes. "What one makes of it depends on other spiritual agencies."[12] These "other spiritual agencies" include the influences of one's mother, father, or other kin (strictly speaking "the prenatal destiny" of such significant others) and the influence of the prenatal destiny that one chooses for oneself before being born. This prenatal decision may be made against having a spouse, bearing children, or being a farmer—in effect, rejecting a normal moral life. Fortes speak of this as "Oedipal fate" in contrast with the "Jobian fulfillment" that comes from recognizing the superior powers of the ancestors and seeking redemption through them. But just as a bad prenatal choice can be revoked by setting up a shrine and making sacrifices to one's ancestors—ritually submitting to and complying with "the norms and customs instituted by them"—a person's positive dispositions may be undermined should he or she neglect or ignore the lineage ancestors.[13]

According to the Yoruba of Nigeria, each person is said to make a choice about his or her preferred destiny before he or she is born. A divinity called Ajàlá, "the potter who makes heads," molds heads from clay, fires them, and places them in a storehouse. Because Ajàlá is an incorrigible debtor whose mind is seldom on his work, many of his heads are badly thrown or over-fired. Ori, the word for the physical head, also connotes the "internal head" (ori-inú), the inner personality "that rules, controls, and guides the life and activities of the person."[14] The act of selecting one's ori is regarded as one of free will. But because of Ajàlá's irresponsible workmanship, many heads turn out to be defective.

Nevertheless, as soon as the choice of a head has been made, one is free to travel to earth where one's success or failure in life will depend largely on the *ori* one picked up in Àjàlá's storehouse.

Ori is, however, only one aspect of human being. *Emi*, which means both the physical heart and the "active life principle," is the imperishable aspect of the person that continues to be reincarnated.[15] *Emi* is given by Olodumare, the supreme being, after Orinsanla, the creator god, has formed the physical body of a person out of clay. The third aspect of a person is called *ese* (leg). Wande Abimbola notes that while a person's destiny derives from his *ori*, the realization of that destiny depends on *ese*, the legs.[16]

A Yoruba tale nicely illustrates this complementarity of *ori* and *ese*: All the *ori* meet together to deliberate on a project they want to bring to fruition. But they fail to invite *ese*. Having made their resolutions, the heads find that without legs they do not have the means to carry out their designs. As Abimbola puts it, "the point of the story is that even if one is predestined to success by the choice of a good *ori*, one cannot actually achieve success without the use of one's *ese*, which is a symbol of power and activity."[17] This "two-sided conception" of human destiny "is accepted by the Yoruba without question. It . . . means that in an inexplicable way, what happens to a person may be simultaneously the result of *Bi ó ti gbà a*—'As he received it (was destined),' and *A-f'-owo-fà*—'that which he brings upon himself.'"[18]

The Igbo also see destiny as a struggle for being. *Chi* is the incorporeal aspect of a person that presides over the prenatal choice of destiny. One's lot or portion on earth reflects a primordial bargain with one's *chi*. As soon as a person is thrown into the world, however, he and his *chi* may find themselves at odds. Thus, a person may fall victim to the demands of an intransigent *chi* or become locked in a struggle to revoke his prenatal choice.[19] In Achebe's novel *Things Fall Apart*, the protagonist, Okonkwo, struggles to overcome his father's legacy of debts unpaid, family neglected, idleness, and faintheartedness. Despite Okonkwo's valiant efforts to be everything his father was not (he becomes a great wrestler and warrior), he fails to protect his ward, Ikemefune, when an Oracle declares that he must be killed and, following this failure, suffers a series of misfortunes and finally hangs himself.

Was Okonkwo's fate presaged in his father's life and in his desperate efforts *not* to follow in his footsteps? Was he or the Oracle responsible for Ikemefune's murder? And to what extent were the advent of colonial rule and mission influence factors in the way this tragedy played out? In answering these questions from a West African point of view, one must consider in more detail the opposing imperatives and competing dispositions that are felt in every human life and the possibility of ever reconciling them. Edo ideas on this subject are particularly illuminating.

It is believed that before birth each individual predestines himself (*hi*) by making a declaration before Osanobua, the creator, setting out a life program and asking for everything needed to carry it through successfully. One's *ehi* (destiny) acts as a kind of prompt at this time and will remain in the spirit world as a guide and intermediary with Osanobua. Misfortune in life is explained as a failure to keep to the chosen life program, a result of having a "bad *ehi*," and a person may implore his *ehi* to intervene and improve his lot. R. E. Bradbury notes that *ehi* "represents the innate potentialities for social achievement with which each individual is believed to be endowed."[20] But while *ehi* implies the absence of personal control over one's fortunes, the head (*uhumwu*) "admits a greater degree of responsibility." The head is the seat of thought, judgment, will, or character; of hearing, seeing, and speaking. It therefore complements *ehi* and, in the past, was the focus of a cult concerned with the headship of families and the rule of the state. The second force that complements *ehi* is the hand (*ikegobo*), which connotes manual skill and successful enterprise. Also the focus of a cult, the hand symbolizes a person's vigor and industry in farming, trading, craftwork, and other undertakings. "It implies personal responsibility and self-reliance in a highly competitive and relatively individualistic society."[21] The English saying "your fate is in your own hands" translates readily into Edo.

The Edo conception of human destiny thus emphasizes the dialectical interplay of prenatal dispositions and understandings (*communis sententia*) and the practical know-how acquired in the course of a person's *social* development. We must be careful, however, not to reduce the predeterminative domain of existence to the prenatal world and so give the impression that the social world is, by contrast, a domain of freedom and fulfillment. With its fixed traditions, conventions, and authority structures, the established social order into which a person is thrown at birth can be just as oppressive and problematic as the innate dispositions decided prenatally. Accordingly, the domain of a person's freedom does not lie over and above either the spirit world from which he comes or the social world into which he is born but squarely between the two. Together they determine the parameters of a person's effective freedom. Praxis is thus a matter of negotiating a path between innate dispositions and social pressures, of accepting or simply living with the often antithetical forces of nature and culture. Throughout Africa, this movement is allegorized as journeying between bush and village.

A common scenario in Kuranko oral narratives involves a young hero who hazards his life on a journey into the wilderness in search of an object, such as a musical instrument or a fetish, that will be of advantage to his community. In his confrontation with wild beings and in his struggles against the temptation to use his gains for selfish ends, the questing hero embodies recurring moral dilemmas in Kuranko social life, such as the competing claims of duty and desire, individuation and association. The resolution of these dilemmas depends on the hero's powers of discernment and judgment, though he is sometimes aided by supernatural helpers or magical objects that occupy a position midway between the social world and the wilderness.[22]

Kuranko rites of initiation (*biriye*) plot a similar course between wildness and sociality, the crucial transformation from childhood to adulthood taking place in a "bush house," the *fafei*, which is burned to the ground when neophytes complete their initiation and return to their village. Initiation is sometimes spoken of as a "taming" (*kan kola*) of the "wild" or "unripe" nature of the child. It is said that an uninitiated child "knows nothing": "a child is just as it was born; it has no social intelligence" (*hankili sa la*). Initiation provides "new understanding" (*hankili kura*); the child becomes a "new person" capable of assuming responsibility for his or her own thought and behavior. Unlike education, the emphasis is on the acquisition of moral responsibility and social nous rather than abstract knowledge. Crucial to this transition is the endurance of pain, *dime*, a word that connotes both emotional suffering and physical hurt. In the bush, cut off from emotional ties with the community, particularly with the mother, the pubescent child is subject to a series of ordeals that are said to simulate the trials of adult life. The

Fate and Freewill

neophyte is urged to control his or her *reaction* to suffering. Mastery of one's reaction to pain—standing stock still, not blinking, not making a sound, not wincing when one is cut—is regarded as the paradigm of all self-mastery. In the Kuranko view, it is only when a person learns to discriminate between the action of pain and his or her reaction to it that he or she gains any measure of control or freedom.[23] *Yiri* (steadiness of body/mind) connotes this detached attitude to an inner state, whether pain, grief, anger, or love. *Kerenteye* (bravery) and *kilanbelteye* (fortitude) suggest moral fiber, an ability to withstand the tides of strong emotions. These virtues are all dependent on the cultivation of an abstract *attitude* that produces consonance between intentions and actions, not abstract *knowledge*, though various adages bring home the importance of this attitude: *Morge kume mir' la i konto i wo l fo le* ("Whatever word a person thinks of, that will he speak," i.e., think before you speak lest you blurt out stupid ideas); *I mir' la koe mi ma, i wo l ke la* ("You thought of that, you do that," i.e., think before you act lest your actions belie your intentions).

In the Kuranko view, the way one comports oneself after leaving the initiation lodge, the *fafei,* is often the way one will comport oneself for the rest of one's life. *A ti wo bo l ka,* the Kuranko say; "one will not leave it." To fail the test of initiation is to remain a child, impetuous, thoughtless, and socially inept, just as one was born (*a danye le wo la,* lit. "how one is made"). In such cases a person may become a butt of jokes and an object of pity, morally excused from responsibility for his or her incorrigible habits. *A ka tala, a saran ta la bole*, people say; "he is blameless; he was born with it." Alternatively, the inscrutable designs of Allah may be invoked, since the Kuranko hold that one's destiny (*sawura*) is ultimately a "gift of Allah," decided before one's birth and quite irreversible: *la tege saraka sa* (no sacrifice can cut it). However, whenever such fatalistic views are offered, whether in terms of prenatal choices as among the Tallensi and Edo or the irrevocable will of Allah as among the Kuranko, they are usually retrospective rationalizations of crises that have befallen people rather than prescriptions for practical conduct. Thus, while the Kuranko aver that certain faculties such as self-possession (*miran*) and intelligence (*hankilimaiye*) or certain traits of temperament (*yugi*) are given by Allah, this does not mean that the mastery and use of such inborn dispositions are similarly given. On the contrary, they are to be regarded as "instrumental possibilities," to use Sartre's phrase, which, though not infinitely malleable, may be opened up to scrutiny, subject to various interpretations, and experienced or reacted to in different ways. This, then, is the domain of choice and of human praxis.

Of all the powers acquired through initiation, none is more important than *hankilimaiye* (social adroitness, common sense, gumption, and moral discernment). As I noted in the preface, this capacity for social skillfulness is valued over the forms of cognitive cleverness and intellectual acuity that the modern West associates with rationality and, by extension, with philosophy. Accordingly, the critical contrasts are not between rationality and irrationality or science and magic but between the degree of emphasis placed on social skills. Just as we might tend to disparage traditional African thought as philosophically unsophisticated, from an African standpoint some of our most celebrated thinkers might be seen as social misfits.

For Kuranko, social intelligence is acquired by listening to elders, and a long life depends on this: *sie tole l to* (long life is in the listening); *si' ban to l sa* (short life ear has not). Social intelligence is associated with the head, so that a fool is someone "without salt in his head" (*kor' sa kunye ma*) or "without brains" (*kun por' sa*) while a socially responsible person has "good thoughts in his head" (*miria nyima a kunye ko*); his "head is full."

Nor is the distinction between *theoria* and praxis as hard and fast as it is in the Western academy. For thought to be "worth its salt," it must have some social and practical benefit; its proof lies in what it produces. It is for this reason that one cannot look for evidence of African philosophy in abstract systems of ideas, hermetically sealed off from life itself, for thought is consummated in skilled practice, from greeting a neighbor to honoring the dead.

Like rites of initiation, African curing rites involve an attempt to harmonize or reconcile the often competing imperatives of "town" and "bush." Among the BaKongo, agitation or "wildness" within a person must be counteracted by the "calming" or "cooling" effects of medicines culled from the domestic domain.[24] This entails an adjustment of the relationship between internal and external fields of being, conceptualized in terms of the contrasts white/black (i.e., self/other) and town/bush. Similar ideas inform medical practice among the Songhai, who often conceptualize disease as an uncontrolled invasion of self or town by "the bush." As Jeanne Bisilliat shows, redressive action necessitates a comparable movement, but one that uses medicines from the "cultivated bush" and involves the controlled, conscious participation of the patient.[25]

According to these African models, "pathways" exist within the human body, as well as between self and society and between society and the wilderness, and the key to well-being lies in a person's ability to control traffic along these pathways. As the image suggests, physical and psychic health is intimately connected with the state of a person's relationship with others in his or her community; it is a result of successfully harmonizing inner compulsion and external rules, of neither succumbing completely to one's "wild" dispositions nor becoming so rigidly rule-bound that one cannot see beyond one's own social role.

In the modes of praxis considered thus far, a person always relies on an ally, mediator, or mentor who is able to tap and tame the wild energies of the bush: bush spirits in Kuranko oral narratives, cult masters associated with powerful bush spirits in Kuranko initiation, and medicine-masters with a command of medicines drawn from the wilderness in Kuranko curing rites. The wilderness is therefore not solely a domain of antisocial powers; it is the source of and a metaphor for the vital energies on which the creation of a viable social order depends. The harmonizing of innate compulsions and social imperatives does not mean overcoming, repressing, or expunging the "wild" but entering into a controlled relationship with it. As Paul Riesman observes in his study of freedom in Fulani social life, "freedom in society is founded on the possibility of each person entering into a direct relation with the bush," a place of solitude where one may lose oneself but also find oneself by gaining in self-mastery and strength.[26]

Perhaps the most important intermediaries between social and extrasocial domains are the diviners. In many West African societies they play a critical role in helping a person redress the imbalance between innate and social imperatives. Among the Kalabari, for example, diviners are able to "diagnose the words" that a person's *teme* (soul) spoke before coming to earth and, by confronting a person with the words, help him or her revoke them. In a ritual known as *bibi bari* (calling back the mouth/speech), the bad words spoken by the *teme* before birth are exchanged for new and better ones.[27] Among the Tallensi, diviners are also able to help a person "exorcise" his or her evil prenatal destiny (*nuor-yin*) by revoking the bad words spoken before birth. But even more significant is the way a person establishes shrines to a unique configuration of "good destiny" ancestors—drawn from both patrilineal and matrilineal forebears—who assist him or her in leading a fulfilling social life. Again, diviners play crucial mediatory roles in communicating the wishes and inclinations of these ancestors to their wards and in advising appropriate sacrifices.[28] In Dahomey, it was believed that a person could tap the antinomian energies of Legba, the trickster, and so change the direction of the fate he or she chose before birth. Alternatively, diviners could help a person establish a shrine to Da, or luck (symbolized for the individual by the umbilicus and cosmologically by the snake and the rainbow), or act as intercessors between a person and his or her "guardian soul," so providing a means of averting predestined misfortune.[29] Among the Edo, the cult of the hand figured significantly in helping a person change his luck, and a man who consulted a diviner about his ill fortune might be advised to "serve his hand" by making offering at the cult shrine.[30]

What I find compelling about these West African philosophies is that all are premised on a compatibilist view of body and mind. One's life is, therefore, a dynamic interplay between what the head decides and what the legs or hands determine to do in response. Thought is never allowed to transcend or override a person's social and physical capacity to abet it or his or her choice to resist it. Every event and every action reflects a unique combination of what we might call nature and nurture, the prenatal and the postnatal, childhood haplessness and adult decisiveness, unconscious dispositions and conscious actions.

10. Center and Periphery

> The name of dialectics says no more, to begin with, than that the objects do not go into their concepts without leaving a remainder, that they come to contradict the traditional norm of adequacy. Contradiction . . . indicates the untruth of identity, the fact that the concept does not exhaust the thing conceived.
>
> —THEODOR ADORNO, *NEGATIVE DIALECTICS*

Of the many themes that have come to characterize existential thought, one of the most compelling is the theme of alienation. Though Karl Marx broached this subject in his critique of the capitalist mode of production, which alienates the worker from the fruits of his labor and undermines his capacity to determine his own destiny, and French existentialism made fashionable cognate ideas of aloneness and estrangement in mass society, my focus in this chapter is alienated thought—the imperfect fit between our lived experience and the ways that we conceptualize, narrate, and represent it. Building on Theodor Adorno's negative dialectics, Jacques Derrida's method of deconstruction,[1] and William James's radical empiricism, I explore this aporia between words and worlds, *nomos* and nature, through the vernacular medium of Kuranko storytelling. Storytelling is a mode of thought, and may be conceptualized as an alternative sovereignty, a negotiated form of ethical and social life that lies at the margins of the state, a space outside of domestication.[2]

Kuranko stories disclose an existential paradox: that it is only through transgressing the boundaries of custom and convention that a person can tap into the vital sources of life itself, without which society becomes an empty shell and personal existence degenerates into the slavish repetition of what has been decided by others at other times. This dialectical tension between what is given and what is sought beyond the margins of the established order plays out in Kuranko stories as a movement between the moral space of the village and the antinomian space of the bush. But this paranomic interplay of duty and desire or constraint and freedom is not only necessary for the viability of the polis; it also answers an existential need in every individual to work out a balance between accepting things as they are and creating a life on his or her own terms—such that a person feels at home in the world.[3]

In Jorge Luis Borges's story "The Garden of Forking Paths," Yu Tsun —a former professor of English at the *Hochschule* at Tsingtao University—reflects on the paradox that while there is possibly no new human experience under the sun, every individual experiences life as if for the first—and last—time. This existential paradox is obliquely related to another: in a riddle whose answer is chess, what is the only prohibited word? The prohibited word is, of course, the word *chess*. By implication, all stories echo the form of a riddle because, unlike discursive writing, fiction prohibits the explicit mention of either its central motif or its biographical sources. In fiction writing, one shows rather than tells, going beyond what can be discursively or preemptively known. As Borges observes, "to omit a word always, to resort to inept metaphors and obvious periphrases, is perhaps the most emphatic way of stressing it."[4]

Such forms of symbolic disguise inspire readers to discover their own meanings in the text. For the writer, techniques of indirection make possible the expression of emotions and thoughts that are not only "too deep for words" but which, if directly articulated, could easily give offense or produce outrage. Like dreams, stories provide us with "intrapsychic alibis," enabling us to deny the role we play in creating them, and allowing us to pass them off as products of tradition rather than personal experience, imagined rather than real, and occurring "far off and long ago" (*wo le yan be la*).[5]

In art, our real-life situations give ground to *contrived* situations involving fantastic characters, magical actions, otherworldly settings, and artificial resolutions. Art, like philosophy, overcomes the limitations of life. Although it takes its raw material from the critical experiences of quotidian life, it organizes this material in ways that could not be achieved in reality—consoling us with the possibility of being actors in a world that all too often overwhelms us, creating the semblance of a just social order, and achieving a fair apportionment of the scarce resources of life itself. To this observation we might add that in every society, classic "fairy tales" put us in touch with the primordial meaning of our humanness. Put otherwise, we might say that fairy tales are concerned with a struggle for existential viability that transcends particular cultural, legal, or moral conceptions of the human. And it is this domain, resisting and remaining outside of "discursive colonization" that defines, for me, the field of ethics.[6]

Riddles and Dilemma Tales

Among the Kuranko, stories are told only at night, when the day's work is done. Whether shared among close family in an isolated farmhouse, besieged by bush and the sound of rain, or with other villagers on a moonlit night in the dry season, stories belong to that penumbral zone between village and bush, day and night, wakefulness and drowsiness. Not only are stories told in these "spaces outside of domestication," but the events they recount, the characters who appear in them, and the places they are located also conjure what lies beyond the pale of moral values, legal codes, and "normal" humanity. Yet, paradoxically, it is through this suspension of the *nomos* that it is finally brought back into focus.

A storytelling session often begins with riddling, and these riddle stories (*sosogoma tileinu*)[7] prepare an audience for the longer and more complex dilemma tales (*tileinu*) that address people's most pressing, yet ordinarily undeclared, existential concerns. The riddles are invariably ridiculous and are told quickly and competitively.

There were once three men. Each claimed to have more lice on his body than either of the others. After boasting for a while, they decided to prove their claims. They sat down. The first man rolled back the waistband of his trousers and began filling a bowl with handful after handful of lice. Soon the bowl was overflowing. But already the lice on the second man had removed his trousers and spread them out in the sun. The second man said to the first man, "Well, what did you see? Did you not see my lice undress me in front of your eyes?" The third man took out a single louse. He then removed the louse's intestines and used them to tie up the other two men. Now, of these three men, which one had the most lice?

The answer is the last man, since he did more with his one louse than the others managed to do with all of theirs!

The mood is now relaxed. People are open to far-fetched scenarios and outlandish events. Nothing is too absurd or too implausible to entertain. And as if to reinforce this sense of having passed from the recognizable and real world of the village into the antinomian space of the bush and of dreams, the storyteller prefaces each tale with a disclaimer—"A long time ago in a far away place"—before going on to disguise the characters as were-animals, paring down their idiosyncratic features and using impersonal terms of address such as "Father," "Uncle," "Elder brother," or "In-law."

The parlor is crowded with men, women, and children. A single hurricane lamp burns on a rickety table and casts flickering shadows on the mud-plastered walls of the room. The storyteller sits on the edge of an iron frame bed, a hand-rolled cigarette held between his fingers. His name is Keti Ferenke Koroma. Keti is his mother's name. Koroma is his clan. He is renowned as the most gifted performer of *tilei* in the Kuranko-speaking area of northern Sierra Leone, and many of his stories—like the first story he tells tonight—are his own creation. In the following story, Keti Ferenke develops a critique of authority that reflects his view that human beings typically make a mess of their lives and bring misery to others when they act impulsively and thoughtlessly, particularly when they are in possession of great power. Social order and social justice can only be guaranteed, therefore, by ensuring that emotions are held in check and the powers of chiefs constrained by extra-human agencies such as djinn, totemic animals, and God. Capricious and inscrutable though these agents might be, they alone can ensure that wrongs are righted, the deserving receive their due, and scarce resources get distributed equitably.

Earlier, I compared riddles to dilemma stories and claimed that the full force of these plays on reality was only felt when their meaning was implicit or oblique. So it was with the vexed question at the core of the story Keti Ferenke told on this particular night: what is the one thing that should never be entrusted to the hands of men?

There was a woman who was greatly admired by many young men. Without bridewealth, none of these men could hope to marry her, so each went in search of what he would need to persuade the girl's father to give his daughter in marriage. One man decided that he would give meat as bridewealth, another that he would give money, and a third that he would give clothes. So each man went his separate way.

The first man spent three years searching for animals to kill for meat. Having failed in his quest, he returned to his natal village, his clothes in tatters, his hopes dashed. The other two men had returned from their quests two years earlier—one bringing money, the other bringing clothes. But they could not give these things to the girl's father because the third man had not returned. They said, "When he comes back and gives what he has brought, we can decide who will marry the woman." They waited two years, during which time the third man was in the bush looking for animals to kill.

Just as he was about to give up his search, he encountered an old woman deep in the bush, surrounded by dried meat. He greeted her, and the old woman greeted him. She then asked, "Why are you wandering so deep in the bush and so far from home?"

The young man said, "My companions and I are rivals for the hand of a young woman. They vowed to bring money and clothes as bridewealth, and I vowed to bring meat, but despite spending three years in the bush, I have found nothing." Then, having seen the meat around the old woman, the young man asked her to give him some. The old woman said, "All right," and told him to sleep.

In the morning, the old woman gave him some dried meat. The young man said, "Eh, grandmother, you are living in this remote place, deep in the bush, yet you have all this meat. Rather than give me some of yours, why not tell me how I can get some for myself?"

The old woman agreed. She explained that she had a tied-up thing. Every morning if she wanted bush cows, she would say, "Bush cows, come!" When they approached her, she would point that tied-up thing at them and say, "Bush cows, I have *nyemakala* this at you," and the animals would die.

That tied-up thing was wrapped in a kerchief. The old woman gave it to the young man on condition that he would bring it back to her after he had married. She said, "Wherever you go, whatever animal you wish to kill, just call it to come. When it comes toward you, say, 'I have *nyemakala* this at you,' and the animal will die." The young man took the fetish and returned to his village.

No one recognized him. His clothes were tattered, and he was emaciated from the years he had spent in the bush. When he told his companions that he had returned, they said that he should rest and meet them in the morning.

At daybreak they called for him and asked what he had brought. They explained that they had waited two years for him to come and asked him to explain his long absence. The man showed his companions the lumps of dried meat that the old woman had given him. They said, "Well, if this is all you have brought, you are not going to marry the woman." The man said, "Wait!" With all the elders watching, he ran to the outskirts of the town, calling as he went, "Bush cows, come!" When the bush cows emerged from the bush, he unwrapped the fetish from the kerchief and said, "I have *nyemakala* this at you." The bush cows fell down dead. The man ordered the villagers to go and fetch the dead animals. While some people began butchering the dead bush cows and distributing the meat, the young man went to the other side of the village and said, "Wild pigs, come!" When they emerged from the bush, he again unwrapped the fetish from the kerchief and said, "I have *nyemakala* this at you." The wild pigs fell dead at his feet. He now went to another side of the village and called to the antelopes. When they came running from the bush, he said pointed the fetish at them and said, "I have *nyemakala* this at you," and they too fell dead at his feet.

The man's companions were afraid. They took the woman and gave her to him.

The man and the woman lived together for a year. But the old woman who had given the fetish to the young man was angry that he had not returned it to her. She went to the village where the young man lived. When she found him, she said, "You left my place a year ago. It was agreed that you would return the fetish to me when you married. But you did not come back, and I have been obliged to journey all this way to find you."

The young man got to his feet. "You obstinate old woman," he said, "why should you come and trouble me with this?" Pointing the fetish at her, he said, "Now I have *nyemakala* this at you!" The old woman fell down dead.

The young man struck fear into the hearts of all. The men who had competed with him to marry the woman called a meeting. But the young man broke in on them. "So you are conspiring against me!" He pointed the fetish at them. "Well then, I have *nyemakala* this at you!" They also fell down dead.

The young man terrorized the village. Wherever he went and whenever he saw people gathered together talking among themselves, he would think they were plotting against him, and he would use his fetish to kill them. He became a burden to the whole world. His father-in-law and mother-in-law, worried for the safety of their daughter, discussed what they might do. But the young man found them talking together. "Ah, my in-laws, so you have met to plot against me. Now I have *nyemakala* this at you!"

Things went from bad to worse. But Allah was watching everything. Finally, Allah said, "This is a terrible thing. I must free people from this curse." Allah transformed himself into a beautiful young woman and came to the young man's village. (Women never fail in their conspiracies against men!)

The woman said, "Your name has traveled far and wide. When I heard about you, I decided I wanted to marry you. Let us sleep together this very night."

The man said, "You are welcome, you are welcome." (Now, we all know that Allah never fails in whatever he decides to do.)

The woman spoke sweet words to the young man. At last she asked him to share the secret of how he killed animals. The young man got out of bed, opened his trunk, and took out the fetish wrapped in the kerchief. He showed it to the young woman.

"So this is what you use for killing animals?" she said.

He said, "Yes."

"Well, you young man, I have *nyemakala* this at you!"

He died immediately. The woman took the fetish wrapped in the kerchief and went back to lakira. It is this same fetish that is in the hands of Allah. Whenever Allah says to a person, "I have *nyemakala* this at you," that person will die. Allah now possesses that thing. No one else.

The Power of the Margins

What exactly is this "tied-up" thing, this fetish, that grants its owner absolute power over life and death? It is ethically ambiguous, for while it empowers its owner to kill animals and potentially sustain the life of an entire community, it also enables that individual to kill those he begrudges or believes to be plotting against him. The word *nyema-kala* encapsulates this ambiguity. *Nyamakala* (Mande) or *nyemakale* (Kuranko) designates the "lower-caste" clans, including leatherworkers, blacksmiths, cobblers, praise-singers, and keepers of chiefly traditions. Although I was once given an ingenious folk etymology of the word that alluded to the roles of praise-singers (*jelebas*) and oral historians (*finabas*) in maintaining protocols of deference and silence in the presence of a chief (*nyema*—a crowd, gathering, or assembly + the verb *a l kala*—to call for silence or to cease speaking), the general consensus among Mande scholars is that the word derives from *nyama* (detritus, rubbish, dung, dead leaves, sweepings from a house) and *kala* (a knot or tuft of grass). *Nyamakala* are thus the "little people, men of no account, commoners, persons of servile origin, people belonging to a caste."[8] But *nyama* also connotes "life energy," including the "personality" or "spirit" of a human being and the genius or supernatural power of a djinn. *Nyama* is associated with the bush rather than the village, nature rather than *nomos*. It is regarded with great ambivalence because while villagers must tap into the "wild" energies of the bush if they are to survive, these energies are potentially destructive. Those that possess *nyama* in abundance—particularly blacksmiths, tradition-keepers, and praise-singers—are seen in a similar light, as they may deploy their *nyama* to either reinforce or undermine the hierarchical structure of society. An unscrupulous praise-singer may inspire his lord and master to rash deeds, an orator may manipulate genealogies to cast doubt on the legitimacy of a chief, and a blacksmith may use his *nyama* for personal gain. In short, their marginality to the moral order of the village places the *nyemakala* clans in a dangerous but potentially empowering relationship with the bush and the wild—spaces outside of domestication.

This logic brings us back to the connotation of *nyama* as rubbish, and the question as to why rubbish should be associated with wild power and dangerous energy. The Kuranko distinction between village (*sue*) and bush (*fera*) is sometimes phrased as a contrast between the ventral and dorsal surfaces of the human body, the belly versus the back. "In the village" (*sue bu lon*, lit. "town belly in") is contrasted with "away from the village" (*sue ko ma*, lit. "town back on"). But the boundary between these spaces is a liminal zone where the dead are buried and rubbish is thrown. This indeterminate space between village and bush is replicated within the village, for the area between the backyards of adjoining households is a similarly liminal space. Although houses are separated by fences of woven elephant grass, the symbolic boundary is defined by the household rubbish heap, where winnowed husks of grain, ash from cooking fires, food scraps, broken calabashes, rusty tinware, scraps of clothing, and sweepings from the house are discarded. This is the *sundu kunye ma* (lit. "behind head on"), and just as the front of the house is associated with the belly, so the rear is associated with the back. Whether houses are circular (with conical thatched roofs) or rectangular (with tin roofs), a gender-based distinction is made between the front rooms and porch, which are men's places (*ke dugu*), and the back rooms and hearths, which are women's places (*musu dugu*). Although West Africanists once identified the male domain with the "politico-jural" and the female domain with the "domestic," both are governed by strict social protocols and can therefore be regarded as belonging to *nomos* rather than nature. The area of the rubbish heap is marginal to both. And like the power associated with *nyama*, the power of the rubbish heap is ambiguous, for the things discarded here are associated with life-giving food, fire, water vessels, and cooking pots yet also belong to the world of the dead—of ash that cannot be brought back to life, of parings and husks that have minimal food value, of broken vessels that have lost their capacity to contain and hold. The liminal character of the *sundu kunye ma* makes it both literally and symbolically "dirty" and "dangerous." As such, it has the power to mediate relations between life and death. This is why infants that die before weaning are often buried in the *sundu kunye ma*. The reasoning is that an unweaned infant has not yet passed completely into the land of the living and may therefore be given another chance at life. In anticipation of a dead infant's return, a mother will slip a sliver of raffia cane under its fingernail, and when her next child is born she will examine its fingernails for traces of its previous, short-lived incarnation. This same logic makes the *sundu kunye ma* an empowering site for cursing thieves and a rich repository of materials for making protective fetishes. A calabash drilled with holes (and with the holes stuffed with cotton wool), a broken cane mat and dead fire stick, a fire coal in salted water, hearthstones or tree bark are often key ingredients, as are bodily wastes (urine, sweat, feces), nail parings, and hair clippings.

The foregoing phenomenology of Kuranko space and place enables us to understand the potency of the "tied-up thing" the young man "borrowed" from the elderly woman in the bush and deployed, first to provide life-sustaining food to the village then to kill whomever questioned his right to possess and exercise absolute power over the life and death of others.

The power is brought from nature into *nomos*, echoing the Kuranko belief that unless villagers enter the bush, exploiting its fertile soils to grow crops, hunting animals to provide meat, and gathering medicinal leaves, the village cannot hope to survive. But unbridled natural energies can just as readily destroy the village. A balance must be struck between being open to the antinomian and being protected from it. This struggle to strike a balance between the domestic and the wild echoes an existential struggle in which individuals seek to transform the given world into a world they actively choose to belong to—a world from which they are not alienated and can call their own. Mikhail Bakhtin recognizes this existential protest against fixed ascriptions of status, role, and hierarchical order in his notion of the carnivalesque while Henri Bergson sees the celebration of organic life as an élan vital that resists the mechanistic routines of everyday life and allows for individual creativity and freedom. But it should be remembered that this vitalist strain in Western *lebensphilosophie*, from Schopenhauer and Nietzsche to Bataille and Deleuze, has its analogues in West African thought and that the critique of Greco-Roman philosophical assumptions in the Western academy can be made from the standpoint of traditional African cosmologies and ritual practices.

Among the Dogon of Mali, the figure of Yourougou is associated with extravagance, disorder, and oracular truth while its opposite, Nommo, represents reason and social order.[9] For the neighboring Bambara, a similar contrast is posited between Nyalé—who was created first and signifies "swarming life," exuberance, and uncontrolled power—and Faro, or Ndomadyiri, who was created next and signifies equilibrium and restraint.[10] For the Kuranko, the contrast between bush and town signifies the same extremes. Because the bush is a source of vital and regenerative energy, the village must open itself up to it perennially. Hunters venture into the bush at night, braving real and imagined dangers in their search for meat. Farmers clear-fell the forest in order to grow the upland rice that is the staple of life. And initiation rites—which take place in the bush and have as their ostensible goal the disciplining and channeling of the unruly energies of children so that after a symbolic death they are brought back to life as moral adults—simultaneously open up the possibility of intense individuation because they encourage each initiate to live the "found" world as though it were of his or her own making.

But while all these transgressions in space and breaks with routine are necessary for the renewal of life, they also imperil the collectivity. Whenever the boundary between town and bush (or their symbolic analogues—day/night, domestic/wild, male/female, adult/child) is crossed, disorder and confusion momentarily reign. Walking through the forest at night, one does not speak for fear that a djinn might steal one's name and use it for bedevilment. During initiations, people fall prey to similar anxieties and consult diviners to see how they may safeguard themselves from witches, who, it is said, can leave their bodies and go forth in the shape of night animals. At such times, parents often send their children to the homes of medicine masters so that they will be protected from the nefarious powers that are abroad while others redouble the protection of their bodies and houses with magical medicines. And day in and day out, role reversals and masquerades give outward expression to this inner disquiet and uncertainty—a consequence, Kuranko aver, of the normal order of things being momentarily in abeyance.

This broaches the question as to how Kuranko manage risk—negotiating the shadow line between closure and openness.

In *Beyond the Pleasure Principle*, Sigmund Freud observed that all organisms, from the lowly amoeba to human beings, need *both* to absorb elements of the world beyond their boundaries *and* to protect these boundaries from invasive and life-threatening forces. Filtering, monitoring, and controlling traffic across body boundaries, either through practical or imaginative strategies, is thus crucial to the life of any organism and gives rise to the recurring human dilemma of how to be open to others yet retain one's own integrity, monitoring and controlling the boundary between closure and openness.[11]

Much of Kuranko ritual and narrative is concerned with how this balance can be negotiated. And from this question arises the riddle: how much wildness (bush) should a person possess, and how much domestication (town) is called for if the wild is going to augment rather than destroy human lives?

The Significance of the Djinn

We have seen how, for Kuranko, bush corresponds to nature and is construed as a force field that lies on the margins of human comprehension and control. It is a source both of the energy that sustains life— in the form of game animals, medicinal plants, and rice (the staple food crop)—and of the powers that can destroy life—in the form of witchcraft, wild animals, and intractable bush spirits. For Kuranko, the paradox of power is that the locus of greatest insecurity and danger is also the place most vital to one's life and livelihood. To phrase this cybernetically, the social system—defined as a domain of nonnegotiable roles, fixed rules, ancestral values, and received wisdom—drifts toward entropy unless it perennially taps into and draws on the vital energies of the bush—the fertility of its soil, its natural resources, and even the genii loci who claim it as their own. But while Kuranko generally conceptualize the bush as an *external* domain, the term also covers *internal* powers such as the "natural gift" of intelligence, the reproductive capacity of women, the potency of men, and the disposition of magnanimity that defines personhood itself (*morgoye*). Indeed, in Kuranko myth, personhood is exemplified not by ancestors but by totemic *animals* that saved the lives of clan ancestors in times of danger long ago. And it is the bush that is the source of life in rituals of initiation. For while initiation is the apotheosis of sublimation, in which instinctual tendencies are brought under strict control—sexuality finding expression in marriage and child-bearing, the body disciplined, the emotions cooled, speech measured, and selfishness transcended—it is also the moment when one encounters, in cult associations, the wild powers of the djinn, who, like totemic animals, are also means of imparting to ordinary human beings extraordinary powers.

The quasi-human figure of the djinn (*nyenne*) embodies what one might call demonic, wild, or libidinal power. All such power is ambiguous: it may work for or against one. In Kuranko terms it is hard to know whether such power will be a good cause (*sabu nyuma*) or a bad cause (*sabu yuge*). One hears plenty of anecdotes about djinn giving a wrestler strength, a dancer grace, a diviner insight, or a musician inspiration, and there are sites associated with djinn in every Kuranko chiefdom, where the unfortunate may offer sacrifices of food in the hope that they will be helped or where the fortunate repay the djinn for help received. Several of the diviners with whom I worked had received their gifts from djinn that appeared to them in dreams during a bout of sickness, and both music and musical instruments are often said to have originally come from the bush. The great Malian musician Ali Farka Touré attributes his genius to the djinn. In his thirteenth year a series of visions and strange experiences transformed his playing, and he entered a new world that he compares with a prolonged sickness or epileptic seizure. "It's different from when you're in a normal state; you're not the person you know anymore."[12] Despite such testimonies, the djinn are capricious, and their help often comes at a price. Sometimes, they simply withdraw their favors and disappear.[13] Sometimes, as in European stories of selling one's soul to the devil, or Columbian stories of "baptized banknotes,"[14] such Faustian pacts bring a sordid boon. Among the Kuranko, a djinn that has done you a favor may demand the life of one of your children or kinsmen in return. As the original inhabitants of the land, the djinn may allow human beings to make their farms on condition they make sacrificial offerings at the beginning of each farm season, but even then a djinn may cause a farmer to cut himself with a machete or injure himself with a hoe. A djinn may possess a person, driving him mad or causing fits of delirium. A djinn may appear in a dream in the form of a beautiful woman (succubus) or handsome man (incubus), but the sexual encounter may lead to impotence or barrenness.

What is at play here is a contest for being that involves a struggle between what is simply given to a person—his or her role, temperament (*yugi*), or birthright—and what a person desires over and above his or her socially prescribed status, role, and identity. The contrast between town and bush implies a contrast between centripetal and centrifugal forces—the first finding expression in custom and convention, the second in antinomian possibilities. The edge of the bush or a forest clearing, like the penumbral zone between day and night, suggests a no-man's-land between the known and the unknown, necessity and desire.[15] While any social system requires dutiful conformity to ancestral protocols, social life would become empty of meaning unless each person realized in himself or herself the capacity to bring the social world into being. But this capacity draws not only on what is tried and true but also on hazardous encounters with extra-social sources of power—bush spirits, wild places, limit experiences.

That one's being has its origin not solely in one's position but in one's disposition, in one's standing within the established order of things, and in one's relationship with forces that have not been tamed, domesticated, or socialized is nowhere better illustrated than in the case of spirit possession, for as innumerable ethnographic studies have shown, it is by allowing oneself to be overcome, taken, infiltrated, or ridden by wild powers that one discovers the resources to go on with life in the face of quotidian hardship and oppression. Thus, in Janice Boddy's compelling account of the Zar cult in northern Arabic-speaking Muslim Sudan, we learn that humans and *zar* spirits exist in parallel but contiguous worlds, the latter "within the realm of nature" and normally invisible to humans, much like the Kuranko djinn.[16] Through possession, Sudanese women are taken out of their everyday lifeworlds, transcending their everyday sense of who they are and seeing the world through new eyes.

When the drums are beating, beating, you hear nothing, you hear from far away, you feel far away. You have left the *midan*, the place of the *zar*. And you see, you have a vision. You see through the eyes of a European. Or you see through the eyes of the West African, whichever spirit it is. You see then as a European sees—you see other Europeans, radios, Pepsis, televisions, refrigerators, automobiles, a table set with food. You forget who you are, your village, your family, you know nothing from your life. You see with the eyes of the spirit until the drumming stops.[17]

As Boddy's work suggests, the world of spirits has become increasingly globalized so that nature marks not merely the boundary between town and bush but between local and global worlds. One also sees the widening of horizons in the changing form of witchcraft fantasies in Sierra Leone. Instead of journeying by night in some ethereal or animal shape and with her coven draining the life from some sleeping victim in another part of the country, contemporary witches imagine traveling by witch airplane across what Rosalind Shaw calls "unbounded and alluring global space."

> They often [describe] a prosperous city where skyscrapers adjoin houses of gold and diamonds; Mercedes-Benzes are driven down fine roads; street vendors roast "beefsticks" (kebabs) of human meat; boutiques sell stylish "witch-gowns" that transform their wearers into animal predators in the human world (no-ru); electronics stores sell tape recorders and televisions (and, more recently, VCRs and computers); and witch airports despatch witch planes—planes so fast, I was once told, that "they can fly to London and back within an hour"—to destinations all around the globe.[18]

Social Imaginaries

The generation and regeneration of life have always been, in the Kuranko social imaginary, a matter of bringing the vital forces of the wild into the precinct of the village—which means transgressing the symbolic boundaries that separate home spaces from the unknown and the beyond. But attitudes toward the outside world are always ambivalent, and this is as true of Kuranko who never leave the security of their natal villages as it is of Kuranko migrants in London. For them, to remain in the village is to doom themselves to a life of toil, limited horizons, and social stasis. But to go abroad means estrangement from close kin and the possibility of losing themselves in a world of strangers. Global space is thus a kind of "bush."[19] In it, one hopes to trap or capture new forms of well being without becoming snared, captured, or lost. Kuranko descriptions of urban life bear an uncanny resemblance to the way that cities were depicted in the social imaginaries of rural England after the Industrial Revolution, when thousands of hopeful migrants left the countryside for the burgeoning new towns. Though the streets of these towns were allegedly paved with gold, they were actually littered with those who had fallen by the wayside, incapacitated, unemployed, rejected, and alienated. Young Kuranko men would ruefully explain to me that city girls would not bother with a man without money and that without contacts one could get nowhere. Though the city was a realm of fabulous opportunities, it was also a place of ambushes and pitfalls in which the vagrant hunter often became the hunted.

Since human sociality emerges at the intersection of free and bound energies or wild and domesticated powers, it is useful to think of the social as "potential space," a space in which human intentions, desires, or dispositions are realized in relation to many possible others, objects, and goals.[20] What we call "culture" is simply the sum total of the *approved* forms and images onto which our will-to-be may fasten or cathect, or, to use Edmund Husserl's term, fill itself in or fulfill itself (*erfülling*). But cultural patterns and artifacts never entirely govern, delimit, or "capture" the existential imperative that often attaches only temporarily to certain objects, remaining mercurial, dissatisfied, and unbound. There is always a "more" and "otherwise" to consciousness, extending beyond the particular names, objects, and people on which it happens to fasten. As Claude Lévi-Strauss puts it, "the mind always has more meanings available than there are objects to which to relate them," thereby creating a gap between the signifying and the signified.[21] Thus, sexual desire may find momentary expression in a fantasy built up around a particular person only for this attachment to be "betrayed" by another fixation. Or the frustrated desire for status in his village may lead a man to fantasize and form alliances with supernatural helpers (bush spirits, totemic animals, foreign benefactors) or to migrate across tribal and international borders in pursuit of wealth, occult powers, magical medicines, or Islamic learning.

In the course of my fieldwork in northeast Sierra Leone, I would occasionally hear rumors of a fabulous town somewhere in the hazy savanna regions to the northeast and known as Musudugu—town or place of women. No men lived there, and the women of the town were famed for their skills in divination, curing, and sorcery. Some said that the medicines the women possessed were the powerful *korté* and anti-*korté* medicines, ordinarily controlled and used by men. Kola traders and seekers would bring reports of miracles accomplished and wealth bestowed, though the town was built on hearsay and fantasy, and no one could confirm that it was actually the mapped Malinké town of Mousadougou, which lies in the Konyor country at the edge of the forests on the border between Ivory Coast and Liberia.

References to the town occur in several Kuranko narratives, and like the similarly marvelous *Town of Women* in Nupe lore,[22] it is said to be located at the edge of the known world or to have existed long ago. Symbolically, however, it gives form to inchoate and contemporary preoccupations about female power that lies *outside* the male space of politico-jural power and is inimical to it.

It would be a mistake to conflate the space of women (*musudugu*) with domesticity, for insofar as the space of men (*kedugu*) is associated with the rule of law, it is men who uphold domestic order and women who possess the "wild" powers associated with the bush. Wildness, however, signifies not only the alleged emotionality and fickleness of women but also their *mediatory* or *indeterminate* positions in the social order. Thus, relationships between brothers-in-law "go through" the sister, a man's relationship with his matrikin "goes through" the mother, and the blessings of one's patrilineal ancestors are contingent on one's mother's behavior. If she is hard working and a faithful and dutiful wife, then her children will receive the blessings of their patrilineal forebears and become *duwe dannu* (blessed children). If she fails in her duty by being lazy, unfaithful, or disobedient, the path along which the patrilineal blessings flow will become blocked, and her children will be cursed. This is why Kuranko say, "A man has many children; a woman bears them; a man's children are in her hands" (*Ke l dan sia; musu don den; ke l den wo bolo*), and observe that you (i.e., your destiny) are in your mother's hands (*i i na le bolo*) or that the book your mother wrote is what you are reading now (*i na l kedi sebene, i wole karantine kedi*)—which is to say that one's actions and disposition are direct reflections of one's mother's actions and disposition.

There is a fascinating parallelism between men's ambivalent attitudes toward women and the vexed relationship between secular and occult power. Ordinarily, these powers are separate and complementary, somewhat like church and state in modern Europe. Indeed, a strict distinction in Kuranko is drawn between the domain of wild powers (*suwage*) associated with magical medicines (*bese*), bush spirits (*nyenne*), and secret societies (*sumafan*) and identified with the bush (*fira*), on the one hand, and, on the other, the domain of custom (*namui* or *bimba kan*) and law (*seriye* or *ton*) associated with secular power (*noé*) and chieftaincy (*mansaye*) and identified with human settlements (*sué*).[23] But though these domains are said to be essentially different, they are, in practice, interdependent, and each is equally vital to the Kuranko lifeworld.[24]

While I would not want to argue that there is a *moral* analogy to be drawn between the youth who joined the Revolutionary United Front and the youth who aspire to leave Sierra Leone for a better life abroad,[25] there is a structural similarity that reflects the moods, mind-sets and imaginings of West African youth who reject farming, rebel against gerontocratic and patrimonial regimes, embrace values associated with Islamic or Euro-American traditions, and form social networks based on personal affinity, shared interests, further education, and personal transformation. All these potentialities are present in traditional West African imaginaries, where corrupt power-holders get their comeuppance, wealth is attained through an alliance with a djinn or benefactor, migration to a fabulous town promises a miraculous change of fortune, love and friendship subvert traditional hierarchies and prescriptions, and the oppressed gain power. Nowadays, however, the bush has become the foreign town.

Consider the situation of Sewa Magba Koroma, a young Kuranko man whom I first met in Freetown in 2002 and who immigrated to England the following year. I spent a lot of time with Sewa, walking around London, meeting other Kuranko friends, getting a sense of what was at stake for them and their struggles with homesickness, racial discrimination, and intimidating rules and regulations.

"You're in another man's land," Sewa once explained to me. "You never know when they [the police] are going to grab you. They'll offer you a free ticket home. You're gone. Just like that." In this city of pitfalls, ambushes, and hidden dangers, there was, however, one place where you could let your guard down and find some sense of security and homeliness. Of Peckham, with its money transfer shops, stores where you could rent African videos, green grocers where you could buy palm oil and cassava leaf and speak Krio, Sewa had said, "This place full na we; we govern this place." Sierra Leoneans referred to Peckham as Kru Town Road after an old quarter of Freetown, and a well-known night spot was called Pardi's, after Paddy's Beach Bar in Freetown's Aberdeen Road.[26] "That's our ground," Sewa said. "That's the place we not scared. The southeast is our stronghold." But outside this neighborhood one had to be vigilant. Just as Sierra Leoneans had evolved their own argot, referring to a Sierra Leonean passport as "potato leaf" (because it is dark green in color) and a residence permit or "stay" as "leather" (because it is harder to get and more valuable than a passport), so they disguised their appearance to avoid becoming targets of local gangs or the police. In Freetown, young men wore American-style basketball trainers; in London they prefer the "normal trainers," hooded jackets, and baggy trousers that young black Londoners wear. "You have to be in the system or else," Sewa told me, explaining that local black gangs often pick on newcomers from West Africa, aggressively demanding "Wot ya got on ya?" and expecting immediate payment. Sewa's tactic was to mimic the cockney "Wot?" and use it repeatedly in response to the locals, hoping they would be fooled into thinking he was one of them and leave him alone.

No doubt many of these tactics of changing one's appearance, hiding one's identity, keeping a low profile, and using a secret language with those one knows and trusts are defensive ruses that have a phylogenetic basis. But this explanation tells us little about the experiential context in which they are deployed—what it feels like to be constantly on the defensive or how real external dangers become translated into imagined fears. Anyone who has moved from a familiar lifeworld and gone to live in a place where he or she is a complete stranger, linguistically inept, economically insecure, and socially stigmatized will immediately identify with Sewa's intense self-consciousness—the suspicion that people were staring at him, that he was under surveillance, that he was somehow in the wrong, without rights or any legitimate identity—though not everyone would share his preoccupation with the power of the police to send him back to his country of origin with no possibility of return, so ending once and for all his dream of improving his lot in life. It was not that Sewa was seeking validation; rather, he was doing everything in his power to avoid the people, situations, and incidents that made him feel as though he was a worthless nobody. In a recent book I argue that human existence plays out as a constant struggle to maximize one's inner recourses or capacities on the one hand and to avail oneself of the external affordances of one's environment on the other.[27] What I admired about Sewa was his capacity for making the most of an environment that not only offered limited opportunities but constantly crossed and humiliated him. That he derived his inner strength from his mother and father was clear to him. They were, as put it, his very life (*ni le wola*). To speak of someone as "being my life," or "being the world to me" is to imply that your own destiny is never simply in your own hands; it is determined by your relationships with significant others and by the ways in which they reflect and care for you, even after they have passed away. In sending his mother photos of himself against the backdrop of the Houses of Parliament, Sewa hoped to inspire in her a validating response, in the same way that enunciating Koranic suras, learned from his father, would end his nightmares and assuage his fears.

At such moments, I was mindful of René Devisch's powerful ethnographic accounts of the Yaka conceptions of health (*-kola*) and well-being (*-syaamuna*) as flowing from a person's vital relationship with a web of forces (*mooyi*), including kinship and community, as well as the ancestral realm. Though this realm is largely beyond ordinary understanding, Yaka aver that the source of life is ultimately maternal and that the most critical relationships in any person's life are with uterine kin. Blockages and disruptions in this flow of forces cause sickness and insanity. So does displacement, and as Devisch shows, maternal images figure as points of anchorage and consolation for migrant youth in the disorienting world of the city, offering them the hope of spiritual connectiveness and renewal.[28]

In many ways, Sewa's situation resembled the situation of these young Yaka men in Kinshasa, for whom matrixial images and sexual attachments were imagined as ways out of the wilderness in which they found themselves adrift. Among strangers, whom Sewa simply called "those people" ("dem people"), one could expect nothing but indifference, disparagement, or outright menace. "They shame me," (*An ya na moliya*), Sewa would say. "They make me feel small" (*An ya na dogoye*). Thus, constant exposure to a negative social environment can easily lead one to feel under attack, fearful of ostracism or deportation, and prey to a nagging guilt that the price of one's own improved chances in life is the loss of one's homeland, one's kith and kin, and one's heritage. At the same time, the impossibility of being accepted into the society in which one has sought asylum translates into a sense that one is worthless, that one is good for nothing, that one is doomed. What kind of thinking enables one to endure such a situation or possibly change it?

In stressful situations, it is possible to think too much for one's own good. One's thinking gets ahead of oneself, throwing up images that inhibit action, ideas that have no relevance, plans that distract one from what can be done in the here and now. Excessive thinking is the source of suffering—a theme that runs through Eastern thought like a red thread. Bringing one's distracted stream of consciousness under some kind of restraint, or even annihilating it, is thus the goal of yogic disciplines for freeing us from our thralldom to the disturbing flux of everyday existence. Neither absorption in oneself nor liberation from oneself has intrinsic value, and it is the critical *relationship* between these hypothetical poles that interests me here. In the same way, thoughts that reproduce the status quo or contravene it may have value depending on the situation at hand. Both conventional wisdom and "wild" forms of thought, affect, and behavior that flout it are equally significant in any such existential space.

The struggle for being first makes its appearance as nebulous yearnings, vague imaginings, and wishful thinking that fasten onto no specific object or, rather, move restlessly from one object to another, much as an infant is curious about everything and anything it can touch or put in its mouth. This is the prototypical expression of what we call undomesticated imagination; it is consciousness in its most opportunistic, promiscuous, and migratory mode, or to invoke the language of Husserl, it is intentionality in its most primordial and preconceptual form. This is the "uncertain, shadowy" existence we sometimes speak of as the private domain that has not yet been transformed "into a shape fit for public appearance."[29] This is also the domain of "intellectually diffuse" experiences or "hazy and unelaborated attitudes" that, as Lévi-Strauss pointed out, are "emotionally intolerable unless they are objectified and integrated in ways that enable us to act and in forms that can be shared."[30]

There is a close affinity here with Jean-Paul Sartre's theory of the imagination. Sartre sees human intentionality as a vital if "undifferentiated" disposition of consciousness toward an external world that always remains to some degree separate from the objects at which it "aims," the people with whom it forms attachments, or the cultural projects whereby it strives to "realize itself."[31] Because the relationship between the thinking subject and the object of his or her thoughts is restive, indeterminate, and unstable, we find ourselves craving things even when satisfied with what we have, conjuring objects that do not strictly speaking exist, or desiring to do things that are not socially acceptable even as we deny the reality of certain objects and experience the reality of others in many different ways. The space of religion and the spaces outside domestication may be compared to the space of dreams, a penumbral domain where consciousness is loosed from the objects, routines, and environs to which it is conventionally tied and freed to entertain or succumb to other modes of objectification. It is a space as haunted by established models and extant memories as it is filled with the aura of imaginary possibilities. Of these possibilities, each representing an incipient or alternative mode of domestication, perhaps the most compelling are the most commonplace: our human capacity for making light of a situation, for transforming work into play, for making music or telling stories, and for finding in laughter, ebullience, and satire a freedom to deny circumstances their power to crush, oppress, and rule us.

This brings me back to the meaning of the riddle in African folklore. We often think of a riddle as a cunningly disguised description of an everyday object. The solution is hidden, or not self-evident. But a riddle can also be construed as a question to which there is no single answer, or as a way of gesturing toward a solution lying beyond the reach of reason—unnameable, unknowable, ineffable. Such are the riddles of existence: When do we think inside the box and when do we think outside it? How can we be at once for ourselves and for others or come into our own without denying the existential imperatives of others with whom we share a common world? What is thinking when it takes the form of a story or informs a ritual practice in which almost nothing is said?

11. Ecologies of Mind

The cybernetic epistemology . . . would suggest a new approach. The individual mind is immanent but not only in the body. It is immanent also in pathways and messages outside the body; and there is a larger Mind of which the individual mind is only a sub-system.

—GREGORY BATESON, *STEPS TO AN ECOLOGY OF MIND*

I want to end this book on the same note with which I began it, by insisting on the primacy of appearances and repudiating the view that causes can be ranked higher than effects and that appearances, as Immanuel Kant claimed, "must themselves have grounds which are not appearances."[1] Hannah Arendt speaks of "the ancient fear" or "nightmare" that has haunted humankind even before philosophy and natural science exacerbated it: the fear that our senses cannot be trusted, that reality and truth lie behind a screen of appearances, and that what seems to us to be solid and incontrovertible is a deception perpetrated by some evil spirit, or simply a dream.[2] It can be argued, however, that even the notion of truth belongs to the world of appearances, even when it purports to lie beyond or beneath it—a phenomenological fact if not an attainable reality—despite the recurring echoes throughout the history of both philosophy and anthropology of the idea that thought can transcend experience and arrive at immutable truths. Thus the uncanny similarity of Parmenides's aspiration to be carried beyond the gates of night and day to a divine way lying "far from the beaten path of men," Bronislaw Malinowski's view that "we cannot possibly reach the final Socratic wisdom of knowing ourselves if we never leave the narrow confinement of the customs, beliefs and prejudices into which every man is born," the migrant's quest for well-being in a place far from home, and the tourist's desire to get away from it all.[3]

Life, from these perspectives, involves a perpetual oscillation between engaging with the world and seeking distance, respite, or release from it. No matter what vernacular idiom is deployed to capture this oscillation—the philosopher's hut versus the open field, the contrast between town and bush, theological images of earth and ether, existential tensions between home and the world—the dilemma persists of how to balance or reconcile these competing imperatives, or discover how one can live with their incommensurability.

To think along these lines is to be immediately reminded of Gregory Bateson's "steps to an ecology of mind."[4] What we call philosophy is only one of many adaptive strategies that human beings have devised for working out a modus vivendi with other human beings and with the extrahuman world that envelops them. As such, ideas emerge, spread, metamorphose, and die out in the same way that other traits do, and all are as potentially vital to our continuing existence as the tools we use, the genes we carry, the families we create, the homes we build, the clothes we wear, the land we farm, and the minerals we mine.

It was this Batesonian way of contextualizing rather than reifying thought that informed my ethnographic fieldwork on southeast Cape York, Australia, in 1993. I wanted to explore Aboriginal relations with their rain-forest and coastal environments, as well as their relations with white Australian society, in terms of the notion of adaptive strategies. And I wanted to know whether conflicts between Aboriginal worldviews and the worldviews of white property developers and eco-activists reflected quite different conceptions of survival—cultural, material, and biological.

The Daintree

On a brief visit to the Daintree River in 1988, I had witnessed confrontations between Greens and roadmakers along the newly bulldozed four-wheel-drive track north of the Daintree crossing. I was well aware of the dismay among conservationists when local Kuku-Yalanji people argued for rather than against the road, claiming a need for better communications between their isolated settlements, even though this might lead to further European incursions into areas used for camping, hunting, and gathering, as well as traditional burial places and sacred sites. The Greens' consternation reflected their commitment to a pervasive "myth of primitive ecological wisdom," which assumes that Aboriginal people live in harmony with, and are closer to nature than, modern Europeans.[5] Arguing against this essentially racist notion, as well as its corollary—that if Aboriginal people seem to abet environmental vandalism it is because they have lost their traditional culture—anthropologist Chris Anderson pointed out that it was local politics, not culture or nature, that led the most vocal and powerful Kuku-Yalanji group to welcome the road because it stood to gain material benefits and consolidate its power in the mission settlement of Wujal Wujal through better access to the outside world.[6] In 1993, my wife and I would discover that the same local politics governed Kuku-Yalanji discourse on a proposed native title claim to the Daintree area.

However, my interest here is not Kuku-Yalanji internal politics per se but the lifeworld of the politically marginalized Kuku-Yalanji family with whom my wife and I and our two-year-old son lived for a year in the Bloomfield rain forest.

As a result of the Queensland government's assimilationist policies, our host family, the Olbars, was forcibly moved in 1970 from their traditional land to a Lutheran mission settlement at Wujal Wujal on the Bloomfield River. In 1992, however, they left the settlement to take up residence on a parcel of their former land that had been purchased for them by the Aboriginal and Torres Strait Island Commission (ATSIC).

Every afternoon we would accompany our hosts on expeditions to the nearby beach at Weary Bay or to the mouth of the Bloomfield River to forage or fish. Unlike my wife, Francine, I lacked the patience for fishing and often preferred to stroll along the beach, listening to the wind in the casuarinas, observing the stingrays moving like cloud shadows beneath the waves, or watching container ships inching forward as slowly as clock hands along the horizon and Torres Strait pigeons flying in from the open sea to feed in the forest. Entranced by what I experienced as the pristine nature of the environment, I commented to Mabel, our host, that it was very beautiful.

My remark was immediately rebutted by a pragmatic set of observations. "This is my *bubu*, my country," Mabel said. And she described the green turtles offshore, the bush yams and *dakay* (mud clams) in the scrub, and said that she hoped it would not be long before she and her family would reclaim all their land and live undisturbed by outsiders in this place that was rightfully theirs.

Mabel's remarks brought home to me the extent to which country, for Aboriginal people, is a *social* reality, steeped in memories of births, deaths, and marriages, of seasonal movements in search of food, and of the traumatic disruptions of colonial history. But it is not passively being on or in the land that gives the land its vitality and meaning, nor are these qualities the result of contemplation. Rather, it is the *vita activa*, the process of living and moving with others on the land and drawing one's livelihood from it, that charges the landscape with vitality and presence. Country embodies the sweat, energy, thought, and feelings of those who invest their labor in it, just as a fabricated object becomes charged with the vitality of the person who shapes it. Like the Ionian theorists of nature in the sixth and seventh centuries, Aboriginal people assume the world of nature to be "saturated or permeated by mind."[7] The ebb and flow of tides, the fury of storms and earthquakes, leaves buffeted and trees broken by high winds all testify to the ways that nature is not only filled with energy and power but "ensouled." Accordingly, relationships between realms that we conventionally separate as natural, cultural, and supernatural are all glossed as *social* relationships, governed by the same principles that obtain in interpersonal life. For the Kuku-Yalanji, such analogical reasoning means that the ecological zones of "sea" and "inland" are also cultural categories—"of the sea" (*jalunji*) and "away from the sea" (*ngalkalji*) connote separate moieties whose members have different essences, and may be identified by their different smells. This logic also explains why sea and inland things must be kept apart. So one is enjoined not to use dugong, turtle, or bullock (which are "meat") as bait for fishing but to use only fish bait to catch fish (the others being "whitefella bait"). And don't use saltwater fish to catch freshwater fish, or vice versa. To infringe any of these *cultural* rules will cause a flood . . . an ungovernable overflowing of *natural* boundaries.

Thus one learns that misfortunes that would in one's own lifeworld be dismissed as accidents or regarded as simply in the "nature of things" actually have social causes. *Someone* must be responsible for them; *someone* must be to blame. The same reasoning explains why "natural" phenomena are so closely and continually examined for their *social* implications, as when a shooting star or a kookaburra laughing at first light are said to signal a death.

This is not to suggest that Aboriginal and Western worldviews imply a difference between erroneous and real understandings of the relation between culture and nature. Rather, they reflect different *practical* priorities. That these worldviews *seem* so incommensurable may be more an artifact of our long-standing habit of exoticizing "primitive" people than a reflection of any empirical reality—a habit still evident in the tendency of many contemporary philosophers of ecology to excoriate global capitalism by urging a recovery of the allegedly more eco-sensitive, sensuous, reciprocal relation between humanity and the natural world that premodern thought is said to epitomize. All such constructions of the other are deeply flawed. In the first place, they inevitably construct nature as benign and narcissistically invoke experiences of the natural world that are pleasing rather than destructive or discomforting to us. The Kuku-Yalanji notion of storms as the malevolent expression of human ill will, of lightning as retributive justice, and of earthquakes and volcanoes as signs of the earth's outrage call this kind of romanticism into question. In the second place, such constructions gloss over the fact that a sensuous experience of connectedness between people and their environment is never permanent or pervasive but always occasional—arising in specific social contexts, tied to specific social purposes, and constrained by cultural ideas and ritual codes. That Mabel Olbar and McGinty Salt, our hosts, made keen observations of the bay whenever we arrived there to fish—remarking on the spoor of a snake in the sand, traces of mullet or herring offshore, the state of the tide, and subtle nuances of the sea, the weather, and the season that entirely escaped my notice—was not because they *participated* in nature but because they were *practiced* in that way of life in that place.

In this sense their participation in the place they called their own was no more "mystical" than the participation of a mechanic, say, in an assemblage of machine parts on which he is working, or a scholar in an engrossing text, or a sculptor in the object she is shaping. All, so to speak, put themselves into what they do, creating thereby the conditions under which they may experience that sense of fusion between body-self and object that we tend to talk about in terms of naturalness, sympathy, and attunement. In short, states of consciousness, as Karl Marx repeatedly observed, are tied to our modes of *interaction* with the world in which we live.

Green Turtle

Two days into our stay, and after long hours working with McGinty and his brother-in-law Babaji to set up our campsite, I went down to the bay alone, stripped, washed and scrubbed myself in the sea, then dressed. The beach was deserted. But as I sat in the shade of a pandanus palm, thinking back on the day and on the fulfillment I had found clearing our campsite with McGinty and Babaji, an aluminum dinghy came slowly inshore from the open sea.

It was Mabel's brothers, Sonny and Oscar, and her brother-in-law Sam. They had been out to Hope Island, hunting green turtles. As they beached the dinghy and drew it up onto the sand, I went down to greet them.

The sea sloshed around my ankles and gently jolted the dinghy. Two boys, Philip and Louie, ran down the beach brandishing their fishing spears as Sam and Sonny hauled the biggest turtle onto the gunwale of the dinghy and tied a rope around its right flipper. Then, as the old man of the sea appeared to gaze about, befuddled, Sam beat its brains out with a sledgehammer.

I watched intently as Sonny began to butcher the turtle.

"We call turtle 'meat' [*minya*], not 'fish' [*kuyu*]," Sam explained. And he told me that great care had to be taken when separating the meat from the carapace, for if the bile is spilled it contaminates the meat and makes it inedible.

In the face of such pragmatism what place did my own unspoken sentiments have, as I watched this beautiful creature—so out of its depth, so out of its element—being hacked open before my eyes? And how might one reconcile the great difference between the Aboriginal and non-Aboriginal sensibilities that collect around such an event? For while many eco-conscious Australians regard the green turtle (*Chelonia mydas*) as both a beautiful and endangered species, Kuku-Yalanji regard its green fat as a delicacy and hunt and eat it with relish.

That evening, Sonny disinterred the cooked turtle from the earth oven he had dug at the outstation, and the fat was shared around. I ate without much appetite, caught between competing cultural persuasions.

GREEN TURTLE

Sam smashes its head in
with the same sledge-hammer
I used this afternoon
to ram our tent pegs home.

A hemisphere turns
turtle; Sonny hacks
its mildewed, sea-marbled
breastplate free.

It recoils from the sky.
Head lolls.
A flipper feebly pushes
Sonny's knife away.

They empty
the long grey rope of its life
onto the sand by the thudding boat
that holds two more

and its carapace is a vessel
filled with a wine lake
in which clouds
float, birds fly, leaves fall.

As the months wore on, I came to understand how Kuku-Yalanji read their environment, learning, for instance, that a hammer bird heard in the cold months means that mullet will be plentiful, that bean trees flowering or the wild tamarind ripening mean that scrub hen eggs can be found, and that the flesh of the parcel apple turning pink means that the liver of the stingrays will also be pink and therefore good to eat, though eating stingrays in the preceding months (October–November) will bring storms. As the wet season approached, I became increasingly fascinated by the family's preoccupation with thunder and lightning. Whereas I saw storms as natural phenomena, our hosts interpreted them in social terms; they were expressions of human malevolence and of tempestuous states of mind. Thus, the phrase *jarramali bajaku* (lit., "exceedingly stormy") is used of people who lose self-control when drunk or drugged, while the term *jarramali* denotes a cyclonic or monsoonal storm, any one of which may embody the ill-will of outsiders. Questions of control thus entail allusions to individual psychology, relations with others, and relations with the elements of nature. Put another way, the "environment" includes social beings, asocial beings, natural species, natural phenomena, and innate "natures."

In Aboriginal communities, one is often struck by people's extraordinary tolerance of aberrant or unruly behavior. I was sometimes reminded of my experience among the Kuranko in Sierra Leone where incorrigible individuals would draw such comments as "He came out of the *fafei* like that" (i.e., even initiation failed to make him mend his ways), "That is how he was made" (*a danye le wo la*), or "He is blameless; he was born with it" (*a ka tala; a soron ta la bole*). But while both Kuranko and Kuku-Yalanji explain dispositions that resist socialization by invoking notions of innateness, there are practical limits to people's tolerance of antisocial behavior that, in both societies, is seen as a form of deafness to social values.

It was Christmas 1993. The heat and humidity was oppressive. Sweat dripped from my forehead onto the pages of my journal as I wrote about the tension that had built up in our camp, breaking on Boxing Day (the day after Christmas) like a storm, with Sonny in a fistfight with his brother-in-law, his elder sister heaping abuse on his head, another sister throwing a couple of punches for good measure, and then the youngest sister Gladys and her husband driving off to Ayton to get away from it all.

Drawn into the family fight and momentarily made scapegoats for the situation, Francine and I also decided to take a break from our field site. Besides, we needed to replenish supplies in Cairns. It was this trip that brought home to me not only the gulf between Kuku-Yalanji and white understandings of the environment and what it means to survive; it sharpened my sense of the existential need to both become deeply involved in the world and to have some way of keeping one's distance from it. In going to Cairns I not only had an opportunity to step back from my research and take stock; I also inadvertently became a tourist.

It so happened that I wandered into the lobby of the Radisson Hotel and found myself in a plastic and plaster rain forest. Although real water trickled through it, splashing gently over real stones, and real goldfish swam in the pool beneath the waterfall, the forest was a replica of the same environment we had only a day before inhabited. Plaster cassowaries, tree kangaroos, frogs, and turtles could be seen in the simulated foliage. Stuffed snakes, crocodiles, and opossums lurked beneath plaster trees that had been festooned with plastic lianas and epiphytes. And strolling through this artificial wilderness, without any apparent awareness of it, were immaculately dressed Japanese tourists, their bodies smelling of soap and shampoo, their skin as polished as porcelain. Other tourists were sitting at tables, discussing plans with travel agents for trips to the reef or rain forest. Still others were setting off, sun-hatted, into the Pier to shop. So different was this world to the Bruegelesque one I had just left that it made me reflect on the itinerant, vagrant, improvised routines that governed our everyday life in the field and echoed an older nomadism—of the perennial search for food and booze; of carousing, loitering, waiting in parks, pubs, parking lots, railway yards, cheap digs, and doss houses; of fights; of splitting up and coming back together. And I thought back to a trip we had made a week earlier to the old sugar mill north of Ayton: the decaying ruins reclaimed by the rain forest, and Lizzie digging for scrub hen eggs, Mabel warning us about the hallucinogenic mushrooms along the path, the danger of falling bloodwood branches, the death adders under the dry leaves . . .

I walked through the hotel into the mall. A paunchy tourist was being photographed with a full-sized photo of Paul Hogan as Crocodile Dundee—akubra hat with plastic croc teeth in the band, a stuffed boa in his hand, the background a painted rain-forest scene. Elsewhere, people were inspecting kitchen towels decorated with Aboriginal motifs, acrylic dot canvases, and painted boomerangs.

I became fascinated by a young couple viewing something on the monitor of their video camera. Their faces were aglow with such delight and vitality that I wondered if the sight of the real thing had been as inspiring for them. Or is it that this kind of joy springs not from the thing-in-itself but from a sense of the command and creative control that a camera gives—a sense that one has captured and subjected to one's own will a miniaturized homologue of a world over which one has, in reality, little mastery? Is this why tourists so often view the world through the lens of cameras and visit museums—because these enable them to arrest and domesticate reality, even at the cost is reducing the world to a collection of lifeless objects?

An analogy is sometimes drawn these days between ethnographic fieldwork and tourism. It's all a question of travel, the argument goes, of boundary-crossing, of hybridity and blurred genres, of the globalization of culture. But this comfortable, Archimedean "view from afar" is all too reminiscent of the armchair anthropology that was eclipsed a hundred years ago by the fieldwork tradition. It's not primarily a question of whether ethnography gives us "truer" insights into other peoples' lives than the tourist gaze; it is a matter of the radically different *experiences* that come from visiting rather than actually living in another society.

This difference may be likened to the difference between magical and political action. The first is a form of play, in which one relates to a homologue of the real world—a toy, a miniature image, a simulacrum—and is thereby safeguarded from the dangers of making direct contact with the object of one's interest, as in a zoo or museum. The second involves *face-to-face interaction* with others *on their terms* and therefore carries the constant risk that one may lose one's stability, security, and identity. Tourism is a vicarious way of relating to the world. It provides, as Orvar Löfgren puts it, "a cultural laboratory where people . . . experiment with new aspects of their identities, their social relations, or their interaction with nature." But this experimentation, Löfgren stresses, is shaped by the "cultural skills of daydreaming and mindtravelling. *Here is an area in which fantasy has become an important social practice.*"[8] To go on holiday is to "get away from it all," not to exchange one set of difficulties for another. Ethnographic fieldwork is not only sustained for a long period, but it also involves direct engagement and social commitment. Though one cannot free one's mind entirely of ethnocentrism and fantasy, an ethnographer is committed to a methodical form of what Hannah Arendt called the "visiting imagination," in which one puts oneself in the place of others, not in order to dream but to work at the task of seeing to what extent one's understanding may be transformed through personal immersion in another way of life.

One may also see the difference between tourism and ethnography in terms of positioning. Like a voyeur, the tourist is always careful to position himself at a safe distance from the action. Virtual travel simply makes this distancing easier. Curious about the Aboriginals, say, whom he sees sitting under the tamarind trees in the park near his hotel, the tourist wants to satisfy his curiosity without getting too involved. He is fascinated, captivated, drawn toward the spectacle, yet he doesn't want to become sullied by an encounter with the other, to be held responsible, to be challenged or obligated in some way, to have his routines and security disturbed. In positioning himself, the tourist uses a camera with a zoom lens to capture an image of the Other. Or he shops for ethnic souvenirs—microcosms of another lifeworld that he will not actually enter—to take home and spin a story around. Or he has his photo taken with a Paul Hogan cutout. Or he watches some tribal theatre or traditional dance, imagining how he might have lived had he been born in another time, in another place.

The urge to travel is born of what Norman O. Brown calls the Oedipal Project—the universal imperative to leave home and create a life for oneself beyond the lifeworld of one's parents.[9] Travel is an archetypal expression of this need to have a home of one's own, to mark out a place for oneself or for one's family in the wider world. As such it can be compared with other minor movements we make in life when we ponder our mundane world from a novel perspective, read philosophy, enter a church or art museum, or try out a new restaurant. But how far one will go geographically or what risks one will run in achieving these separations from quotidian life differs from person to person and from society to society. In Aboriginal Australia, a young neophyte would travel the Dreaming tracks of his ancestors as part of his initiation, enlarging the horizons of his world to encompass a geo-mythological space-time of staggering extent. In West Africa, the bush that lay beyond the perimeter of one's natal village was a metaphor for the hazards of life outside the secure circle of hearth and home. This is why initiation takes place in the bush. Venturing into the bush or migrating to places beyond one's village defines what it means to come into one's own, to become a man. In my own case, growing up in a small, rural New Zealand town, I felt the allure of foreign places from an early age. I yearned to escape the narrow confines of a world in which I felt anomalous and unfulfilled. I read travel books, feeding my imagination with exotic narratives about darkest Africa, wild men of Borneo, cannibals in the South Seas, and desert islands. At university, many of my contemporaries did drugs, but I was sustained by the dream of displacement—discovering somewhere else on earth, utterly unlike the place in which I had been born and raised, where I might undergo an initiatory rebirth and become the person I craved to be. But it took many years of traveling—to Australia, India, Europe, Central Africa—before I realized that travel alone could not effect the changes I had in mind. A deeper and more prolonged immersion in some alien environment would be needed for this metamorphosis to occur—and it was not until I discovered ethnography that I found the means by which philosophy could achieve a deep engagement with the world rather than remain isolated on some Olympian Height or Ivory Tower, far from the madding crowd.

Notes

Introduction

1. "How do we form or understand boundaries in reality and in our minds, between ourselves and others, within communities, or between man and God? Do borders only separate, or can they act as unifiers?"

2. Carla Mantilla Lagos, "The Theory of Thinking and the Capacity to Mentalize: A Comparison of Fonagy's and Bion's Models," *Spanish Journal of Psychology* 10, no. 1 (2007): 189.

3. Claude Lévi-Strauss, "The Concept of Primitiveness" (1966), in *Man the Hunter*, ed. Richard B. Lee and Irven Devore (Chicago: Aldine, 1968), 351.

4. This existential bias toward praxis finds expression in James Scott's use of the classical Greek notion of *mētis* to emphasize common knowledge over the general abstract knowledge that tends to foster and legitimate social hierarchies. Scott thereby directs our attention to the life skills, practical wisdom (*phronesis*), improvisation, and skepticism that circumvent rather than entrench state power (James Scott, *Seeing Like a State: How Certain Schemes to Improve the Human Condition Have Failed* [New Haven, Conn.: Yale University Press, 1998], 6–11, 311–313).

5. Peter Fonagy and Mary Target, *Psychoanalytic Theories: Perspectives from Developmental Psychopathology* (New York: Brunner-Routledge, 2003); Wilfrid Bion, *Attention and Interpretation: A Scientific Approach to Insight in Psycho-Analysis and Groups* (London: Tavistock, 1975).

6. Kurt Gray, Liane Young, and Adam Waytz, "Mind Perception Is the Essence of Morality," *Psychological Inquiry* 23 (2012): 106.

7. Maurice Merleau-Ponty, *Phenomenology of Perception* (1962), trans. Colin Smith (London: Routledge, 1989), 348.

8. Bernard Stiegler, *Acting Out*, trans. David Barison, Daniel Ross, and Patrick Crogan (Stanford, Calif.: Stanford University Press, 2009), 3, emphasis in original. Stiegler attributes his insight to Gilbert Simondon.

9. Marjorie Grene, "Positionality in the Philosophy of Helmuth Plessner," *Review of Metaphysics* 20, no. 2 (1966): 250–277. For Max Scheler, this oscillation between being open-hearted and narrow-minded is characterized as a movement between love and hate. Both these philosophical anthropologists may have drawn crucial insights from Freud's argument that all organisms, from the lowly amoeba to human beings, need to both absorb elements of the world beyond their boundaries and protect these boundaries from invasive and life-threatening forces (Sigmund Freud, *Beyond the Pleasure Principle* [1920], trans. James Strachey [1953; New York: W. W. Norton, 1989], 30–35). Because the boundary (*grenz*) can never be permanent, Plessner refers to this process whereby an organism constantly renegotiates its boundaries as *Begrenzung* (Grene, "Positionality," 255).

10. Maurice Merleau-Ponty, "The Metaphysical in Man" (1947), in *Sense and Non-Sense*, trans. Hubert L. Dreyfus and Patricia Allen Dreyfus (Evanston, Ill.: Northwestern University Press, 1964), 97.

11. Natasha Dow Schüll, *Addiction by Design: Machine Gambling in Las Vegas* (Princeton, N.J.: Princeton University Press, 2012), 2.

12. Chaos theory echoes this Benjaminian point of view: "Chaotic systems are characterized by an extreme sensitivity to initial conditions, small differences being susceptible of having major and unpredictable consequences. And yet, despite the unpredictability, nonlinearity and non-periodicity of chaotic systems, they are also characterized by long-term regular patterns of alternation and oscillations. Although these systems never repeat themselves and never take a path that has already been taken, they nevertheless look familiar, as the paths taken have structures that are similar to previous ones" (Quentin Gausset, *Constructing the Kwanja of Adamawa [Cameroon]: Essays in Fractal Anthropology* [Berlin: LIT Verlag, 2010], 12). Gausset is drawing on the work of James Gleick, *Chaos: Making a New Science* (London: Heinemann, 1988).

13. Walter Benjamin, cited by Theodor W. Adorno, "A Portrait of Walter Benjamin" (1981), in *Prisms*, trans. Samuel Weber and Shierry Weber (Cambridge, Mass.: MIT Press, 1983), 231.

14. This tension informed the "rationality debate" in the early 1970s in which philosophers, notably Peter Winch, argued for different rationalities rather than perpetuate some a priori distinction between primitive irrationality and modern rationality. The debate echoed the sixteenth-century ecclesiastical debate over whether primitive people had souls. In my view, the burning

question is whether and when moderns *are* rational and whether the violence of the Spanish conquest of the Americas calls into doubt the nature of the conquistadors' souls.

15. Immanuel Kant, *Logic* (1880). See Michel Foucault, *Introduction to Kant's Anthropology*, trans. Roberto Nigro and Kate Briggs (Los Angeles: Semiotext(e), 2008), 74–75.

16. "Philosophy has to come down from the heavens and take up human causes, Herder urges; it must become 'immediately useful for the people (a philosophy of sound understanding. . . . What new fruitful developments would not arise if only our whole philosophy would become anthropology" (John H. Zammito, *Kant, Herder, and the Birth of Anthropology* [Chicago: University of Chicago Press, 2002], 176).

17. Richard Rorty, *Philosophy and the Mirror of Nature* (Princeton, N.J.: Princeton University Press, 1979), 368, 377. Adorno contrasts "systematic philosophizing" with an "open philosophy" that "seeks its contents in the unlimited diversity of its objects" (Theodor W. Adorno, *Lectures on Negative Dialectics: Fragments of a Lecture Course 1965/1966*, ed. Rolf Tiedemann, trans. Rodney Livingstone [Cambridge: Polity, 2008], 81).

18. Hannah Arendt, *The Life of the Mind* (New York: Harcourt Brace, 1971), 10.

19. Alain Badiou, *Conditions*, trans. Steven Corcoran (London: Continuum, 2008), 4–5.

20. Theodor W. Adorno, *Critical Models: Interventions and Catchwords*, trans. Henry W. Pickford (New York: Columbia University Press, 1998), 5–6.

21. Jonathan Lear, *Open Minded: Working Out the Logic of the Soul* (Cambridge, Mass.: Harvard University Press, 1998), 3–4.

22. Martin Heidegger, *Being and Time* (1927), trans. John Macquarrie and Edward Robinson (San Francisco: Harper & Row, 1962), 76.

23. Ralph Ellison, *Invisible Man* (1952; New York: Modern Library, 1994).

24. Donna Haraway, *When Species Meet* (Minneapolis: University of Minnesota Press, 2008). See also Stanley Cavell, Cora Diamond, John McDowell, Ian Hacking, and Cary Wolfe, *Philosophy and Animal Life* (New York: Columbia University Press, 2009).

25. Plato, *The Republic*, trans. Francis M. Cornford (Oxford: Clarendon Press, 1941), 222–230.

26. Plato, *The Republic*, trans. Desmond Lee (1955; London: Penguin, 2003), 345.

27. Rorty, *Philosophy and the Mirror of Nature*, 41–45.

28. *Penumbra*, from the Latin *paene* (almost) + *umbra* (shadow). The penumbral connotes a phenomenologically indeterminate zone "between regions of complete shadow and complete illumination," "an area in which something exists to a lesser or uncertain degree," and "an outlying or peripheral region"

(*The American Heritage Dictionary*). See Michael Jackson, *The Palm at the End of the Mind: Relatedness, Religiosity, and the Real* (Durham, N.C.: Duke University Press, 2009), for a fuller elaboration of this motif.

29. Mark C. Taylor, *Field Notes from Elsewhere: Reflection in Dying and Living* (New York: Columbia University Press, 2009), 2.

30. Arendt, *The Life of the Mind*, 6.

31. Scott, *Seeing Like a State*.

32. Michael Herzfeld, *Anthropology Through the Looking-Glass: Critical Ethnography in the Margins of Europe* (Cambridge: Cambridge University Press, 1987).

33. John Dewey, *Experience and Nature* (London: Allen & Unwin, 1929), 251.

34. Iris Murdoch, "Philosophy and Literature: A Dialogue with Brian Magee," in *Men of Ideas: Some Creators of Contemporary Philosophy* (Oxford: Oxford University Press, 1978), 231, 232, 235.

35. Pierre Bourdieu, *Pascalian Meditations*, trans. Richard Nice (Cambridge: Polity, 2002), 2.

36. Diana Allan, *Refugees of the Revolution: Experiences of Palestinian Exile* (Stanford, Calif.: Stanford University Press, 2014).

37. Lotte Buch Segal, "The Burden of Being Exemplary: National Sentiments, Awkward Witnessing, and Womanhood in Occupied Palestine," *Journal of the Royal Anthropological Institute* 21 (2015): 33.

38. Veena Das, "Ordinary Ethics," in *A Companion to Moral Anthropology*, ed. Didier Fassin (Oxford: Blackwell-Wiley, 2012), 139.

39. John Dewey, *How We Think* (1910; Buffalo, N.Y.: Prometheus Books, 1991), 12.

40. Michel de Montaigne, *The Essays: A Selection*, trans. M. A. Screech (Harmondsworth, UK: Penguin, 2004), 17. Montaigne's observations call to mind Arendt's theme of natality and its sharp contrast with Heidegger's preoccupation with mortality and being-unto-death. For an exposition of this contrast, see Miguel Vatter, "Natality and Biopolitics in Hannah Arendt," *Revista de Ciencie Política* 26, no. 2 (2006): 137–159.

41. Dewey, *Experience and Nature*, 7.

42. Veena Das, *Life and Words: Violence and the Descent Into the Ordinary* (Berkeley: University of California Press, 2007).

43. Michael Jackson and Thomas S. Wentzer, "Joint Statement," in *Anthropology and Philosophy: Dialogues on Trust and Hope*, ed. Sune Liisberg, Esther Oluffa Pedersen, and Anne Line Dalsgård (New York: Berghahn, 2015), 59–60.

44. Hannah Arendt to Karl Jaspers, Palenville, 29 August 1957, in Hannah Arendt and Karl Jaspers, *Correspondence, 1926–1969*, trans. Robert Kimber and Rita Kimber (Orlando, Fla.: Harcourt Brace, 1993), 317–318.

45. Joshua Greene argues, "Our own moral brains, which do a reasonably good job of enabling cooperation within groups (Me vs. Us), are not nearly as good at enabling cooperation between groups (Us vs. Them)" (*Moral Tribes: Emotion, Reason, and the Gap Between Us and Them* [New York: Penguin, 2013], 148).

46. Greene, *Moral Tribes*, 353.

47. Bettina Bergo, "Emmanuel Levinas," in *Stanford Encyclopedia of Philosophy* (2011), http://plato.stanford.edu/entries/levinas/.

48. http://ebolaliberiakwankewlai.blogspot.com/2014/10/etu-in-suokoko-bong.html; http://www.npr.org/blogs/goatsandsoda/2015/02/12/385528882/the-ebola-diaries-trying-to-heal-patients-you-cant-touch.

49. Aristotle, *The Nichomachean Ethics*, trans. David Ross (New York: Oxford University Press, 1980), 212.

50. Hannah Arendt, *The Human Condition* (Chicago: University of Chicago Press, 1959), 52.

51. Charles Hallisey uses a Buddhist perspective in arguing against the view that ethics is necessarily tied to ideas of choice, individual freedom, and autonomy. In support of this view that moral action is often unconscious, if not unintentional, Hallisey provides this example: "There was a Protestant village in France during the Second World War that got involved, at great risk to themselves, in protecting Jewish refugees. The people who participated were extremely inarticulate when asked why they did what they did. They said, 'Someone knocks on the door, you open it. You don't think about it. You open the door.' How did they become so good? They said, 'I don't feel so good. I didn't decide to do anything. I just opened the door.' It's a kind of spontaneousness, like when you see a toddler wandering too close to the edge of the subway platform. Even when it's not your own child, you reach over and pull him back. And you don't say, 'Oh, let me make a decision here. Should I do this or not?' Someone knocks on the door, you open it" ("To Answer, When Compassion Knocks," 1 September 2014, http://hds.harvard/edu/news/2014/09/01/answer-when-compassion-knocks#).

52. Jane Bennett, *The Enchantment of Modern Life: Attachments, Crossings, and Ethics* (Princeton, N.J.: Princeton University Press, 2001), 3.

53. Knud Løgstrup, *Beyond the Ethical Demand* (Notre Dame, Ind.: University of Notre Dame Press, 2007).

54. Adorno, *Lectures on Negative Dialectics*, 12.

55. Edmund Husserl, *Ideas: General Introduction to Pure Phenomenology* (1931), trans. W. R. Boyce Gibson (New York: Collier Macmillan, 1962), 93, 99–100.

56. Husserl, *Ideas*, 103. This is precisely where Levinas parted company with Husserl.

57. Pierre Clastres conceived this relation as one between (primitive) society and the state—where "primitive society" serves as a summary metaphor for the human variety of languages and lifeways that are written off, suppressed, or disguised by whoever has power to determine the dominant discourse, the prevailing ethos, and the approved behaviors of the status quo.

58. João Biehl, *Vita: Life in a Zone of Social Abandonment* (Berkeley: University of California Press, 2005), 88, 90, 24.

59. Katherine Boo, *Behind the Beautiful Forevers* (New York: Random House, 2012), 253–254.

60. Shalom Auslander, *Hope: A Tragedy* (New York: Riverhead Books, 2012), 1.

61. "Constellation is not system. Everything does not become resolved; everything does not come out even; rather, one moment sheds light on the other" (Theodor W. Adorno, *Hegel: Three Studies*, trans. Shierry Weber Nicholsen [Cambridge, Mass.: MIT Press, 1993], 109).

62. Theodor W. Adorno, *Negative Dialectics*, trans. E. B. Ashton (New York: Seabury Press, 1973), 9.

1. Analogy and Polarity

1. G. E. R. Lloyd, *Polarity and Analogy* (Cambridge: Cambridge University Press, 1966).

2. George Eliot, *Middlemarch* (1874; Harmondsworth, UK: Penguin, 1985), 111.

3. Michel Foucault, *The Order of Things* (London: Tavistock, 1970), 29. Walter Benjamin makes an identical observation in his essay on the mimetic faculty. "The sphere of life that formerly seemed to be governed by the law of similarity was comprehensive; it ruled both microcosm and macrocosm" ("On the Mimetic Faculty," in *Walter Benjamin: Selected Writings*, ed. Michael W. Jennings, Howard Eiland, and Gary Smith [Cambridge, Mass.: Belknap Press of Harvard University Press, 1999], 2:720).

4. Foucault, *The Order of Things*, 29.

5. Cited in Foucault, *The Order of Things*, 19, emphasis added.

6. Michael Jackson, *Allegories of the Wilderness: Ethics and Ambiguity in Kuranko Narratives* (Bloomington: Indiana University Press, 1982), 16–17.

7. Foucault, *The Order of Things*, 19.

8. E. E. Evans Pritchard, *Nuer Religion* (Oxford: Clarendon Press, 1956), 128, 131–132.

9. Foucault, *The Order of Things*, 22, citing Oswald Crollius's *Traite des signatures*.

10. Geneviève Calame-Griaule, *Ethnologie et langage: la parole chez les Dogon* (Paris: Gallimard, 1965), 27.

11. Marcel Griaule, "The Dogon of the West Sudan," in *African Worlds*, ed. D. Forde (London: Oxford University Press, 1954), 95–98.

12. Calame-Griaule, *Ethnologie et langage*, 27–57.

13. Foucault, *The Order of Things*, 23.

14. Cited by Claude Lévi-Strauss, *The Savage Mind* (London: Weidenfeld & Nicolson, 1966), 61.

15. Foucault, *The Order of Things*, 26.

16. Foucault, *The Order of Things*, 22.

17. Foucault, *The Order of Things*, 22–23.

18. C. Ronan, ed., *The Shorter Science and Civilization in China: An Abridgement of Joseph Needham's Original Text*, vol. 1 (Cambridge: Cambridge University Press, 1978), 95. Janet Gyatso makes a very similar point in her monumental study of Tibetan medicine's "intricate intellectual history," in which Buddhist ways of knowing accompany an evolving scientific and empirical tradition "operating apart from Buddhist revelation" (*Being Human in a Buddhist World: An Intellectual History of Medicine in Early Modern Tibet* [New York: Columbia University Press, 2015], 17).

19. Ronan, *The Shorter Science and Civilization in China*, 104.

20. Recent research casts doubt on the story of Kekulé oneiric inspiration (Malcolm W. Browne, "The Benzene Ring: Dream Analysis," http://www.nytimes.com/1988/08/16/science/the-benzene-ring-dream-analysis.html.)

21. Lévi-Strauss, *The Savage Mind*, 15–16.

22. Jacob Needleman, *A Sense of the Cosmos: The Encounter of Modern Science and Ancient Truth* (New York: Doubleday, 1975), 6.

23. Foucault, *The Order of Things*, 25–30.

24. René Descartes, "Discourse on Method" (1637), in *The Philosophical Works of Descartes*, trans. E. S. Haldane and G. R. T. Ross (Cambridge: Cambridge University Press, 1931), 1:92.

25. Maurice Merleau-Ponty, "Eye and Mind" (1961), trans. Carleton Dallery, in *The Primacy of Perception and Other Essays on Phenomenological Psychology, the Philosophy of Art, History and Politics* (Evanston, Ill.: Northwestern University Press, 1964), 177, 176.

26. Maurice Merleau-Ponty, *Phenomenology of Perception* (1945), trans. Colin Smith (London: Routledge, 1962), 354, 352.

27. Hannah Arendt, *The Life of the Mind* (New York: Harcourt Brace, 1978), 104.

28. Joseph Needham, "Time and Eastern Man," *Royal Anthropological Institute Occasional Paper* 21 (1965): 1.

29. H. A. Bunker and B. D. Lewin, "A Psychoanalytic Notation on the Root GN, KN, CN," in *Psychoanalysis and Culture*, ed. G. B. Wilbur and W. Muensterberger (New York: International Universities Press, 1965), 363–367.

30. For an account of Bacon's ambivalence toward magic and alchemy, see B. Farrington, *The Philosophy of Francis Bacon* (Liverpool: Liverpool University Press, 1966), 51–55. As for Newton, M. Keynes refers to him as "the last of the magicians . . . whose deepest instincts were occult, esoteric, semantic" (Keynes, *Essays in Biography* [London: Hart-Davis, 1951], 311).

31. The enlightenment antipathy to anthropomorphism and myth is discussed at length in Horkheimer and Adorno's *Dialectic of Enlightenment*, trans. J. Cumming (New York: Herder & Herder, 1972).

32. Michel de Montaigne, "On the Cannibals" (1595), in *The Essays: A Selection*, trans. M. A. Screech (Harmondsworth, UK: Penguin, 2004), 82.

33. Montaigne, "On the Cannibals," 83.

34. John Locke, *Essays on the Law of Nature (1663–1664)*, ed. W. von Leyden (Oxford: Clarendon, 1954), 141.

35. Michel Foucault, *The Archaeology of Knowledge*, trans. A. M. Sheridan-Smith (London: Tavistock, 1972), 192.

36. Ernst Cassirer, *The Philosophy of the Enlightenment* (1932), trans. F. C. A. Koelin and J. P. Pettegrove (Princeton, N.J.: Princeton University Press, 1951), 33.

37. Alain Badiou, *The Adventure of French Philosophy*, trans. Bruno Bosteels (London: Verso, 2012), 87.

38. Jadran Mimica, *Intimations of Infinity: The Cultural Meanings of the Iqwaye Counting System and Number* (Oxford: Berg, 1988), chapter 6.

39. Mimica, *Intimations of Infinity*, 104.

40. Ludwig Wittgenstein, *Philosophical Investigations* (1953), trans. G. E. M. Anscombe (Oxford: Blackwell, 1958), 227.

41. Helen Verran, *Science and an African Logic* (Chicago: University of Chicago Press, 2001).

42. Justin L. Barrett, "Exploring the Natural Foundations of Religion," *Trends in Cognitive Science* 4, no. 1 (2000): 29.

43. Wittgenstein, *Philosophical Investigations*, 11. See Michael Jackson, "Thinking Through the Body," in *Paths Toward a Clearing: Radical Empiricism and Ethnographical Inquiry* (Bloomington: Indiana University Press, 1989), 142.

44. Carla Stang, *A Walk to the River in Amazonia: Ordinary Reality for the Mehinaku Indians* (New York: Berghahn, 2009), 126–127.

45. Stang, *A Walk to the River*, 142.

46. Gregory Bateson, *Steps to an Ecology of Mind: Collected Essays in Anthropology, Psychiatry, Evolution and Epistemology* (Frogmore, St. Albans, Herts: Paladin, 1973), 49–50.

47. "Metaphor consists in giving the thing a name that belongs to something else; the transference being either from genus to species, or from species

to genus, or from species to species, or on grounds of analogy." Aristotle, *The Art of Poetry*, trans. W. Hamilton Fyfe (Oxford: Clarendon, 1940), 56–57.

48. Cited by Johannes Fabian, *Time and the Other: How Anthropology Makes Its Object* (New York: Columbia University Press, 1983), 108.

49. James Edie, *Speaking and Meaning: The Phenomenology of Language* (Bloomington: Indiana University Press, 1976), 173.

50. Richard Rorty, *Philosophy and the Mirror of Nature* (Princeton, N.J.: Princeton University Press, 1979), 12.

51. John Dewey, *The Quest for Certainty: A Study of the Relation of Knowledge and Action* (1929; New York: Perigee, 1980), 23.

52. Fabian, *Time and the Other*, 108.

53. Sigfried Giedion, *Space, Time, and Architecture: The Growth of a New Tradition* (Oxford: Oxford University Press, 1941), 31.

54. Christine Helliwell, "Good Walls Make Bad Neighbours: Public and Private Space in a Dayak Longhouse," *Oceania* 62, no. 3 (1992): 179–192.

55. This pattern has changed dramatically over the past fifty years. Most villages are now aligned along roads or streets so that houses have easy vehicle access. Moreover, most houses are rectangular, not round, with corrugated iron (pan) roofs rather than thatch.

56. Marshall McLuhan and Quentin Fiore, *The Meaning Is the Massage: An Inventory of Effects* (Harmondsworth, UK: Penguin, 1967), 68.

57. Marshall McLuhan, *The Gutenberg Galaxy: The Making of Typographic Man* (London: Routledge & Kegan Paul, 1962).

58. David Riesman, "The Oral and Written Traditions," in *Explorations in Communication*, ed. E. Carpenter and M. McLuhan (London: Jonathan Cape, 1970), 114.

59. William Ellis, cited in David Farrier, *Unsettled Narratives: The Pacific Writings of Stevenson, Ellis, Melville, and London* (New York: Routledge, 2007), 106.

60. Laura Bohannan, "Political Aspects of Tiv Social Organization," in *Tribes Without Rulers,* ed. J. Middleton and D. Tait (London: Routledge & Kegan Paul, 1970), 37, 38.

61. Meyer Fortes, *The Web of Kinship Among the Tallensi* (Oxford: Oxford University Press, 1949), 10.

62. Fortes, *The Web of Kinship*, 10–11.

63. Giambattista Vico, *The New Science of Giambattista Vico*, trans. T. G. Bergin and M. H. Fisch (Ithaca, N.Y.: Cornell University Press, 1968), xx–xxi.

64. E. E. Evans-Pritchard, *The Nuer* (Oxford: Clarendon, 1940), 202, emphasis added.

65. John Dewey, *Experience and Nature* (London: Allen & Unwin, 1929), 170; A. Korzybski, *Science and Sanity* (New York: Science Press, 1941).

66. Martin Heidegger, "Building, Dwelling, Thinking" (1952), in *Poetry, Language, Thought*, trans. Albert Hofstadter (New York: Harper & Row, 1975), 145–161.

67. Jacques Derrida and F. C. T. Moore, "White Mythology: Metaphor in the Text of Philosophy," *New Literary History* 6, no. 1 (1974): 23.

68. Yi-Fu Tuan, *Space and Place: The Perspective of Experience* (Minneapolis: University of Minnesota Press, 1977), 25.

69. Gaston Bachelard, *The Poetics of Space* (1958), trans. Maria Jolas (Boston: Beacon Press, 1969), 72.

70. See Fabian, *Time and the Other*, 198, 108; Rorty, *Philosophy and the Mirror of Nature*, 39; David Howes, *Sensuous Relations: Engaging the Senses in Culture and Social Theory* (Ann Arbor: University of Michigan Press, 2003); Paul Stoller, "Eye, Mind and Word in Anthropology," *L'Homme* 24, no. 3–4 (1984): 91–114; and Paul Stoller and Cheryl Olkes, "Bad Sauce, Good Ethnography," *Cultural Anthropology* 1, no. 3 (1986): 336–352.

71. A. Seeger, *Nature and Society in Central Brazil: The Suya Indians of Mato Grosso* (Cambridge, Mass.: Harvard University Press, 1981), 87, 91, 119. For comparable ethnographic details on scent "as the main way [the Amazonian Mehinaku] understand the potency of all things, and the way these potencies are transferred and interact," see Stang, *A Walk to the River*, 38.

72. René Devisch, "Le corps sexué et social ou les modalités d'échange sensoriel chez les Yaka du Zaïre," *Psychopathologie Africaine* 19 (1983): 5–31.

73. René Devisch, "Symbol and Psychosomatic Symptom in Bodily Space-Time: The Case of the Yaka of Zaire," *International Journal of Psychology* 20, no. 4–5 (1985): 597, 596.

74. Gananath Obeyesekere, *Imagining Karma: Ethical Transformation in Amerindian, Buddhist, and Greek Rebirth* (Berkeley: University of California Press, 2002), 1.

75. John Stuart Mill, *Autobiography and Literary Essays* (1824), ed. J. M. Robson and J. Stillinger, in *Collected Works of John Stuart Mill*, vol. 1 (Toronto: University of Toronto Press, 1981), 141.

76. Mill, *Autobiography and Literary Essays*, 151, 153.

77. Friedrich Nietzsche, *Beyond Good and Evil: Prelude to a Philosophy of the Future* (1886), trans. R. J. Hollingdale (Harmondsworth, UK: Penguin, 1973), 17.

78. George Steiner, *After Babel* (Oxford: Oxford University Press, 1973), 223, 224–225.

79. C. F. Jayne, *String Figures: A Study of Cat's Cradle in Many Lands* (New York: Scribner's, 1906), 3; W. C. Handy, "String Figures from the Marquesas and Society Islands," *Bernice P. Bishop Museum Bulletin* 18 (1925): 3–7.

2. Identity and Difference

1. Clifford Geertz refers to this question as anthropology's "recurrent dilemma" (*Interpretation of Cultures: Selected Essays* [New York: Basic Books, 1973], 22). See also George Stocking on the "dialectic between the universalism of 'anthropos' and the diversitarianism of 'ethnos' or, from the perspective of particular historical moments, between the Enlightenment and the Romantic impulse" (*The Ethnographer's Magic and Other Essays in the History of Anthropology* [Madison: University of Wisconsin Press, 1992], 347).

2. Émile Durkheim, *The Elementary Forms of Religious Life* (1912), trans. Karen E. Fields (New York: Free Press, 1995), 45, 15–16, 9.

3. Malinowski wrote his first drafts of this work in 1916–1917.

4. Bronislaw Malinowski, *Coral Gardens and Their Magic*, vol. 2, *The Language of Magic and Gardening* (1935; Bloomington: Indiana University Press, 1965), 8.

5. Malinowski, *Coral Gardens and Their Magic*, 2:237–238.

6. Bronislaw Malinowski, *Coral Gardens and Their Magic*, vol. 1, *Soil Tilling and Agricultural Rites of the Trobriand Islands* (1935; Bloomington: Indiana University Press, 1965), 226–227.

7. Bronislaw Malinowski, *Argonauts of the Western Pacific: An Account of Native Enterprise and Adventure in the Archipelagoes of Melanesian New Guinea* (London: Routledge & Kegan Paul, 1922), 401, emphasis added.

8. Michael W. Young "Writing His Life Through the Other: The Anthropology of Malinowski," *Public Domain Review*, 22 January 2014.

9. Claude Lévi-Strauss, *The Savage Mind* (1962), trans. (London: Weidenfeld & Nicolson, 1966), 3. These observations echo Max Gluckman's comments on traditional African theories of causation and "the logic of witchcraft," which emphasize the *interplay* of human agency and extra-human forces (*Custom and Conflict in Africa* [Oxford: Basil Blackwell, 1970], 83–85).

10. Lévi-Strauss, *The Savage Mind*, 22.

11. Lévi-Strauss, *The Savage Mind*, 269.

12. George Devereux, *From Anxiety to Method in the Behavioural Sciences* (The Hague: Mouton, 1967).

13. Recent research in the field of attention theory is relevant here. See Jeffrey W. Sherman, John K. Kruschke, Steven J. Sherman, Elise J. Percy, John V. Petrocelli, and Frederica R. Conrey, "Attentional Processes in Stereotype Formation: A Common Model for Category Accentuation and Illusory Correlation," *Journal of Personality and Social Psychology* 96, no. 2 (2009): 305–323.

14. Claude Lévi-Strauss, *The Raw and the Cooked* (1964), trans. J. and D. Weightman (London: Cape, 1970), 15.

15. Susan Buck-Morss, *The Origin of Negative Dialectics: Theodor W. Adorno, Walter Benjamin, and the Frankfurt Institute* (New York: Free Press,

1977), 129. John Cage comments perceptively, "The disintegration of harmonic structures is commonly known as atonality. All that is meant is that two necessary elements in harmonic structure—the cadence, and modulating means—have lost their edge. Increasingly, they have become ambiguous" (*Silence: Lectures and Writings* [Middleton, Conn.: Wesleyan University Press, 1961], 63).

16. Claude Lévi-Strauss, *Totemism* (1962), trans. Rodney Needham (Boston: Beacon Press, 1963), 89.

17. Bronislaw Malinowski, "The Problem of Meaning in Primitive Languages," in *The Meaning of Meaning: A Study of Influence of Language Upon Thought and of the Science of Symbolism*, ed. C. K. Ogden and I. A. Richards (New York: Harcourt, Brace & World, 1923), 296–336.

18. Sherman et al., "Attentional Processes in Stereotype Formation."

19. Susan Sontag, "The Power of Principle," adapted from a speech at the presentation of the Rothko Chapel Oscar Romero award to Ishal Menuchin, chairman of Yesh Gvul, *Guardian*, 26 April 2003.

20. Joe Sacco, "On Satire—a Response to the Charlie Hebdo Attacks," *Guardian*, 9 January 2015, http://www.theguardian.com/world/ng-interactive /2015/jan/09/joe-sacco-on-satire-a-response-to-the-attacks.

21. Rabbi Michael Lerner, "Mourning the Parisian Journalists yet Noticing the Hypocrisy," *Huffington Post*, 9 January 2015, http://www.huffingtonpost .com/rabbi-michael-lerner/mourning-the-parisian-jou_b_6442550.html.

22. Bronislaw Malinowski, *A Diary in the Strict Sense of the Term* (London: Routledge, 1967).

23. "Who's Afraid of the Ivory Tower? A Conversation with Theodor W. Adorno," trans. Gerhard Richter, *Monatshefte* 94, no. 1 (Spring 2002): 15; originally published in *Der Spiegel* 23, no. 19 (5 May 1969): 204–209.

24. "Who's Afraid of the Ivory Tower," 18.

25. Theodor W. Adorno, "Resignation," *Telos* 35 (Spring 1978): 165–168.

3. Relations and Relata

1. William James, *The Varieties of Religious Experience* (1902; New York: Signet, 1958), 377.

2. Martin Heidegger, *Being and Time* (1927), trans. John Macquarrie and Edward Robinson (San Francisco: Harper & Row, 1962), 73–74.

3. William James, *Essays in Radical Empiricism* (1904; Cambridge, Mass.: Harvard University Press, 1976), 21.

4. James, *Essays in Radical Empiricism*, 21.

5. William James, *Principles of Psychology* (1890; New York: Dover, 1950), 1:243, 245, emphasis added.

6. "This is obtained through a certain balance between the inner and outer horizon," writes Merleau-Ponty. To achieve this "optimum distance" we must neither see the object too close, "divorced from any background against which it can stand out" or from "too great a distance" (*Phenomenology of Perception*, trans. Colin Smith [London: Routledge, 1962], 302).

7. John Dewey reiterates James's argument in *Experience and Nature* (1925; New York: Dover, 1958), 11, emphasizing that "the conception of experience as the equivalent of subjective private consciousness set over against nature, which consists wholly of physical objects, has wrought havoc in philosophy." Michael Oakeshott concurs. "'Experience' stands for the concrete whole which analysis divides into 'experiencing' and 'what is experienced.' Experiencing and what is experienced are, taken separately, meaningless abstractions; they cannot, in fact, be separated" (*Experience and Its Modes* [Cambridge: Cambridge University Press, 1933], 9).

8. James, *Principles of Psychology*, 2:325.

9. Carl Jung, "Symbols of Transformation," *The Collected Works*, vol. 5, trans. R. F. C. Hull (New York: Routledge & Kegan Paul, 1956), 18.

10. James, *Essays in Radical Empiricism*, 12–13.

11. Jung, "Symbols of Transformation," 11.

12. Ronald McIntyre and David Woodruff Smith, "Theory of Intentionality," in *Husserl's Phenomenology: A Textbook*, ed. J. N. Mohanty and William R. McKenna (Washington, D.C.: Center for Advanced Research in Phenomenology, and University Press of America, 1989), 148.

13. James, *Principles of Psychology*, 1:239; James, *Principles of Psychology*, 1:488.

14. James, *Principles of Psychology*, 1:352–373, 487.

15. James Joyce, *Ulysses* (1922; London: Picador, 1998), 350–351.

16. Analogues of these Joycean innovations may be found in the fiction of Malcolm Lowry, William Faulkner, and Virginia Woolf.

17. Vike Martina Plock, "Bodies," in *Cambridge Companion to Ulysses*, ed. Sean Latham (Cambridge: Cambridge University Press, 2014), 195.

18. Plock, "Bodies," 195–196. This blurring of the line between animality and humanity is so explicit and pervasive in some human societies that it has become fashionable in contemporary anthropology to call into question "modernist" assumptions about the essential difference between animality and humanity or persons and things. But the fallacy of this so-called ontological turn is that no distinction is made between *cultural* modes of *representing* reality (worldviews, epistemologies) and *personal* modes of *experiencing* reality. Being and thought are conflated. It is assumed that lived experience conforms to, and can be inferred from, the ways in which people think about the world and that these modes of thought are unchanging from situation to situation or moment to moment.

19. James, *Principles of Psychology*, 1:371.

20. Michael Jackson, *Between One and One Another* (Berkeley: University of California Press, 2012), 2–3.

21. Joyce, *Ulysses*, 62.

22. Charles Piot, *Nostalgia for the Future: West Africa After the Cold War* (Durham, N.C.: Duke University Press, 2010).

23. Arthur Kleinman, Yunxiang Yan, Jing Jun, Sing Lee, Everett Zhang, Pan Tianshu, Wu Fei, and Guo Jinhua, *Deep China: The Moral Life of the Person: What Anthropology and Psychiatry Tell Us About China Today* (Berkeley: University of California Press, 2011), 5.

24. William James, *A Pluralistic Universe* (1909; Cambridge, Mass.: Harvard University Press, 1977).

25. Stephen A. Mitchell, *Hope and Dread in Psychoanalysis* (New York: Basic Books, 1993).

26. Philip M. Bromberg, *Standing in the Spaces: Essays on Clinical Process, Trauma, and Dissociation* (Hillsdale, N.J.: Analytical Press, 1993), 186.

27. This model of multiple selfhood is not to be confused, however, with multiple personality disorder (now known as dissociative identity disorder), in which, as Philip Bromberg puts it, the normally "flexible multiplicity of relatively harmonious self-states . . . becomes a rigid multiplicity of adversarial self-states" (*Awakening the Dreamer: Clinical Journeys* [Hillsdale, N.J.: Analytical Press, 2006], 191).

28. Michel de Montaigne, "On the Inconstancy of Our Actions," in *The Essays: A Selection*, trans. M. A. Screech (Harmondsworth, UK: Penguin, 1993), 128, 129, 131.

29. Herman Melville, *The Confidence Man: His Masquerade* (1857; Harmondsworth, UK: Penguin, 1990), 84–85.

30. Virginia Woolf, *Orlando* (New York: Harcourt Brace, 1928), 308–309, cited in Bromberg, *Awakening the Dreamer*, 52.

31. Fernando Pessoa, *The Book of Disquiet* (1998; Harmondsworth, UK: Penguin, 2003), 327–328.

32. James, *Principles of Psychology*, 1:294, 291, emphasis in original.

33. Michael Jackson, *Excursions* (Durham, N.C.: Duke University Press, 2007), 102.

34. G. A. Bradshaw, Allan N. Schore, Janine L. Brown, Joyce H. Poole, and Cynthia J. Moss, "Elephant Breakdown: Social Trauma: Early Disruption of Attachment Can Affect the Physiology, Behaviour and Culture of Animals and Humans Over Generations," *Nature* 433 (2005): 807.

35. George Devereux, *Ethnopsychoanalysis: Psychoanalysis and Anthropology as Complementary Frames of Reference* (Berkeley: University of California Press, 1978), 74–77.

36. Pessoa, *The Book of Disquiet*, 254.

37. Michael Herzfeld, *The Social Production of Indifference: Exploring the Roots of Western Bureaucracy* (New York: Berg, 1992).

38. Hannah Arendt, *The Human Condition* (Chicago: University of Chicago Press, 1958), 95, 169.

39. I am riffing here on Barbara Myerhoff's theme of "re-membering" as a strategic means whereby a person re-aggregates and reorders the self by summoning prior and prospective selves, and collaborating with significant others in generating new forms of selfhood ("Life History Among the Elderly: Performance, Visibility, and Remembering," in *A Crack in the Mirror: Reflexive Perspectives in Anthropology*, ed. J. Ruby [Philadelphia: University of Pennsylvania Press, 1982], 99–117). More recently, Michael White has used Myerhoff's work on re-membering in the context of narrative therapy, mediating a client's creative construction of alternative "multi-voiced" modes of self-identity (*Maps of Narrative Practice* [New York: W. W. Norton, 2007], 136–139).

40. Philip Bromberg, *Awakening the Dreamer* (Mahwah, N.J.: Analytic Press, 2006), 68.

41. James, *Principles of Psychology*, 1:487.

42. I am indebted to Devaka Premawardhana for this crucial insight.

43. In Arendt's terms, this is an expression of natality, the "startling unexpectedness" that is "inherent in all beginnings and in all origins" and occurs "against the overwhelming odds of statistical laws and their probability." This is why "the new . . . always appears in the guise of a miracle" (*The Human Condition*, 177–178).

44. Mitchell, *Hope and Dread in Psychoanalysis*, 101. Jaan Valsiner and Rene van der Veer make a similar observation. "The personal core of the selves system is fortified through this constant adaptation—the selves are there not to keep, but to constantly abandon, in the sense of novel versions of the selves system" (*The Social Mind: Construction of the Idea* [Cambridge: Cambridge University Press, 2000], 261–262).

45. This kind of opportunistic switching between direct action and strategic inaction brings to mind Aristotle's distinction between "active" and "passive" agency (*Metaphysics* 5.12), the first term referring to a subject's action on the world that changes it in some way, the second to its being subject to the actions of others—suffering, receiving, or being moved or transformed by external forces. Arendt speaks of this contrast between being an actor and being acted on as a difference between being a "who" and a "what" (*The Human Condition*, 181–186).

46. Pessoa, *The Book of Disquiet*, 91, 30.

47. James, *The Varieties of Religious Experience*, 377; James, *Essays in Radical Empiricism*, 35.

48. William James, *Pragmatism* (1907; Indianapolis, Ind.: Hackett, 1981), 92; Hannah Arendt, "Understanding and Politics" (1994), in *Essays in*

Understanding, 1930–1954: Formation, Exile, and Totalitarianism (New York: Harcourt Brace, 1994), 321.

49. James, *Pragmatism*, 87, emphasis in original.

50. Cited by H. N. Gardiner, "The First Twenty-Five Years of the American Philosophical Association," *Philosophical Review* 35 (1926): 150.

51. James, *Radical Empiricism*, 146.

4. Matters of Life and Death

1. Theodor W. Adorno, *Negative Dialectics* (1966), trans. E. B. Ashton (New York: Seabury Press, 1973), 13, 34.

2. Adorno, *Negative Dialectics*, 3, 361.

3. Primo Levi, *The Drowned and the Saved* (1986), trans. R. Rosenthal (London: Abacus, 1989), 36.

4. Vincent Crapanzano, *The Harkis: The Wound That Never Heals* (Chicago: University of Chicago Press, 2011), 6, 7, 9.

5. Edward Said, "Reflections on Exile," *Granta* 13 (1984): 159.

6. Crapanzano, *The Harkis*, 12.

7. Hannah Arendt, *The Life of the Mind* (New York: Harcourt Brace, 1971), 175.

8. Friedrich Nietzsche, *Thus Spoke Zarathustra* (1887), trans. Walter Kaufmann (Harmondsworth, UK: Penguin, 1978), 313.

9. Frank B. Lindeman, *Plenty-Coups: Chief of the Crows* (Lincoln: University of Nebraska Press, 1962), 311, cited in Jonathan Lear, *Radical Hope: Ethics in the Face of Cultural Devastation* (Cambridge, Mass.: Harvard University Press, 2006), 2.

10. Lear, *Radical Hope*, 6, 7.

11. Yakir Englander, "On the Danger of Peace Work," *Huffington Post*, 23 July 2015, www.huffingtonpost.com/yakir-englander/on-the-danger-of-peace-work_b_7597660.html.

12. Michael Jackson, *Between One and One Another* (Berkeley: University of California Press, 2012), 82–83.

13. Rodney Frey, *The World of the Crow Indians: As Driftwood Lodges* (Norman: University of Oklahoma Press, 1987), xv, xvii, 155–159, 179.

14. David Carrasco, personal communication, March 2015.

15. Knud Løgstrup, *Beyond the Ethical Demand* (Notre Dame, Ind.: University of Notre Dame Press, 2007), 68.

16. Hannah Arendt, *The Human Condition* (Chicago: University of Chicago Press, 1958), 178.

17. Hannah Arendt, *Men in Dark Times* (Harmondsworth, UK: Penguin, 1973), 106.

18. Alain Badiou, "For a Tomb of Gilles Deleuze," in *The Adventure of French Philosophy*, trans. Bruno Bosteels (London: Verso, 2012), 339.

19. Fred Myers, *Pintupi Country, Pintupi Self: Sentiment, Place, and Politics Among Western Desert Aborigines* (Washington, D.C.: Smithsonian Institution Press, 1986), 146; cf. Fred Myers, "Burning the Truck and Holding the Country: Pintupi Forms of Property and Identity," in *We Are Here: Politics of Aboriginal Land Tenure*, ed. Edwin N. Wilmsen (Berkeley: University of California Press, 1989), 18.

20. Karl Jaspers, *Philosophie*, vol. 3 (Berlin: Julius Springer, 1932), 122.

21. Wilfred Bion, *Attention and Interpretation: A Scientific Approach to Insight in Psycho-analysis and Groups* (London: Tavistock, 1975).

22. Peter Fonagy and Mary Target, *Psychoanalytic Theories: Perspectives from Developmental Psychopathology* (New York: Brunner-Routledge, 2003).

23. George Lakoff argues that this same tension between patriarchal control and maternal care finds expression in American political ideologies. While liberals emphasize the responsibility of the state to care for its citizens, conservatives emphasize the state's responsibility to protect the country and its constitution (*Moral Politics: What Conservatives Know That Liberals Don't* [Chicago: University of Chicago Press, 1996], 62–63). Cf. Ghassan Hage, "The Spatial Imaginary of National Practices: Dwelling-Domesticating/ Being-Exterminating," *Environment and Planning D: Society and Space* 14 (1996): 463–485.

24. Ernst Bloch and Theodor W. Adorno, "Something's Missing: A Discussion Between Ernst Bloch and Theodor W. Adorno on the Contradictions of Utopian Longing," in *The Utopian Function of Art and Literature: Selected Essays*, trans. Jack Zipes and Frank Mecklenburg (Cambridge, Mass.: MIT Press, 1988), 1–17.

25. Philippe Rospabé, "Don archaïque et monnaie sauvage," in *MAUSS: Ce que donner veut dire: don et interet* (Paris: Éditions la Découverte, 1993), cited in David Graeber, *Debt: The First 5,000 Years* (New York: Melville House, 2011), 133.

5. Ourselves and Others

1. Georg Simmel, *The View of Life: Four Metaphysical Essays with Journal Aphorisms* (1918), trans. John A. Y. Andrews and Donald N. Levine (Chicago: University of Chicago Press, 2010), 13, 61.

2. Hannah Arendt, *The Human Condition* (Chicago: University of Chicago Press, 1958), 88.

3. Jonathan Lear, *Radical Hope: Ethics in the Face of Cultural Devastation* (Cambridge, Mass.: Harvard University Press, 2006), 4–5.

4. I follow J. F. M. Hunter's interpretation of what Wittgenstein actually meant by the phrase "form of life." Form of life implies "something typical of a human being," "one of life's forms," in which case concepts, language games, everyday experiences, and behaviors are all forms of life, to be placed on a par as variant ways of being (J. F. M. Hunter, "'Forms of Life' in Wittgenstein's 'Philosophical Investigations,'" *American Philosophical Quarterly* 5, no. 4 (1968): 235.

5. Clare Winnicott, "D. W. W.: A Reflection," in *Between Reality and Fantasy: Transitional Objects and Phenomena*, ed. Simon A. Grolnick and Leonard Barkin (Northvale, N.J.: J. Aronson, 1978), 15–33.

6. Oliver Sacks, "My Own Life," *New York Times*, 19 February 2015, http://www.nytimes.com/2015/02/19/opinion/oliver-sacks-on-learning-he-has-terminal-cancer.html.

7. Thom van Dooren, *Flight Ways: Life and Loss at the Edge of Extinction* (New York: Columbia University Press, 2014), 4.

8. Van Dooren, *Flight Ways*, 4–5.

9. Eduardo Kohn, *How Forests Think: Toward an Anthropology Beyond the Human* (Berkeley: University of California Press, 20), 1.

10. Karl Marx, *Pre-capitalist Economic Formations* (1859), trans. Jack Cohen (London: Lawrence & Wishart, 1964), 81.

11. Arjun Appadurai, ed., *The Social Life of Things: Commodities in Cultural Perspective* (New York: Cambridge University Press, 1988); Eduardo Viveiros de Castro, *From the Enemy's Point of View: Humanity and Divinity in an Amazonian Society*, trans. Catherine V. Howard (Chicago: Chicago University Press, 1992); Bruno Latour, *We Have Never Been Modern* (1991), trans. Catherine Porter (New York: Harvester Wheatsheaf, 1993); Jane Bennett, *Vibrant Matter: A Political Economy of Things* (Durham, N.C.: Duke University Press, 2010).

12. Denis Johnson, *Train Dreams* (New York: Farrar, Straus and Giroux, 2002), 63–64.

13. Michael Jackson, *Paths Toward a Clearing: Radical Empiricism and Anthropological Inquiry* (Bloomington: Indiana University Press, 1989), 102–118.

14. Lucien Lévy-Bruhl, *Les fonctions mentales dans les sociétés inférieures* (1910), trans. Lilian A. Clare as *How Natives Think* (1926; Princeton, N.J.: Princeton University Press, 1985). Rane Willerslev, *Soul Hunters: Hunting, Animism, and Personhood Among the Siberian Yukaghirs* (Berkeley: University of California Press, 2007), 106.

15. "Cocker Spaniel Saves Baby from Crawling into the Sea in Turkey," https://www.youtube.com/watch?v=8r8riGW3KMc.

16. Emmanuel Levinas, *Difficult Freedom: Essays on Judaism*, trans. Seán Hand (Baltimore: Johns Hopkins University Press, 1990), 153.

17. Michael Jackson, "Meaning and Moral Imagery in Kuranko Myth," *Research in African Literatures* 13, no. 1 (1982): 168.

18. Curiously enough, a Warlpiri informant called Minjina recounted the same story to A. Capell in 1952, and with the same mimetic mastery that Zack possessed. Capell speaks of Minjina's "wealth of eloquence that only a recording machine could have preserved, and of action which would have demanded a ciné camera" ("The Wailbri Through Their Own Eyes," *Oceania* 23, no. 2 [1952]: 130). Minjina was the paternal grandfather of the Aboriginal painter Michael Jagamara Nelson (Vivien Johnson, *The Art of Clifford Possum Tjapaltjarri* [East Roseville, NSW: Gordon & Breach Arts International, 1997], 12).

19. Maurice Merleau-Ponty, *The Visible and the Invisible* (1964), trans. Alfonso Lingis (Evanston, Ill.: Northwestern University Press, 1968), 123, 122.

20. Willerslev, *Soul Hunters*, 190–191.

21. William James, *The Principles of Psychology* (New York: Dover, 1950), 1:506–507; Harriet Martineau, *Miscellanies* (Boston: Hillard, Gray, 1836).

22. Victor Turner, *The Forest of Symbols* (Ithaca, N.Y.: Cornell University Press, 1967), 106.

23. Michael Jackson, *Life Within Limits: Well-being in a World of Want* (Durham, N.C.: Duke University Press, 2011), 38–45.

24. Willerslev, *Soul Hunters*, 46–47.

25. Leslie Marmon Silko, "Notes on the Deer Dance," in *The Delicacy and Strength of Lace: Letters Between Leslie Marmon Silko and James Wright*, ed. Anne Wright (Saint-Paul, Minn.: Greywolf Press, 1986), 9–10.

26. Patricia Vinnecombe, *People of the Eland: Rock Paintings of the Drakensberg Bushmen as a Reflection of Their Life and Thought* (Pietermaritzburg, SA: University of Natal Press, 1976), 180. Vinnecombe's insights are reminiscent of Walter Buckert's argument that hunting rituals involve expiation for the guilt of killing of an animal. A classical example is the annual Athenian slaying of the ox (Bouphonia) followed by a trial for the murder of the animal, with the axe and knife found guilty and cast into the sea (Buckert, *Homo Necans: The Anthropology of Ancient Greek Sacrificial Ritual and Myth*, trans. Peter Bing [Berkeley: University of California Press, 1983], 20).

27. Eduardo Kohn, "How Dogs Dream: Amazonian Natures and the Politics of Transspecies Engagement," *American Ethnologist* 34, no. 1 (2007): 7.

28. Deborah Bird Rose, *Dingo Makes Us Human: Life and Land in an Aboriginal Australian Culture* (Cambridge: Cambridge University Press, 1992), 176–177. A similar attitude prevails among the Evenki of Siberia. "Evenki dogs are not respected [often neglected and never fed enough], but people cannot imagine life without them" (Tatiana Safonova, and István Sántha, "Stories About Evenki People and Their Dogs: Communication Through Sharing Contexts," in *Animism in Rainforest and Tundra: Personhood, Animals, Plants,*

and *Things in Contemporary Amazonia and Siberia*, ed. Marc Brightman, Vanessa Elisa Grotti, and Olga Ulturgasheva [New York: Berghahn, 2012], 92).

29. A. M. Homes, *The Mistress's Daughter* (New York: Viking, 2007), 69–70.

30. Marcel Mauss, *The Gift* (1950), trans. Ian Cunnison (London: Cohen & West, 1954), 10–12.

31. David Carrasco, *City of Sacrifice: The Aztec Empire and the Role of Violence in Civilization* (Boston: Beacon, 1999), 73–74.

32. I know of only one instance of this sacrifice, known as *baramawulan saraké*. In 1979, chief Kulio of Sambaia told me that his ancestor, Mali Yan (tall) Jallo—a Fula—had migrated to present-day Sierra Leone some eleven generations ago. Mali Yan's three sons, Samba, Bubu, and Kalo settled in different areas (Sambaia, Buiyan, and Kalian). The country that Fula Manse (Fula chief) Bubu entered was already inhabited by the Kargbo. But the Kargbo were living in caves to escape the depredations of Tegere (Temne) warriors. The Kargbo asked Fula Manse Bubu to help them drive the Temne away. With the help of his younger brother, Kalo, and a renowned warrior, Morogbe Kundu Togele, Bubu succeeded in repulsing the Temne. As a reward, the Kargbos offered Bubu land to settle, though they would first have to consult with their allies and "brothers," the Sisé of Sambadugu. After much deliberation, the Kargbo and Sisé decided to make Fula Manse Bubu protector and lord of the land but only on condition that he make a sacrifice to the land. Fula Manse Bubu asked his wife, Ma Hawa, to give their daughter as a human sacrifice. The girl stood in a pit (*baramawulan*), her head inside a copper receptacle, gold in her mouth, and was buried alive. In addition, "one hundred of everything" had to be distributed among the populace. The Kargbo now declared, *m'bol fa ma kin fa*, meaning "my hands and my feet are yours." Fula Manse Bubu released an arrow into the air that fell to earth in a straight line, signifying that the sacrifice had been accepted by the ancestors and a covenant made. Bubu then built his courthouse on the spot where the arrow landed and gave part of his chiefdom to Morogbe Kundu.

33. Carrasco, *City of Sacrifice*, 179, 148. In "The Other Mexico," Octavio Paz writes that the real rivals of the Aztecs are not to be found in the East (he first suggests the Assyrians) but in the West, "for only among ourselves has the alliance between politics and metaphysics been so intimate, so exacerbated, and so deadly: the inquisitions, the religious wars, and above all, the totalitarian societies of the twentieth century" (*The Labyrinth of Solitude and Other Writings*, trans. Lysander Kemp [New York: Grove Press, 1985], 307–308).

34. This notion of sapping the energy, draining the blood, or consuming the vital organs of a healthy and potent person in order to augment one's own flagging powers finds expression in the widespread fantasies of human sacrifice.

35. Godfrey Lienhardt, *Divinity and Experience: The Religion of the Dinka* (Oxford: Oxford University Press, 1961), 234, 23.

36. Wilhelm Dilthey, *Selected Works*, vol. 1, *Introduction to the Human Sciences*, trans. Rudolf Makreel and Frithjof Rodi (Princeton, N.J.: Princeton University Press, 1989), 227, 50.

6. Belief and Experience

1. I am thinking particularly of the Cartesians of the second generation—Nicolas Malebranche, Arnold Geulincx, Géraud de Cordemoy—who considered mind and matter to be wholly different substances. Since one could not, therefore, act on the other, some supernatural agency had to be postulated as the cause of what appears to be an interaction (as when *"I move my hand"*). See Richard N. Coe, *Beckett* (Edinburgh: Oliver & Boyd, 1964), 27–31.

2. Raf Sanchez and Peter Foster, "You Rape Our Women and Are Taking Over Our Country," *Telegraph*, 18 June 2015, http://www.telegraph.co.uk/news/worldnews/northamerica/usa/11684957/You-rape-our-women-and-are-taking-over-our-country-Charleston-church-gunman-told-black-victims.html.

3. Michael Jackson, "The Witch as a Category and as a Person," in *Paths Toward a Clearing: Radical Empiricism and Ethnographic Inquiry* (Bloomington: Indiana University Press, 1989), 88–101.

4. Tine M. Gammeltoft, *Haunting Images: A Cultural Account of Selective Reproduction in Vietnam* (Berkeley: University of California Press, 2014).

5. James Scott, *Seeing Like a State: How Certain Schemes to Improve the Human Condition Have Failed* (New Haven, Conn.: Yale University Press, 1998), 316, emphasis in text.

6. Lotte Buch Segal, "The Burden of Being Exemplary: National Sentiments, Awkward Witnessing, and Womanhood in Occupied Palestine," *Journal of the Royal Anthropological Institute* 21, no. S1 (May 2015): 30–46.

7. Michael Jackson, "Emmanuel," in *The Wherewithal of Life: Ethics, Migration, and the Question of Well-Being* (Berkeley: University of California Press, 2013), 24–45.

8. Jean-Paul Sartre, *The Family Idiot: Gustave Flaubert, 1821–1857*, vol. 2, trans. Carol Cosman (Chicago: University of Chicago Press, 1987), 174; James C. Scott, *Weapons of the Weak: Everyday Forms of Peasant Resistance* (New Haven, Conn.: Yale University Press, 1987).

9. This existential understanding of religion is not incompatible with new cognitive approaches to religion that focus on the ordinariness rather than extraordinariness of religious beliefs. "Regardless of metaphysical claims, what we observe as religion is still a constellation of human phenomena communicated and regulated by natural human perception and cognition. . . . Religious

concepts may be more 'natural' than they seem" (Justin L. Barrett, "Exploring the Natural Foundations of Religion," *Trends in Cognitive Science* 4, no. 1 [2000]: 29).

10. Kate Connolly, "Angela Merkel Comforts Sobbing Refugee but Says Germany Can't Help Everyone," *Guardian*, 16 July 2015, http://www.the guardian.com/world/2015/jul/16/angela-merkel-comforts-teenage-palestinian -asylum-seeker-germany.

11. Gary Younge, "Farewell to America," *Guardian*, 1 July 2015, http://www .theguardian.com/us-news/2015/jul/01/gary-younge-farewell-to-america.

12. Steven Feld, "Pygmy POP: A Genealogy of Schizophonic Mimesis," *Yearbook for Traditional Music* 28 (1996): 5–6.

13. Christine J. Walley, *Exit Zero: Family and Class in Postindustrial Chicago* (Chicago: University of Chicago Press, 2013), 161.

14. Norbert Elias, *The Civilizing Process: The History of Manners and State Formation and Civilization*, trans. Edmund Jephcott (Oxford: Blackwell, 1994); Jonas Frykman and Orvar Löfgren, *Culture Builders: A Historical Anthropology of Middle-Class Life*, trans. Alan Crozier (New Brunswick, N.J.: Rutgers University Press, 1987), 126–153.

15. Elisabeth Lasch-Quinn, "From Inwardness to Intravidualism," *Hedgehog Review* 13, no. 1 (2011): 43–51.

16. Ivan Illich, *Tools for Conviviality* (London: Caldar & Boyars, 1973); Michael Jackson, *The Other Shore: Essays on Writers and Writing* (Berkeley: University of California Press, 2013), ix.

17. Hubert Marcuse, "The Affirmative Character of Culture" (1932), in *Negations: Essays in Critical Theory*, trans. Jeremy J. Shapiro (Boston: Beacon Press, 1968), 120.

18. Julia Prewitt Brown, *The Bourgeois Interior: How the Middle Class Imagines Itself in Literature and Film* (Charlottesville: University Press of Virginia, 2008).

19. T. S. Eliot argued that while metaphysical poets like John Donne sought to unify sensations and ideas, feelings, and thoughts, the early seventeenth century saw these modalities of experience become increasingly separated, creating an increasing division between ratiocination and emotionality and giving rise to genres of writing that defined their identities in mutually exclusive terms.

7. Persons and Types

1. F. Scott Fitzgerald, *The Rich Boy* (1926; London: Hesperus Press, 2003), 3.

2. Pumla Gobodo-Madikizela, *A Human Being Died That Night: A South African Story of Forgiveness* (Boston: Houghton Mifflin, 2003), 14-15.

3. Gobodo-Madikizela, *A Human Being Died*, 19–20.

4. Gobodo-Madikizela, *A Human Being Died*, 32.

5. Gobodo-Madikizela, *A Human Being Died*, 34.

6. Michel de Montaigne, "On the Inconstancy of Our Actions" (1595), *The Essays: A Selection*, trans. M. A. Screech (London: Penguin, 1993), 128.

7. Montaigne, "On the Inconstancy of Our Actions," 128.

8. Montaigne, "On the Inconstancy of Our Actions," 131.

9. Dave Grossman, *On Killing: The Psychological Costs of Learning to Kill in War and Society* (New York: Little, Brown, 2009).

10. Gobodo-Madikizela, *A Human Being Died*, 39, 114.

11. Gobodo-Madikizela, *A Human Being Died*, 125.

12. In January 2015, "in the interests of nation-building and reconciliation" and because he had expressed remorse over his crimes and helped authorities recover the remains of some of his victims, justice minister Michael Masutha ordered de Kock's release on parole.

13. William James, *Pragmatism* (1907; Indianapolis, Ind.: Hackett, 1981), 92.

14. Bronislaw Malinowski, *Magic, Science, and Religion, and Other Essays* (London: Souvenir Press, 1974), 146.

15. George Devereux, "Mohave Coyote Tales," *Journal of American Folklore* 61 (1948): 238.

16. Cited by Stephen Matterson, introduction to Herman Melville's *The Confidence Man: His Masquerade* (London: Penguin, 1990), xvii.

17. Melville, *The Confidence Man*, 84–85.

18. Walter Benjamin, "The Storyteller: Reflections on the Work of Nicolai Leskov" (1936), in *Illuminations*, trans. Harry Zohn (New York: Schocken, 1969), 84, 91.

19. The Senegalese fire finch (*tintingburuwe*) habitually flits and nests around houses, and it is this association with domestic space that may explain why the souls of dead infants are said to inhabit the fire finch while awaiting possible reincarnation, for a small child does not enter the public domain for some time after its birth.

20. This circumlocution conveys the idea that women prepare the best food for their lovers.

21. The Seli is the largest river draining the southern area of Kuranko country. In referring to a local river, the locus of the story ceases to be mythical and is suddenly brought closer to home.

22. *Bal'fole*, lit. *balanje* (xylophone)-hitter, by implication a praise-singer, a *jeleba*.

23. The Kuranko phrase *ko manni a nyorgo manni* means literally "something happened, its partner [i.e., the same thing, its counterpart] also happened."

24. *Kemine gbana* is an unmarried young man, an idler, a drifter. Here the term is used as a synonym for a commoner, someone of inconsequential status.

8. Being and Thought

1. Michel Foucault, *The Order of Things: An Archaeology of the Human Sciences* (1966), trans. (London: Tavistock 1974), 387.

2. http://www.theguardian.com/books/australia-culture-blog/2014/feb/28 /eleanor-catton-creation-is-a-completely-divine-concept.

3. Interview by Jade Filton for Livemusic.fm, London, 30 November 2010, in "Dark Dark Dark Live at the Lexington (plus interview)," uploaded 5 January 2011, https://youtu.be/N-7hKVyQcmA.

4. Cited in Tomás R. Villasante, *Las ciudades hablan: identidades y movimientos sociales en seis metrópolis latinoamericanas* (Buenos Aires: Editorial Nueva Sociedad, 1994, 264).

5. Karl Popper, *Objective Knowledge: An Evolutionary Approach* (New York: Oxford University Press, 1979).

6. As Gillian Tan reminds us, Bateson's ecology of mind implied that "*purposive consciousness*, which sought the shortest path at the expense of a finely tuned appreciation of interconnectedness, was only one small part of mind" ("An Ecology of Religiosity: Re-Emphasizing Relationships Between Humans and Nonhumans," *Journal for the Study of Religion, Nature and Culture* 8, no. 3 [2014]: 318).

7. William James, *Pragmatism* (1907; Indianapolis, Ind.: Hackett, 1981), 30.

8. Michael Jackson, *Being One and One Another* (Berkeley: University of California Press, 2013).

9. Gillian Rose, *Love's Work: A Reckoning with Life* (New York: Schocken Books, 1995), 135–139, 128.

10. Rose, *Love's Work*, 97–98.

11. Jorge Semprún, *Literature or Life* (1994), trans. Linda Coverdale (New York: Viking, 1997), 41, 42.

12. Albert Camus, *The Myth of Sisyphus*, trans. Justin O'Brien (London: Hamish Hamilton, 1955), 98–99.

13. Sol Reader, "Agency, Patiency, and Personhood," in *A Companion to the Philosophy of Action*, ed. Timothy O'Connor and Constantine Sandis (Oxford: Blackwell, 2010), 200–208.

14. E. M. Foster, *A Room with a View* (1923; New York: Knopf, 2011), 50.

15. Forster, *Room with a View*, 41.

16. Walter Benjamin, "The Task of the Translator" (1923), in *Illuminations: Essays and Reflections*, trans. Harry Zohn, ed. Hannah Arendt (New York: Schocken Books, 1968), 71.

17. *Manfred*, act 1, scene 1.

9. Fate and Freewill

1. Jean-Paul Sartre, *Saint-Genet: Actor and Martyr*, trans. B. Frechtman (New York: George Braziller, 1963), 49–50.

2. Jean-Paul Sartre, "Itinerary of a Thought," *New Left Review* 58 (1969): 45.

3. Albert Camus, *The Myth of Sisyphus*, trans. Justin O'Brien (London: Hamish Hamilton, 1955), 7.

4. Maurice Merleau-Ponty, *The Phenomenology of Perception* (1945), trans. Colin Smith (London: Routledge & Kegan Paul, 1962), 358.

5. Rachel Perkins and Marcia Langton, eds., *First Australians: An Illustrated History* (Melbourne: Miegunyah Press, 2008), 29.

6. Perkins and Langton, *First Australians*, xxv.

7. Bruce Pascoe, "How It Starts," in Perkins and Langton, *First Australians*, 120.

8. Pascoe, "How It Starts," 129.

9. Pascoe, "How It Starts," 163.

10. Friedrich Nietzsche, *Twilight of the Idols* (1889), trans. R. J. Hollingdale (Harmondsworth, UK: Penguin, 1968), 23.

11. James Faubion, "Paranomics: On the Semantics of Sacral Action," in *The Limits of Meaning: Case Studies in the Anthropology of Christianity*, ed. Matthew Engelke and Matt Tomlinson (New York: Berghahn, 2006), 205.

12. Meyer Fortes, *Oedipus and Job in West African Religion* (1959; rev. ed., Cambridge: Cambridge University Press, 1983), 15.

13. Fortes, *Oedipus and Job*, 23.

14. E. B. Idowu, *Olodumare: God in Yoruba Belief* (London: Longmans, 1962), 170.

15. Segun Gbadegesin, *African Philosophy: Traditional Yoruba Philosophy and Contemporary African Realities* (New York: Peter Lang, 1991), 41.

16. W. Abimbola, "The Yoruba Concept of Personality," in *La Notion de personne en Afrique noire*, ed. G. Dieterlen (Paris: Centre National de la Recherche Scientifique, 1973), 85.

17. Abimbola, "The Yoruba Concept of Personality," 86.

18. Idowu, *Olodumare*, 183.

19. Chinua Achebe, *Morning Yet on Creation Day: Essays* (London: Heinemann, 1975).

20. R. E. Bradbury, *Benin Studies*, ed. P. Morton-Williams (London: Oxford University Press, 1973), 263.

21. Bradbury, *Benin Studies*, 265.

22. Michael Jackson, *Allegories of the Wilderness: Ethics and Ambiguity in Kuranko Narratives* (Bloomington: Indiana University Press, 1982).

23. During his fieldwork among the Jelgobe Fulani, Paul Riesman noted that feelings of pain were rarely indulged or expressed to solicit sympathy. "It

was the same with all pain, physical and mental: people talked about it freely and objectively, so to speak, but they did not express it by that language of intonation and gesture which is familiar to us." According to Riesman, this equanimity was the result of neither repression nor stoicism but of control. "To name pain and suffering in a neutral tone is to master them, because the words do not escape thoughtlessly but are spoken consciously" (*Freedom in Fulani Social Life* [Chicago: University of Chicago Press, 1977], 147, 148).

24. J. M. Janzen, *The Quest for Therapy in Lower Zaire* (Berkeley: University of California Press, 1978), 203.

25. Jeanne Bisilliat, "Village Diseases and Bush Diseases in Songhay: An Essay in Description with a View to a Typology," trans. J. B. Loudon, in *Social Anthropology and Medicine*, ed. J. B. Loudon, ASA Monograph 13 (London: Academic Press, 1976), 590.

26. Riesman, *Freedom in Fulani Social Life*, 257.

27. Robin Horton, "The Kalabari World-View: An Outline and Interpretation," *Africa* 32 (1962): 205; Robin Horton, "Social Psychologies: African and Western," in Fortes, *Oedipus and Job*, 56.

28. Fortes, *Oedipus and Job*, 23.

29. Fortes, *Oedipus and Job*, 8–9.

30. Bradbury, *Benin Studies*, 264.

10. Center and Periphery

1. Derrida's deconstruction and Adorno's negative dialectics are remarkably similar. "The logocentrism of Greek metaphysics will always be haunted . . . by the 'absolutely other' to the extent that the *Logos* can never englobe everything. There is always something which escapes, something different, other and opaque which refuses to be totalized into a homogeneous identity" (Jacques Derrida, "Deconstruction and the Other," interview with Richard Kearney, in *Dialogues with Contemporary Continental Thinkers: The Phenomenological Heritage*, ed. Richard Kearney [Manchester: Manchester University Press 1984], 117).

2. Ghassan Hage, personal communication, 2014.

3. Michael Jackson, *At Home in the World* (Durham, N.C.: Duke University Press, 1995).

4. Jorge Luis Borges, "The Garden of Forking Paths" (1958), trans. Donald A. Yates, in *Labyrinths: Selected Stories and Other Writings* (Harmondsworth, UK: Penguin, 1970), 53.

5. George Devereux, "Art and Mythology, Part 1: A General Theory," in *Studying Personality Cross-Culturally*, ed. B. Kaplan (New York: Harper & Row, 1961), 378.

6. Mattijs van de Port, *Ecstatic Encounters: Brazilian Candomblé and the Search for the Really Real* (Amsterdam: Amsterdam University Press, 2011), 28.

7. *Sosogoma* (riddle) derives from the verb *ka sogo*, "to point out" or "indicate."

8. Denise Paulme, "Blood Pacts, Age Classes and Castes in Black Africa," in *French Perspectives in African Studies: A Collection of Translated Essays*, ed. Pierre Alexandre (London: Oxford University Press, 1973), 90–91.

9. G. Calame-Griaule, *Ethnologie et langage: la parole chez les Dogon* (Paris: Gallimard, 1965).

10. Dominque Zahan, *The Bambara* (Leiden: E. J. Brill, 1974), 15.

11. Sigmund Freud, *Beyond the Pleasure Principle* (1922), trans. James Strachey (New York: Norton, 1989), 30–35.

12. Ali Farka Touré, sleeve notes to *Radio Mali* (World Circuit CD WC8044, 1996).

13. For specific cases, see Michael Jackson, "Imagining the Powers That Be: Society Versus the State," in *Excursions* (Durham, N.C.: Duke University Press, 2007), 48–49, and Michael Jackson, *Life Within Limits: Well-Being in a World of Want* (Durham, N.C.: Duke University Press, 2011), 120–121.

14. Michael Taussig, *The Devil and Commodity Fetishism in South America* (Chapel Hill: University of North Carolina Press, 1980).

15. Among the Bambara the term *sako*, which connotes social necessity, translates as "death matter" while the complementary term *dunko*, connoting inward personal desire, translates as "depth matter" (Youssouf Cissé, "Signes graphiques, représentations, concepts et tests relatifs a la personne chez les Malinké et les Bambara du Mali," in *La notion de personne en Afrique noire, Paris 11–17 Octobre, 1971*, ed. Colloque International sur la Notion de Personne en Afrique Noire [Paris: Éditions du Centre National du Recherche Scientifique, 1973], 148–149; Kone, personal communication).

16. Janice Boddy, *Wombs and Alien Spirits: Women, Men, and the Zar Cult in Northern Sudan* (Madison: University of Wisconsin Press, 1989), 3.

17. Boddy, *Wombs and Alien*, 350.

18. Rosalind Shaw, *Memories of the Slave Trade: Ritual and the Historical Imagination in Sierra Leone* (Chicago: University of Chicago Press, 2002), 202.

19. In contemporary Anglophone Cameroon, "any place where there is money can be called 'bush'" (e.g., the West or *white man kontri*), and the dream of migration is known as "bushfalling" (Maybritt Jill Alpes, "Bushfalling: The Making of Migratory Expectations in Anglophone Cameroon," in *The Global Horizon: Expectations of Migration in Africa and the Middle East*, ed. Knut Graw and Samuli Schielke [Leuven: Leuven University Press, 2012], 43).

20. D. W. Winnicott, *Playing and Reality* (Harmondsworth, UK: Penguin, 1974), 113–116.

21. Claude Lévi-Strauss, *Structural Anthropology* (1958), trans. Claire Jacobson and Brooke Grundfest Schoepf (New York: Basic Books, 1963), 184.

22. S. F. Nadel, "Morality and Language Among the Nupe," in *Language in Culture and Society: A Reader in Linguistics and Anthropology*, ed. Dell Hymes (New York: Harper & Row, 1964), 265.

23. *Suwage* connotes both witchcraft and anti-witchcraft powers—an indication of the ambiguity surrounding the domain of extrasocial forces.

24. A direct analogy is with the public spheres of men and women (*ke dugu* and *musu dugu*), for while these are strictly separated, they too are functionally complementary.

25. In a recent book, however, I recount conversations with a young Kuranko man who made no ethical distinction between these alternatives courses of action (Jackson, *Life Within Limits*, 77–87).

26. Nigerians referred to Peckham as "Little Lagos."

27. Michael Jackson, *Existential Anthropology: Events, Exigencies, and Effects* (New York: Berghahn, 2005), xiv–xv.

28. René Devisch, "Frenzy, Violence and Ethical Renewal in Kinshasa," *Public Culture* 7 (1995): 593–629.

29. Hannah Arendt, *The Human Condition* (Chicago: University of Chicago Press, 1958), 50.

30. Lévi-Strauss, *Structural Anthropology*, 171–172.

31. Jean-Paul Sartre, *The Imaginary: A Phenomenological Psychology of the Imagination*, rev. and introduction by Arlette Elkaïm Sartre, trans. Jonathan Webber (London: Routledge, 2004), 30. I find Georg Groddeck's notion of the "it" helpful here—the nebulous, pre-objective, and amorphous life force that precedes specific symbolic or cultural expressions of identity so that we may say not only "I live" but "I am being lived" and, methodologically, set greater store by abstaining from immediate interpretation than by rushing to judgment (Georg Groddeck, *The Meaning of Illness: Selected Psychoanalytic Writings*, trans. Gertrud Mander [London: Hogarth Press, 1977], 132–157).

11. Ecologies of Mind

1. Immanuel Kant, *Critique of Practical Reason*, cited in Hannah Arendt, *The Life of the Mind* (New York: Harcourt Brace, 1978), 24.

2. Hannah Arendt, *The Human Condition* (Chicago: Chicago University Press, 1958), 277–279. Henri Ellenberger traces this "unmasking trend" back to the seventeenth-century moralists (*The Discovery of the Unconscious* [New York: Basic Books, 1970], 537). Nevertheless, this assumption that "understanding consists in reducing one type of reality to another" finds ubiquitous

expression in the suspicion that "true reality is never most obvious, and that the nature of truth is already indicated by the care it takes to remain elusive" (Claude Lévi-Strauss, *Tristes Tropiques* (1955), trans. John and Doreen Weightman [London: Jonathan Cape, 1973], 57–58).

3. Parmenides, cited by Hannah Arendt, *The Life of the Mind* (New York: Harcourt Brace, 1978), 23; Bronislaw Malinowski, *Argonauts of the Western Pacific: An Account of Native Enterprise and Adventure in the Archipelagoes of Melanesian New Guinea* (London: Routledge & Kegan Paul, 1922), 518.

4. Gregory Bateson, *Steps to an Ecology of Mind* (Frogmore, St. Albans, Herts: Paladin, 1973).

5. Kay Milton, *Environmentalism and Cultural Theory: Exploring the Role of Anthropology in Environmental Discourse* (London: Routledge, 1996), 109–114.

6. Christopher Anderson, "Aborigines and Conservation: The Daintree-Bloomfield Road," *Australian Journal of Social Issues* 24, no. 3 (1989): 214–227.

7. R. G. Collingwood, *The Idea of Nature* (Westport, Conn.: Greenwood Press, 1944), 3.

8. Orvar Löfgren, *On Holiday: A History of Vacationing* (Berkeley: University of California Press, 1999), 6–7. Löfgren speaks of two basic philosophies of travel, one based on an urge to "see the world," the other on a desire "to get away from it all," and he shows how these philosophies gather momentum from the eighteenth century to the twentieth century, with ever-changing ideas of how the craving for elsewhere can be most comfortably, fashionably, and excitingly consummated.

9. Norman O. Brown, *Life Against Death: The Psychoanalytical Meaning of History* (London: Routledge & Kegan Paul, 1959), 118.

Index

Abimbola, Wande, 174
Aboriginal societies, 53, 86, 93,
    210–11, 213; Daintree and, 204–8;
    land and, 170–71, 205–6
abstract: knowledge, 108; metaphors
    as concrete images of abstract
    ideas, 36
absurdity, 13, 22, 134
Abu Ghraib prison, 59
Achebe, Chinua, 173, 174
action: active life principle or *emi*,
    174; activity, passivity, and,
    78–79, 156, 229n45; life of mind
    and, 122–25; *vita activa*, 10–11,
    122, 206
Adorno, Theodor, 6, 7, 10, 52, 62,
    82, 217n17; "constellations" and,
    22, 220n61; influence, 83; nega-
    tive dialectics and, 23, 25, 51, 57,
    181, 240n1
aemulatio, 28–29
Aeschylus, 173
"affirmative culture," 136

Africa. *See* West Africa
agency, patiency, and, 22, 25, 154,
    158, 163
alienation, 25, 48, 181
Allan, Diana, 13
alternity, 49–50
American Philosophical Associa-
    tion, 80
analogical reasoning, 22, 27, 206
analogy, 27, 29, 37, 198, 212, 222n47
"ancient fear," of human existence,
    203
Anderson, Chris, 205
animals: in folktales, 149, 150; green
    turtle, 208–9; human-animal
    relationships, 103, 105–13, 123,
    185–87, 227n18, 233n28, 237n19;
    hunting rituals, 233n26; Kuranko
    people and totemic animals, 107,
    192; with post–traumatic stress
    disorder, 74; sacrifice of, 114,
    118; at Warlpiri Dreaming sites,
    108–9; witchcraft and, 117, 118

anthropology: defined, 19–20; Herder with, 6; philosophical anthropology, 4, 10–11, 14, 19, 23, 51, 62, 63, 118; philosophy and border between, 1, 3, 4, 5, 6, 14–15; positioning and, 5; sociocultural anthropology, 23, 51; truth and, 9

anthropos, ethnos and, 11–12, 225n1

antipathy, 30, 222n31

anti-witchcraft powers (*suwage*), 116, 197, 242n23

apartheid, 138–42

Apsáalooke people. *See* Crow people

Arden, Elizabeth, 54

Arendt, Hannah, 4, 6, 7, 80, 82, 89, 100; with fear, 203; Holocaust and, 140; on Jaspers, 16; on love, 18; natality and, 229n43; "visiting imagination" and, 212–13; with *vita activa* and *vita contemplativa*, 10–11, 122

Argonauts of the Western Pacific (Malinowski), 54

Aristotle, 67, 71, 229n45; with friendship, 18; on metaphors, 38

art, 1, 2; inwardness and, 66; with life and overcoming limitations, 182–83; life imitating, 145; in Magdalenian caves, 10; role of, 9–10; work of art, life and afterlife, 165

atonality, 23, 51, 56, 225n15

attention: directed attention, 66; selective attention, 56, 158

attitudes, toward self, 57, 135

Auschwitz, 82

Auslander, Shalom, 21

Aztec people, 115, 234n33

Ba-Benzélé people, 133

Bach, Johann Sebastian, 8

Bachelard, Gaston, 44, 45, 46

Bacon, Francis, 33, 35

Badiou, Alain, 7, 90, 91

Bakhtin, Mikhail, 190

BaKongo people, 178

Bambara people, 190, 241n15

Bangura, Yebu, 117

Bateson, Gregory, 37, 203, 204, 238n6

Baudelaire, Charles, 162

beauty magic, 54

Bedtime Stories, 133

Begrenzung, 216n9

being: being a part of and being apart from world, 118–19, 160–61; being-thought, 154–57; beliefs and, 122; *Dasein*, 7, 63, 94; having and, 113–14; knowing and, 166; "potential being," 94

beliefs: being and, 122; change and, 124; impossible, 120–21; life of mind and action, 122–25; in magic, 30; seeing and believing, 46

Belon, Pierre, 30

Benjamin, Walter, 5, 61, 146, 164, 216n12, 220n3

Bennelong, 169–70

Bennett, Jane, 18–19

ben-Zakkai, Yohanan (Rabbi), 85–86

Bergson, Henri, 63, 110, 190

Beyond the Pleasure Principle (Freud), 191

Biehl, João, 20

big house (*wharenui*), 44

Bion, Wilfred, 96–97

birth defects, 124

Bisilliat, Jeanne, 179

Bloch, Ernst, 98

Boddy, Janice, 194

Bodin, Jean, 35

Englander, Yakir, 85
enlightenment, 11, 66–67, 222n31
Enlightenment, the, 33, 34, 36, 154, 168, 225n1
episteme, 30, 32, 34, 105, 155–56
ese (leg), 174
Essays in Radical Empiricism (James), 63, 80
Essays on the Law of Nature (Locke), 34
Ethics (Spinoza), 93
ethics, life and, 18–19
ethnography: "ethnographic theory of language," 53; power of, 15; role of, 5, 7, 21, 212
ethnos, anthropos and, 11–12, 225n1
eudaimonia, 71
Euripides, 173
Evans-Pritchard, E. E., 43
Evenki people, 233n28
evil, 122, 203; good and, 24, 61, 137, 140; witchcraft and, 129
exile, 83
existence: *dukkha* or unsatisfactoriness of existence, 48; in Shatila Camp, 13. *See also* human existence
existentialism: domestic and wild, struggle between, 190–91; human existence, paradox of, 182
experience, 227n7; consciousness and, 95; as double-barrelled, 65, 77; of life and death, 90, 92, 93; lived experience, 167; thinking transforming, 2
Experience and Nature (Dewey), 227n7
extinction, 94, 102

face-to-face relationships, in West Africa, 75
fairy tales, 183

Faku, Pearl, 138, 139
Fang people, 30
fantasy, 5, 212
fate: colonial history with freedom and, 169–72; freedom and, 25; freewill and, 172; "Oedipal fate," 173; West African thought and, 172–80
Faubion, James, 172
fear: "ancient fear" of human existence, 203; brain and, 160; death and fear of pain, 21
"Fearful Sphere of Pascal, The" (Borges), 27
Feld, Steven, 133
female power, 196–97
fire finch, 237n19
Fischer, Dick (father), 86
Fischer, Peter, 86–87
Fitzgerald, F. Scott, 24, 137, 142
Fleming, Alexander, 31
folktales, 60, 159; Na Nyale, story of, 146–52; stereotypes and, 144–45; with types, 143–44. *See also* storytelling
Fonagy, Peter, 97
food, 56, 75, 99, 101, 114, 147; food magic, 54; human sacrifice and, 115; for lovers, 237n20; sacrifices and, 193
Forster, E. M., 163–64
Fortes, Meyer, 42–43, 173
Foucault, Michel, 6, 155–56; history of thought and, 35; with similitude, modes of, 27–30
Franco, Roberto, 77–78, 79
Frankfurt School, 11
freedom: colonial history with fate and, 169–72; fatality and, 169; fate and, 25; limits of, 97; social life and, 179; West African thought and, 172–80

freewill: fate and, 172; Yoruba people and, 173–74

Freud, Sigmund, 45, 130, 191, 216n9

Frey, Rodney, 87–88

friendship, 41, 98, 101, 170; ethic of, 18; folktales and, 146; love and, 165–66, 198

Fulani people, 179, 239n23

Galileo, 32

Gammeltoft, Tine, 124

gardening magic, 53, 54

"Garden of Forking Paths, The" (Borges), 182

Geertz, Clifford, 225n1

genealogy, 7, 42

Genet, Jean, 167–68

genius, 38, 153, 157, 188, 193

Geulincx, Arnold, 235n1

Giedion, Sigfried, 39–40

gifts, 49, 114, 193

giver: receiver and, 47, 114; witchcraft and, 115, 116–17

global space, as bush, 195

Gluckman, Max, 225n9

Gobodo-Madikizela, Pumla, 138–42

good: evil and, 24, 61, 137, 140; "good destiny" ancestors, 180; higher good and individual good, 143

Goya, Francisco de, 8

Green, John, 170–71

Green, Mary (wife), 170–71

Greene, Joshua, 16, 219n45

green turtle, 208–9

Groddeck, Georg, 242n31

Gyatso, Janet, 221n18

Hadot, Pierre, 14

Halbwachs, Maurice, 162

Hallisey, Charles, 219n51

Hancock, Herbie, 133

happenchance, life and, 163–66

Haraway, Donna, 8

Harkis people, 82–83

hate, 18, 101, 152, 216n9

Haunting Images (Gammeltoft), 124

having, being and, 113–14

Headhunters, 133

Heaney, Seamus, 132

Hegel, Georg Wilhelm Friedrich, 6, 8, 34

Heidegger, Martin, 6–7, 9, 43, 63, 218n40

Helliwell, Christine, 40

Herder, Johann Gottfried, 6, 217n16

Herzfeld, Michael, 11–12, 75

Histoire de la nature des oiseaux (Belon), 30

history: fate and freedom with colonial, 169–72; of thought, 34–35

Hogan, Paul, 211, 213

Holocaust, 82, 84, 106, 140, 162, 219n51

Homer, 69

Homes, A. M., 113

house, 223n55; big house or *wharenui*, 44; boundaries, 189–90; carved house or *whare whakairo*, 44; as metaphor, 43–46

How Forests Think (Kohn), 103

human existence: "ancient fear" of, 203; invisibility and, 8; paradox of, 182; struggle of, 4–5, 21, 94, 135–36, 154; truth and, 11

humanities, embourgeoisement of, 134–36

humans: as good and evil, 140; human-animal relationships, 103, 105–13, 123, 185–87, 227n18, 233n28, 237n19; sacrifice, 115, 234n32, 234n34

Hume, David, 67, 68

Hunter, J. F. M., 232n4

hunting, 103, 112, 120, 190, 205, 208; Kuranko people and, 107, 109–11, 190–91; rituals, 233n26; Yaka people and, 48
Husserl, Edmund, 18, 19, 21, 67, 196, 219n56

ideas, 27; concepts, 94–96; Mehinaku people and, 37; metaphors as concrete images of abstract, 36; of self, 19; storytelling and, 159, 160; with truth, 14, 79, 143
identical (idem), 52
Igbo people, 174
illumination, 10, 217n28
imagination, 98, 131; life and, 16; theory of, 201; "visiting imagination," 212–13
individuals: higher good and individual good, 143; murderers and individuality, 141; types and, 139, 143, 144
individuation, 3–4, 176, 191
Industrial Revolution, migrants in, 195
infinity, 36, 82
initiation: rites of, 176–78; sexuality and, 192
inspiration, 156–60
intentionality, 18, 67, 201
"intrapsychic alibiing," 144
Invie, Nora Marie, 156–57
invisibility, 8, 116, 158, 194
inwardness: bourgeoisie with, 135, 136; consciousness and, 66, 70; outward appearances and inward feelings, 125–30
ipse (unique), 52
Iqwaye people, 36
Islam, 58, 122, 196, 198
ityo (patrilineage), 42
Ivory, James, 164

Jackson, Heidi, 41
Jakamarra, Zack, 108–9, 233n18
Jallo, Mali Yan, 234n32
James, William, 7, 10, 23, 63, 69, 111; American Philosophical Association and, 80; consciousness and, 67; experience and, 65, 77; on philosophy, 160; pluralistic universe and, 79; radical empiricism, 63, 64, 80, 181; self and, 73; on truth, 143
Japaljarri, Barnaby, 89–90
Japanangka, 108
Jaspers, Karl, 10, 16, 94
jelebas (praise-singers), 150, 188, 237n22
"Jobian fulfillment," 173
Johnson, Denis, 105
Joyce, James, 67–69, 70, 153
jukurrpa (the Dreaming), 46, 91, 93, 157
Jung, Carl, 65
Jupurrurla, Paddy Nelson, 108

Kalabari people, 179
Kant, Immanuel, 6, 7, 12, 67, 112, 203
kanyininpa (possession of physical objects), 91
Kargbo people, 234n32
Keats, John, 23, 49, 51
Kekulé, Friedrich August, 31–32
kemine gbana (unmarried young man), 238n24
Keynes, M., 222n30
Kierkegaard, Søren, 126
Klemm, Gustav, 6
knowing: being and, 166; etymology, 33; as seeing, 39
knowledge: abstract, 108; magical, 31–32; similitude and, 27–30
Kohn, Eduardo, 103, 112–13

ori (physical head), 173–74
others, 102; inscrutability of, 130–31; living with otherness, 104–5; reciprocity for self and, 131–34; self and, 53–54, 74
Ouédraogo, Ibrahim, 75–76, 129–30
outwardness, 125–30
overconsumption, 135

pain, 21, 177, 239n23
Palestine, 13, 132
Paracelsus, 28, 31
Parmenides, 7, 203
passivity, activity and, 78–79, 156, 229n45
Patañjali, 66
patiency, agency and, 22, 25, 154, 158, 163
patrilineage (*ityo*), 42
Paz, Octavio, 234n33
peace of mind, 5, 124–25
penumbral zone, 10, 183, 193, 202, 217n28
People of the Eland (Vinnecombe), 112
persons: de Kock, 138–42; distance without reification, 142–45; types and, 24, 137
perspective, print technology and, 41–42
Pessoa, Fernando, 73, 74, 79
phenomenology, 44, 51, 95–96, 190
Phenomenology of Mind (Hegel), 8
Phenomenology of Perception (Merleau-Ponty), 3–4
Phillip, Arthur, 169–70
philosophical anthropology, 14, 23, 51, 62, 63, 118; individuation and, 4; role of, 19; *vita activa* and, 10–11

philosophy, 10, 12, 160, 217n16; anthropology and border between, 1, 3, 4, 5, 6, 14–15; common sense and, 22; literacy and, 41–42; storytelling with social science and, 137; of travel, 213–14, 243n8; truth and, 7, 82
physical head (*ori*), 173–74
Picasso, Pablo, 157
Pintupi people, 91, 92
pirlirrpa (life force), 90, 91
placenta, land and, 86
Plato, 2, 5, 9, 11, 12, 34
Plenty Coups (Crow chief), 84, 85, 87
Plessner, Helmuth, 4, 216n9
pluralism: paradox of, 4, 52; pluralistic universe, 72, 79
politics, 82, 231n23
Popper, Karl, 158
positioning, anthropology with, 5
possession of physical objects (*kanyininpa*), 91
post–traumatic stress disorder (PTSD), 74, 128
"potential being," 94
"potential space," 196
power: of boundaries, 187–92; djinn and, 192–95; of ethnography, 15; female, 196–97; wild powers, 192, 194, 197; witchcraft and antiwitchcraft powers or *suwage*, 116, 197, 242n23
praise-singers (*jelebas*), 150, 188, 237n22
praxis, 48, 168–69, 176, 178, 179, 215n4
pregnancy, women and, 30, 86, 124, 129
premodern thought, 22, 27, 55, 207

pretending: "pretend mode," 3, 97; storytelling as, 145
primary intersubjectivity, 1, 4, 18
"primitive peoples," 7, 220n57; Aboriginal societies, 53; divination and, 157–58; South American Indians as, 33–34
primitive thought, 8, 55
Principles of Psychology (James), 63
print technology, perspective and, 41–42
psychoanalysis, 7, 153
psychology, 63, 64, 77, 79, 128
PTSD (post–traumatic stress disorder), 74, 128
public spheres, of men and women, 242n24
pure consciousness, 19
purposive consciousness, 238n6

al-Qaida, 59
al-Qaisi, Ali Shallal, 59
queue (*nongo*), 42

racism, 77, 121, 138–42, 167
radical empiricism, 65–70; concepts and, 95; James and, 63, 64, 80, 181
Radical Hope (Lear), 84
"rationality debate," 216n14
Reader, Sol, 162
receiver, giver and, 47, 114
reciprocity, for self and others, 131–34
recognition, 74, 111, 132–33
Reem, 132
relationships, 4, 11, 22, 75, 91; friendship, 18, 41, 98, 146, 165–66, 198; giver and receiver, 47, 114; human-animal, 103, 105–13, 123, 185–87, 227n18, 233n28,

237n19; relations, over relata, 64, 79; Tallensi people with, 42–43
religion, 235n9; Buddhism, 21, 219n51, 221n18; Islam, 58, 122, 196, 198; violence with, 58–60, 61
remembering, recognition and, 132–33
resignation, 60–62
Revolutionary United Front, 90, 198
"Rich Boy, The" (Fitzgerald), 24, 137
riddles, 183–87, 202
Riesman, David, 42
Riesman, Paul, 179, 239n23
ritual, 1, 2, 14, 103; hunting, 233n26; Kuranko rites of initiation, 176–78; ritualized redistribution of life, 113–18; with words, 179
Roof, Dylann Storm, 121
Room with a View, A (film), 164–65
Room with a View, A (Forster), 163–64
Rorty, Richard, 7, 38, 39
Rose, Gillian, 161–62
Rospabé, Philippe, 98
Rubenstein, Helena, 54
Runa people, 112

Sacco, Joe, 58–59, 60
Sacks, Oliver, 101
sacrifice: animals, 114, 118; food and, 193; human, 115, 234n32, 234n34; witchcraft and, 115, 116, 117–18
Said, Edward, 83
sako (death matter), 241n15
Salt, McGinty, 207, 208
samadhi, 66
San people, 112
Sartre, Jean-Paul, 4, 7, 127, 167, 178; imagination, theory of, 201; praxis and, 168–69

Scheler, Max, 63, 216n9
Schoenberg, Arnold, 23, 51
Schopenhauer, Arthur, 13, 190
science, 36, 61, 155; with discoveries as accidental, 31–32; magic and, 30, 55. *See also* social science
Scott, James, 11, 125, 127, 215n4
seeing: believing and, 46; knowing as, 39
selective attention, 56, 158
self, 4, 19, 64, 83, 228n27, 229n44; attitudes toward, 57, 135; dissociation and, 74, 109–11, 127; migrant consciousness and multiple, 70–79; *miran* or self-possession, 92, 177; others and, 53–54, 74; reciprocity for others and, 131–34; *samadhi* and, 66
Seli River, 148, 237n21
Semprún, Jorge, 162
sex, 48, 49, 60, 68, 196, 200; djinn and, 193; initiation and sexuality, 192; women and sexuality, 47
Sexual Life of Savages (Malinowski), 54
shadow, light and, 10
shamanism, 10, 48
Shatila Camp, 13
Shaw, Rosalind, 195
Silko, Leslie Marmon, 111–12
similitude, 27–30
Simmel, Georg, 51, 100, 105, 119
singular universal, 4
Sisé people, 234n32
slum dwellers, 20–21
social boundaries, 98
social imaginaries, Kuranko people and, 195–202
social intelligence, 176, 178
social life: of concepts, 94–96; flow of, 93; freedom and, 179

social science, 34, 38, 63, 79, 137, 153
sociocultural anthropology, 23, 51
Socrates, 7, 38, 203
"something happened, its partner also happened" (*ko manni a nyorgo manni*), 237n23
Songhai people, 178–79
Sontag, Susan, 58
Sophocles, 172, 173
sound, light and, 40
South American Indians, 33–34
"sovereign expressions of life," 19, 89
Soyinka, Wole, 173
space, 39, 202; bush as global space, 195; lived space, 40–41; power and female space, 196–97
speech, language and, 53–54
Spinoza, Baruch, 93, 154
Spiritual Canticle, 156
Stang, Carla, 37
staring (*opia*), 128–29
Steiner, George, 49–50
Steps to an Ecology of Mind (Bateson), 203
stereotypes, 24, 56, 137, 141; folktales and, 144–45; witchcraft, 122; women, 146
Stiegler, Bernard, 4
Stocking, George, 225n1
stone, magic, 86–87
storytelling, 1, 2, 14, 137; dilemma tales and riddles, 183–87; divination, inspiration, and, 157–60; folktales, 143–52, 159; Kuranko people and, 25, 143–52, 159, 176, 179, 181–82, 183–87
stream of consciousness, 67–68
Stream of Thought, The (James), 63
struggle. *See* human existence

Victoria (Queen of England), 170
View of Life, The (Simmel), 100
Vinnecombe, Patricia, 112, 233n26
violence, 15, 167, 216n14; colonial history and, 170–71; de Kock with, 138–42, 145, 237n12; in folktales, 146–52; against Kuranko people, 90, 91–92; peace of mind and, 124–25; racism and, 121; terrorism, 58–60, 61, 62
vision: ocular metaphor, 38, 39; *opia* or staring, 128–29; visual-spatial thinking, 8
"visiting imagination," 212–13
"Vita" (Biehl), 20
vita activa. See life
vita contemplativa. See life
Von Humboldt, Alexander, 6

Wagner, Richard, 56–57
Walley, Christine, 133–34
Warlpiri people, 45–46, 89–90, 91, 92; dreaming and, 108–9, 157; human-animal relationships and, 108–9, 113; with life, flow of, 93
Weaver, Harriet Shaw, 153
West Africa, 135; with face-to-face relationships, 75; with thinking, distrust of, 3; thought, 172–80, 190
wharenui (big house), 44
whare whakairo (carved house), 44
White, Michael, 229n30
Whitehead, A. N., 23, 63
wild: domestic and, 113, 117, 190–92; initiation and, 176; wild powers, 192, 194, 197

Willerslev, Rane, 105, 110, 111
Winch, Peter, 216n14
Winnicott, D. W., 101
witchcraft, 115–18, 122, 129, 225n9; *suwage* and anti-witchcraft powers, 116, 197, 242n23; travel and, 195
Wittgenstein, Ludwig, 7, 10, 36, 232n4
women, 47, 237n20, 242n24; of Mousadougou, 196–97; pregnancy and, 30, 86, 124, 129; stereotypes, 146
Woolf, Virginia, 73
words, ritual with, 179
Wordsworth, William, 49
world: being a part of and being apart from, 118–19, 160–61; *mitwelt* or world of other people, 102
writing: inspiration and, 160; role of, 135

Xenophon, 39

Yaka people, 46, 47–48, 200
Yarralin people, 113
Yellowtail, Tom, 88, 89
yoga, 66
Yoruba people: freewill and, 173–74; with numeration, systems of, 36
Younge, Gary, 132
Yu Tsun, 182

Zar cult, 194

GPSR Authorized Representative: Easy Access System Europe, Mustamäe tee
50, 10621 Tallinn, Estonia, gpsr.requests@easproject.com

www.ingramcontent.com/pod-product-compliance
Lightning Source LLC
Chambersburg PA
CBHW031535260326
41914CB00032B/1812/J